Welcome Home!

Welcome Home!

*Stories of Fallen-Away
Catholics Who Came Back*

Compiled by
St. Joseph Communications

Edited by Victor R. Claveau

IGNATIUS PRESS   SAN FRANCISCO

Cover art by Christopher J. Pelicano
Cover design by Roxanne Mei Lum

© 2000 Ignatius Press, San Francisco
All rights reserved
ISBN 0-89870-792-7
Library of Congress catalogue number 99-68652
Printed in the United States of America ∞

"Welcome one another, therefore,
as Christ has welcomed you,
for the glory of God."
(Romans 15:7)

This book is dedicated to the Glory of God,
the Father, Son, and Holy Spirit,
and to His Holiness Pope John Paul II,
by the goodness of God
Prince of Pastors in the Universal Church,
Infallible Teacher of the Christian Faith,
with affection and admiration.

Acknowledgments

Special thanks to Dan Gallio, Michael Wick,
Kit O'Brien, Brother Charles Madden, and
Peter Ptak (Catholic Creative Services)
who helped bring this
worthy project to completion.

The Publisher and
St. Joseph Communications
thank the contributors who had the
courage to lay bare their lives
and share with the world their trials
and their joys.

Contents

Preface

"If a man has a hundred sheep and one of them goes astray, will he not leave the ninety-nine in the hills and go in search of the stray?" (Mt 18:12).

This year marks the twenty-first anniversary of the founding of the Catholic audio tape apostolate, St. Joseph Communications. This event has given me the opportunity to reflect on all the blessings the Lord has bestowed upon us and accomplished through this, His work. My co-workers and I have calculated that St. Joseph's has distributed more than two million audio tapes during these twenty-one years, with a library of more than fifty thousand titles. All of the tapes have been selected to move the hearts of listeners to grow in love and knowledge of the doctrines and practices of the Catholic Church and of Sacred Scripture. Many of our customers have written or called us, telling us how these tapes, as well as our family and parish conferences, have changed their lives and the lives of their friends and family. We praise God that the seeds we have been casting have been falling on fertile soil.

Some of these communications are truly remarkable. They describe how the Lord has been able to inspire fallen-away Catholics to return to the Faith of their childhood—and return with fervor. Often He has used St. Joseph Communications materials to touch their hearts.

Several years ago it occurred to me in prayer that others would benefit from knowing of these stories. Thus began the process that has led to this book, *Welcome Home!*

There are so many fallen-away and non-practicing Catholics in our "post-Christian" American society. The reasons Catholics leave the Faith are legion. But many "reverts" (cradle Catholics who have returned to the Faith) talk of being poorly catechized in their youth or of having an unfortunate experience with a priest or religious. In their lack of knowledge or even resentment they were susceptible to seeking spiritual nourishment in other Christian denominations or in the many non-Christian spiritualities that abound in our pluralistic culture. Many others simply became "cultural Catholics" — sacramentalized but not evangelized. They gradually drifted away from even a ritualized participation in the life of the Church and settled into a sort of spiritual limbo. Often these, the lukewarm, are the hardest to reach.

Yet human nature is such that we are irresistibly drawn to the truth. When presented in its fullness and with enthusiasm, Catholic truth is a magnet, and the Holy Spirit is its hidden power. The stories in *Welcome Home!* attest to this power.

Ironically, many of the writers were quite satisfied — socially and, in many ways, spiritually — with their membership in evangelical and fundamentalist churches. They anguished over leaving their congregations, friends, and even their livelihood to return to the Catholic Church. Many Protestant ministers have had to give up paycheck and professional status to "come home". For some, such as Sue Sowden, returning to the Church was a great relief. For years she wandered like a nomad from one spirituality to the next—Twelve Step programs, Mormonism, secular humanism, New Age, fundamentalism—only to rediscover what she already possessed. Then there are Catholics such as Rick Strom, who never really renounced the Faith, but only after being tested to the limit through injury and adversity did he fully embrace it.

There is one common denominator, though, among the writers of *Welcome Home!* To paraphrase Archbishop Fulton Sheen, few hate the Catholic Church for what she teaches, but millions hate it for what they *think* she teaches.

The defining moment of illuminating grace almost always came when our storytellers began to examine Catholic teaching *for themselves.* As police officer Jesse Romero attests, "Hearsay testimony is inadmissible in a court of law, and all of my anti-Catholic biases were hearsay." Practically all Catholics who leave the Church for other denominations or spiritualities are un-catechized Catholics. They really don't know what the Church teaches or why, particularly in the area of human sexuality. Instead, they have accepted the biased interpretations of anti-Catholic writers and preachers, or they view the Church from the lens of the secular media, often hostile to even the idea of religious faith. Only through personal study of the early Fathers or the *Catechism of the Catholic Church,* through examining the writings of Pope John Paul II or other magisterial documents, reading the testimonies of other converts and reverts, or listening to Catholic apologetical tapes was the light of Catholic truth able to banish the darkness of their biases. "So that is why the Church teaches what it does!" is the general response. The truth is shockingly self-evident; but we must seek out the truth first and be open to it interiorly through the help of the Holy Spirit.

I believe if you have *Welcome Home!* in your hands right now you have been brought to this point by the Holy Spirit. Perhaps you have left the Church of your youth and are contemplating returning. Perhaps a friend or family member gave you *Welcome Home!* and you are just being polite in breezing through its contents (you are sure, of course, that the stories will only confirm your darkest suspicions about the "unbiblical" teachings of the Church). Perhaps you are in deep pain because children who left the Catholic Faith that you cherish are involved in a fundamentalist church or even a cult. How do you reach them? Can they be reached?

All I would suggest is that you ask the Holy Spirit to guide you at this point. Keep an open mind. Maybe you will recognize your story; maybe not. Nonetheless, grace has brought you here. And the Good Shepherd, who is busy seeking out the lost and weary, is looking to bring you — or your loved ones — back to the fold. There is absolutely no doubt about that.

And when He finds you, no matter where you have been, He will always say, "Welcome home!"

Terry Barber
President, St. Joseph Communications

Foreword

In the twilight of his priesthood, a certain elderly Benedictine monk would express to his confreres his feelings of heartache over the apparent disintegration of the Catholic Church and religious life in America in recent decades. His concerns were not without cause. In his youth this kindly monk had entered into a mystical marriage with the Bride of Christ, and he had loved and served her with every fiber of his being. In his lifetime he had seen Christ's Mystical Body, the one true Church of Christ, wounded by a storm of rebellion. In a mystical way, the Church had been bloodied as Our Lord's mortal body had been at the time of His Passion. In heart and soul this faithful priest had been wounded by the loss of faith in Christ's Eucharistic Presence, the widespread abuse of the Church's liturgy, and a growing infidelity among countless consecrated souls.

He had witnessed over thirty years the contempt for the apostolic authority of the Church by a vast number of her own children and their rejection of her Christ-given right to teach authoritatively in matters of faith and morality. He had lamented the public confrontation directed against the Magisterium of the Church and the successors of St. Peter by large numbers of Catholic clergymen, religious, theologians, and prominent lay persons. They seemed to revel in intellectual pride while asserting their supposed "right" to attack timeless truths that have the Spirit of Christ as their origin. He mourned and prayed for those souls who seemed to see no contradiction in their abandonment of the moral law in favor of the popular mores of the day. Their well-publicized dissent helped to bring about the general acceptance of the sexual revolution, which served to sever the divinely ordained links between marriage, human sexuality, and the sanctity of human life. Affirmed by nothing more than the results of the latest opinion polls, these dissidents contributed generously, he felt, to the spiritual and moral decay of American social order, the predictable corrosion of family life, and the rise of the "culture of death".

For three decades this Benedictine had watched the decline of a once magnificent system of Catholic education, which began to wither like a severed branch after it was cut off from the life-giving vine of sound Catholic doctrine in the later sixties and early seventies. Moral relativism and religious ignorance had become the norm for the better part of two generations of poorly catechized Catholic youth as a result.

With many of his peers, he had long ago foreseen the destructive consequences of the spiritual bankruptcy that had ensued and the inevitable exodus of formerly faithful Catholics from their parishes. They had fallen away in increasing numbers as the Mass, the priesthood, prayer, sin and repentance, and the universal call to holiness of life came to be viewed as irrelevant. As the intellectual confusion called Modernism spread more widely throughout the Church in America, more and more ordinary Catholics began to look elsewhere for a Divine Savior they felt they had never truly come to know. Week after week, year after year, they left their churches on Sunday mornings uninstructed and uninspired, often perplexed by the watered-down presentation of their Faith by pastors from the pulpit. Those were the days when priests maintained a silence regarding the hard truths of Roman Catholicism and sought popular acceptance in the preaching of modern psychology, all the while failing to communicate the divinely revealed mysteries of salvation.

Over the years this tired veteran confessor tried to console Catholic parents who agonized because sons and daughters had cast off their Faith with less consideration than they would have given their worn-out jeans. Many of these children came to reject Christ and transcendent values in the shallow pursuit of the so-called "American Dream". In sorrow he offered Masses for the conversion of others, who had left the Church to seek fulfillment in Protestant fundamentalism, religious cults, and the New Age movement, unaware that they were leaving behind a treasure of immeasurable value, having been baptized into the one Church possessing the fullness of divinely revealed truth and all of the divinely established means of salvation.

The repeated assurances of his Benedictine brothers that the Holy Spirit will never depart from the Church and that the gates of hell will not prevail against it provided the monk with little solace. God's words to the prophet Hosea, "My people perish for want of knowledge" (Hos 4:6), seemed to be fulfilled again in his time. But let us never forget that God unfailingly raises up heroic souls in times of crisis in the Church, and never has Satan long succeeded in suppressing Catholic truth.

It is my firm belief that history will repeat itself. During this critical period in the history of the Church, Christ will once again rise up to calm the winds and waves of the present storm. Undoubtedly, the Holy Spirit is even now raising up a new Gideon's Army to defend the Kingdom of God on earth. Among the warriors in this modern legion will be devout men and women from the ranks of both the clergy and the laity who have made the long journey back to the Church that is One, Holy, Catholic, and Apostolic.

That they are now among the Church's staunchest defenders should not be surprising to anyone. The joy of reconciliation often leaves love deeper than it was before the break. Surely, God will make use of the newly enkindled fire within them to inflame the hearts of many cradle Catholics who have grown indifferent toward the incomparable spiritual treasure we possess. All of us can benefit from the knowledge that Christ, the Good Shepherd, never abandons any who stray.

I have no doubt that those who read *Welcome Home!* will take from these intriguing conversion stories a renewed spirit of confidence and devotion. In it they will also find an informative source of Catholic apologetics that will especially attract those who have shared similar life experiences in their sincere search for truth and reconciliation with the Church of their youth, which is indeed the Covenant Family of God where the One who is Truth Itself abides forever.

Father Bill Casey, C.P.M.
Father General, Fathers of Mercy
South Union, Kentucky

"Those Strong Feet
That Followed After"

Father John Corapi, S.O.L.T.

Those of us who have been baptized in the name of the
Father, and of the Son, and of the Holy Spirit are living
tabernacles, temples of the Holy Spirit, children of God,
His adopted sons and daughters. He cares for each of us
in a way that is difficult to comprehend. He is with us
always, whether on the highest mountain or in the deepest pit of despair. I pray that I will never lose sight of the
wonder and depth of His love and mercy.

It is an honor for me to be able to share my story with
you. You may consider it a somewhat fantastic testimony,
but I assure you that God in His mercy has touched numerous other lost children even more dramatically than
He touched me.

On the day of my ordination, the founder of the religious order of which I am a member said to me, "Remember, from this day forward you receive blessings by
giving blessings." I fervently desire that my relating some
of my life's experiences will be a blessing for you. Keep

in mind that I give glory to God for all the good, and I take full responsibility for all the bad.

Whenever I travel and speak to groups, most of the people don't really know me. They see a religious dressed in a habit. They see a priest. Some may know a little about me, but not much. Most have no idea of the extraordinary way that God has worked in my life. I suppose that my story, my testimony, is different, maybe even radically different.

It's a humbling thing, you know. I think my guardian angel often reminds me who my listeners and readers are — God's children, temples of the Holy Spirit, tabernacles of the Father, Son, and Holy Spirit. And since that's who you are, then with what thanksgiving and reverence I come before you!

St. Paul once said to his beloved Timothy, "Never be ashamed to give your testimony." Giving my testimony is the hardest thing in the world for me to do. I don't like doing it. So, we are going to do the hardest thing first. I'm going to tell you about my life — not because my life is so important, but because sometimes God chooses to act through instruments.

I remember hearing the great Archbishop Fulton Sheen say that two thousand years ago Jesus rode into the city of Jerusalem on the back of a jackass. He continues to do it! We are well aware of that. God can ride into your heart even on the back of a jackass. He does it all the time. I know he's done it through me, unworthy as I am.

Forty-nine years ago I was born in a small town in upstate New York. My earliest memories are of a time when I was probably between five and seven years old. I don't recall exactly when it was, but I do know that it must have been in the month of May, for the lilacs were in bloom. I had gone to May devotions that evening with my family. We had said the Rosary in our parish, Our Lady of Mount Carmel. I came home, and I was in the back yard of my grandmother's house. She lived right across the street, and I was at peace with the world. When you are a child and you still have your innocence, there's a certain peace and joy that the world hasn't spoiled yet.

You know, the world has a way of sowing cynicism and discouragement into our hearts, but when you are young, and I was young, you still have the joy and the peace of youth, of innocence. Having just come from church, I had even more peace. We had prayed to Our Lady, prayed the Holy Rosary, and I was in the back yard smelling the lilacs. I have always loved the smell of the lilacs. All of a sudden I became aware of a young woman, a very beautiful young woman. She looked at me. I didn't recognize her. She smiled, and she said but one word, my name, "Johnny". I was rather embarrassed, as little boys often are, and I turned away. When I turned back she was gone, which was not unusual. People came and went at my grandmother's house all the time.

Among those early youthful memories, I can recall that I always wanted to "be somebody". Do you know what I mean by that? The human spirit longs to be somebody, to be special. We want to have the approval of our friends, of the rest of the world. God didn't make us for dust. God made us for greatness, and that greatness He sowed into the very fabric of the human spirit.

We may not be aware of a desire to be special, but even

from my earliest years I knew that I was different. Every one of us is different. Every one of us is unique, precious, and unrepeatable—a masterpiece of the Most High God. So I knew somehow that my life would be different. I knew that I was called to be somebody. I had that great longing in my heart.

As I grew up, in the beginning I tried to accomplish this goal through athletics, through football mostly. For a while it looked as though I would succeed. My friends looked up to me. I was a good football player. I progressed in my abilities. But then, just when I thought I was becoming somebody, I had an accident and hurt my shoulder. I couldn't play football anymore and my poor, youthful mind was crushed. My heart was broken. Why? Because now I was nobody, all over again.

Time went on, and a couple of years later I healed. The Vietnam War came along. I was eighteen years old, and I had feelings of idealism, a certain patriotism, and I thought, "Well, I'll go to serve my country."

In those days I had a good more zeal than brains, and that probably is what animated me, but patriotism is not a bad thing. It's a good thing. Maybe I didn't understand all of the ins and outs, the political ramifications of the war, but I know my intentions were good. I loved my country, and I thought, "Well, maybe I can become a somebody through a military career."

I entered the Army with, of all things, an enlistment commitment with the special forces, the Green Berets. I remember going off to the Army, leaving my small home town. I had never been away. Everything in my home town was familiar to me. I was comfortable there, and for an eighteen-year-old boy to leave everything that's comfortable and familiar is not an easy thing. I remember getting on the bus with stirrings of idealism and patriotism. I wanted to serve my country; in those days not knowing, of course, that we have no lasting home here. Our country lies beyond time, beyond space.

Yet, I had those stirrings in my heart to serve my country, and off I went. I went through all the training to become a soldier, a very specialized kind of soldier. I finished it all, and at the end I was injured again, in a helicopter accident. Just when I thought once again I was becoming somebody, I was reduced to nothingness, nobody.

The Army sent me off to Germany to a miserable desk job. I didn't know what penance was in those days, but for me to sit at a desk, that was indeed penance! So I sat out the Vietnam War in Heidelberg, Germany, pushing a pencil. I returned home and decided I'd go back to college. I didn't know what else to do, and so I thought, "Well, maybe in business I can make my mark on the world. Maybe I can do something worthwhile in the field of business." After all, that's where money is to be made, and everyone had been shouting at me for years that if you want to be somebody (and I had wanted to be somebody since I was a little boy), then you have to go for the gusto, go for the greenbacks.

So I went after worldly success with a vengeance. I finished college and went off to, of all places, Las Vegas. I had a best friend who was there, and I joined a CPA firm, a large one. We did work for major hotels and casinos. So I began to operate in the glittery, high-profile world of Las Vegas. My clients were the Las Vegas Hilton, the

Flamingo, the Tropicana, and others. I began to like my new life. There's a certain heady and seductive element in that worldly kind of a life, especially for the young. I was a young man, and I liked the excitement. Pretty soon, rather famous people came into my life. Some of them would recognize me on the floor of the casinos. Elvis Presley was still around, playing at the Hilton in those days. Frank Sinatra would come. Glen Campbell. Many of the well known people would come in and out of those casinos. I liked the atmosphere. It got into my mind and into my blood.

As I became more and more known, I developed a taste for affluence and for power. I liked being seen with famous people. When you don't really know who you are (and most people do not), sometimes you need to feed your ego by being associated with people who are somebody. It makes you feel good, builds you up.

So I went through life that way for some time. Eventually I left Las Vegas and went to California. Why? Because I wanted to make big money. Making good money wasn't enough. I wanted to be very wealthy. There was a gold rush going on in California. In the '70s it was called real estate, and I wanted to cash in on that second gold rush.

I moved to Los Angeles, and I entered the very fast-paced, heady world of commercial and residential income real estate brokerage. The poor boy from the little town in upstate New York who had always wanted to be somebody found himself in a very cutthroat kind of competitive world, and he wanted to make good.

I can remember my young partner and I—he was eighteen when he started with me, right out of high school

—we used to sit down, have dinner, and convince each other that we were going to become successful. We would psyche each other up. Within a year and a half we were doing very well indeed, so well that we didn't need to stay with the real estate brokerage firm we were working for. I founded my own company in Beverly Hills, Century City, and Encino in the San Fernando Valley, near Los Angeles.

We began to be more and more successful and to have movie stars and rock stars introduced to us. I invested their money for them and made them a lot of money. Back in the '70s in California anybody's granny could, and often did, become a millionaire. It wasn't that hard.

So I became very wealthy. Finally, there came a certain turning point. At the end of one year I bought a new Ferrari. I had made a lot of money that year, and my accountant—by then I had my own accountant, my own lawyers—and my accountant told me, "You need to go invest some money. You've made too much money. You need some tax shelter. Do it quickly."

I bought a nice, shiny, red Ferrari, and I had mine before Magnum PI had his, too! I remember I used to drive down Rodeo Drive in Beverly Hills, and I'd put my cowboy hat on, and I had my "shades", and I was "cool". I'd drive down the street and people's heads would turn, and they would look and they would say, "That must be somebody."

I liked that because that's what I had lived for since I had been a little boy. We have the seeds of greatness within us, but usually we don't know what that greatness is. We don't know in whom we can become great. We don't really know our identity. That's why today we have this thing called an "identity crisis". Everybody is suffering from an identity crisis. It's been written about in psychology journals, sociology books.

Priests have identity crises. They don't know who they are. They leave their vocations. Religious sisters have identity crises. They don't know if their vocation is "relevant" or not, and so they go off in search of who knows what. Married people don't know if their vocation as spouses and parents is relevant in a rapidly changing world. They race off to this, that, and the other thing in crisis, identity crisis. It's painful, and it's real. The reason for the crisis is that they don't know who they are.

I didn't know who I was. I just knew that I was called to be something special. All human beings in their heart know that. So I began to grow in wealth, in success, in notoriety; I was running with the fast-lane crowd, going to all the "in" places, parties of the movie stars, parties of the rock stars, and my morals eroded away over the years.

From the time I was about sixteen or seventeen years old I thought I knew it all. I didn't listen to my parents. I didn't listen to my grandparents. I didn't listen to the parish priest. I just went my way. Funny thing, God will let you go your way. He really will. He'll let you go your way, and then one day you will wake up and find out that it wasn't the right way, and that there's only one way — the One who is the Way.

So I went from bad to worse. I began to dine with the rich and famous, to drink with them, to party with them, and to sin with them. I remember one evening in particular. I was in the Hollywood Hills at a party in a big mansion, and an up-and-coming beautiful young actress took me aside. She said, "Come with me. I want to introduce you to my best friend."

She took me into a room in the back of the house. She opened her purse, took out a gold container, and opened it up, and inside there was a white powder. She said, "Meet my best friend, cocaine." Then I began a slide down a slippery slope that would pass through hell itself on its way to something better.

From that evening on, my life began to crumble. When you dance with death, death will have its way with you. When you enter into the works of Satan, you find out that he is a cruel master indeed. So I entered into this bondage, this bondage of sin. Our Lord said, "He who sins becomes the slave of sin." And so it was that the shackles tightened, and those chains weighed me down; and I limped through life, sick in my heart—starting out in innocence, ending in shame and misery.

My life went from bad to worse, and finally one day I found myself in a hospital, almost dead. After three years of living that way, physically bankrupt, emotionally bankrupt, spiritually dead, I was taken into a Veterans Administration hospital. There for one full year I found out something, perhaps but a dim intimation—of what it means to be separated from God. That's the definition of hell.

I began to experience a kind of living hell. God let me feel separation from all that is really meaningful: separation from goodness, separation from truth. All my friends deserted me. You know, very often you find out that those who hold themselves up as friends are not. When things go wrong, they desert you like rats off a sinking ship. So it was with most of my friends.

In the end I was left with no one. Everyone deserted me except my mother. In a very real way, my story is the story of a mother, but not just one mother. In a sense, it is the story of three mothers—like the Trinity, one God but three Divine Persons. This mother is one, and yet she manifested herself as three—first, my own mother, Veronica (her name is kind of close to Monica, and not so different in the way her life unfolded either). It's a story of my natural mother. It's a story of my holy mother, the Catholic Church. It's the story of our Blessed Mother. It's a story for mothers and of mothers—for spiritual mothers, for those who engender life in souls, for natural mothers.

So I lay in that hospital, and I suffered. I had a long time to think as the darkness closed in on me. I remember the worst day of my life—I felt totally despondent, bereft of any hope. Remember where I came from. I was a poor boy. I grew up in a very poor neighborhood, and all I wanted was to be somebody, to gain a little respect, to make my family proud of me, to be something in the world, to make my mark. I didn't start out with evil intentions. Almost never does someone start out with evil intentions. We start out good. Then, by degrees, sin holds sway.

One day, when I was in despair and wanting to die, the staff put me into a little room. They felt, perhaps, that I was suicidal, although I never attempted suicide. It was the worst day of my life. I lay there on an examination table, locked in that little room, waiting, waiting. Looking up at the ceiling, I remember crying out from the depths of my soul, "Lord, how, how could it have come to this? How could I be here?"

I wonder how many millions of people have asked that throughout history? "How could I be here in prison, in the gutter, in a hospital, in the pits? How could I be here?" At that moment the door of the room opened, and a nurse came in. She was a young woman, very beautiful, vaguely familiar. She looked at me. She smiled, a very peaceful smile. She said but one word, "Johnny". She went out, and for some reason, the scent of lilacs came into the room. I thought she was wearing perfume. I didn't think anything of it. I really didn't. My mind had drifted back to those early years, those years of innocence, those years of peace and joy; because for many years I had not had any peace or any joy or any innocence.

My whole life seemed to be, in a sense, running away from something, a running *to* something. The words of the poet Francis Thompson come back to me as I think of it:

I fled Him, down the nights and down the days;
I fled Him, down the arches of the years;
I fled Him, down the labyrinthine ways
    Of my own mind; and in the midst of tears
I hid from Him, and under running laughter.
    Up vistaed hopes, I sped;
    And shot, precipitated,
Adown Titanic glooms of chasmèd fears,
    From those strong Feet that followed, followed
    after . . .

I had been running to the siren song of the world—the seductive song of riches, prestige, power—running toward an illusion. Some call it the American Dream. I ran after it with a vengeance, and I caught up with it, only to find out that it is a nightmare. I ran to that, and I ran away from the Only One who can give us peace or joy. Eventually I was released from the hospital. Having lost everything, I ended up on the streets. It is one thing to be born poor and to live poor. It is quite another thing to be born poor, to become wealthy, and then to lose everything through your own stupidity and negligence and to find yourself in the street. That's where I ended up. I was a street person—no place to live, nothing to eat, nothing!

Most of us have not walked in the streets desolate, homeless, hungry. Let me tell you something, my dear friend. The next time you see one of those people in the streets, you'd better begin to see Jesus Christ and not run to the other side of the street. You don't know where that person, who at that moment is desperate, is headed, because God isn't finished with him yet.

He's not finished with you yet, and He wasn't finished with me yet. I wandered about hopeless and homeless. I remember I used to sit sometimes on a park bench in the affluent area of the San Fernando Valley where I had made my fortune. In an earlier time I would sit there to watch the ducks come in and out, reveling in my success. Now I was sitting on the same park bench in the depths of despair.

Eventually I received, through a friend, a letter from my mother. My mother is the only one who didn't abandon me. You mothers, I'm talking to you. You grandmothers, I'm talking to you. You know who you are. A mother never abandons her child. My mother didn't abandon me, and I received a letter in which she said, "Son, why don't you just say a Hail Mary every day? You've tried everything else." She enclosed a prayer card that had the Hail Mary on one side and a picture of Our Blessed Mother on the other. I thought to myself, "Well, I have tried everything else, why not this?"

So I began to say one Hail Mary a day. I had to read the words from the prayer card. I didn't remember how to say a Hail Mary! Now, I grew up Catholic, and I went to Catholic school, but I had been away from the Faith so long that I didn't remember even how to say a Hail Mary. At least in my day, the sisters had taught us how to say our prayers. It is not the same everywhere today, unfortunately. I have been in many places and talked to many children who have had ten and twelve years of so-called Catholic education and who don't even know how to say a Hail Mary. That's another story.

Anyway, I read from the prayer card, "Hail Mary, full of grace, the Lord is with thee . . ." Once a day. None of this religious fanaticism for me. Once a day, that's it. I did it for a while, and within a month another letter came, and my mother said, "Son, why don't you just give it up. Throw in the towel. Come home." And I did.

Grace was at work. I went home, but I was in misery. It's a rough thing to be born poor, to become rich, to become even more poor, and to go home a loser. All I wanted to do was to be somebody, and going home a loser was a bitter pill to swallow. I went home, and I remember that for a period of about a month I went into the depths of a darkness I can't even begin to express. I was so sick in my spirit.

I began to say the Rosary, a little bit at a time. I began to read the Bible then, a little bit every day. Then one night that oppressive depression, that despondency, that despair pressed down on me and about crushed the life out of me. That night I fell upon my knees. It wasn't the first time I had fallen down on my knees and prayed, but nothing had ever happened before.

Nothing *is* going to happen until you give up sin. You can pray until you are blue in the face, but until you are ready to let go of the sin, God is not going to work in your life. But I guess God knew that I really had sin beaten out of me, for, when I prayed that night, something changed. I lay down on my bed, and I cannot explain this, and I will not try. I lay down that night and fell into a deep peace. That's all I can tell you. It was a deep, penetrating, all-pervasive, beautiful peace.

I had no visions. I heard no voices. All I can tell you is that peace which surpasses all understanding bathed me in its light and its beauty. I couldn't move all night. I was absolutely immobilized. I couldn't twitch a muscle, nor did I want to. For eight hours or more I lay in my bed, arms crossed, immovable, external faculties suspended; not able to speak or move or blink an eye, just resting in a peace that really is beyond all understanding.

In the morning I was released from this peace, and I realized that my life was a disaster. I realized that my whole life had been running away from the Only One who could help me.

I slept, methinks, and woke.
And, slowly gazing . . .
    I shook the pillaring hours
And pulled my life upon me; grimed with smears,
I stand amidst the dust o' the mounded years—
My mangled youth lies dead beneath the heap.
My days have crackled and gone up in smoke.

I was in touch with reality for the first time, but the reality that transcended all reality was that I knew one thing and not from the outside in. I knew that one thing from the inside out. I knew God's name. God's name is Mercy! Though your sins be as scarlet, they can be washed whiter than snow in the Blood of the Lamb. I knew that in an intuitive and immediate way, and I cried and I cried tears of repentance and joy, for I knew the Lord God is God, indeed!

He is real and He is not an abstraction someplace in outer space. God is real, He is here, He knows you, and He has called you by name, as He called me by name in His infinite mercy and love.

That was the morning of June 24, 1984, the feast of the birth of St. John the Baptist, my patron saint. That year it happened to be the Feast of Corpus Christi as well. It was Sunday. I went to my mother, and, as nonchalantly as I could, I said to her, "Well, Mom, I think I'd like to go to confession." Now, you have to understand that this poor woman had prayed for me for twenty years! Just as nonchalantly she tried to say, "Well, all right, son. That's fine." And I said, "But I'm not going around here." After all, I'd been a big-time sinner. I was not just going to go to confession in any old place.

She said, "All right", and she took me to the Shrine of the North American Martyrs, which is not far from my home town. It's the place where SS. Isaac Jogues and René Goupil were martyred, the birthplace of Blessed Kateri Tekakwitha—holy ground! So I went there. It's about an hour from home, and we were walking on the grounds, and I was scared to death because I had to go to confession. Scared to death! I saw a priest, and the moment of truth had come. I went up to him and said, "Father, I would like to go to confession." He was in a hurry. He had to go to celebrate Mass, but he said, "Fine, there's a priest on the front porch of the office. He'll hear your confession!"

I walked in the direction he had pointed out, and, sure enough, on the porch of the kind of a log cabin that is the office of that shrine, there was an elderly priest in a rocking chair. He was saying the Rosary, and that was kind of a sign to me because now I had been saying the Rosary for a little while. It comforted me. I went up to him and said, "Father, will you please hear my confession?" He didn't know what he was getting into. He said, "Why, certainly." So, right there, at the Martyr's Shrine, I made my confession. "Bless me, Father, for I have sinned. It's almost twenty years since my last confession." Then a lifetime of sin and deception and poison poured out. Immediately after it was finished and he had raised his hand in absolution, he looked at his watch, and he said, "Amazing; it is exactly 3:00 P.M., the Hour of Mercy, the hour when Our Blessed Lord died on the Cross for you. Yet there's even more than this. I sense something powerful for the Church is happening. Something amazing. I don't know what it is." I said, "Oh, Father, I know." He said, "Tell me. What is it?" I said, "I'm called to be a priest!"

Now you have to understand, that poor man had just heard my confession and possibly had brain damage from the experience. He was an old man. He kind of swayed in his rocking chair, and he said, "Well, all things are possible with God."

So it began—a journey that had, of course, started at the first moment of my conception, when the journey of every life begins; a journey that had taken many twists and turns through many a dark and perilous valley. I was at least on the right road.

Time went by, and I found myself first in a monastery, then in a seminary, and then on my way to Europe. I was to be ordained a priest by Pope John Paul II and to receive a doctorate in Sacred Theology from one of the greatest Catholic universities in the world. You see, when God forgives, unlike us very often, He forgets. When God forgives, there aren't any boundaries or limits to what His mercy can do. When God goes to work in a life, watch out! Fasten your seat belts because you are going for a ride. It is wilder than any fiction, wilder than any *Star Wars* movie. Reality is far, far more exciting than fiction.

So it began. I remember the day of my of ordination. Sixty-two of us processed into St. Peter's Basilica. When we came to the front, we went to our places, and, as I turned my head as I was sitting down, I recognized a certain religious habit. It was Mother Teresa of Calcutta. She was about eight feet from me, right behind me. She had one of her sisters on either side of her. I believe three men of her Order were being ordained that day with us. I had Mother Teresa behind me, and I had Pope John Paul II on the altar, and at that moment I thought I was in a pretty good spot. So began the three-hour magnificent liturgy of ordination of the Roman Catholic Church.

When my time came I walked up, and I knelt down before the successor of St. Peter, Pope John Paul II. His hands came down upon my head, and I remembered. I knew where I had been. I thought: I've been through the darkness, but I know where I am now. God has brought me out into His own marvelous light. So we walk from glory to glory in that light, headed toward our destiny, which is truly to "be somebody" in Jesus Christ.

This is the answer to the identity crisis—the only answer to the painful, agonizing questions of the human heart. "Who am I? Where did I come from? Where am I going?" Your identity and mine is the Lord of Lords and the King of Kings. There isn't any authentic human identity outside of Him. Finally, I knew that, indeed, I am somebody in Jesus.

The Pope ordained me a priest, and, at the end of that beautiful ceremony, as we were processing out, ten thousand people were cheering wildly. St. Peter's Square was filled with more than one hundred thousand people, and there were three choirs singing beautifully. I call it my wedding day. You know, we priests are married, too. In Scripture Jesus is called the "bridegroom". He's the only priest, the High Priest. We are ordained into His priesthood. His spouse is the Church. My bride is the mystical, beautiful bride of Jesus Christ, the Church. I love my bride!

Just as Jesus shed His blood on the Cross that His bride might be sanctified, so any priest in his right mind must be willing to shed his very blood for the sanctification of his beloved bride, the Church.

As we processed out, filled with that joy and that peace beyond imagination, with the choirs singing and the crowds cheering, out of the corner of my eye I caught sight of a woman, a young woman, a beautiful young woman, a beautiful young woman who was vaguely familiar; and although I could not stop, she smiled at me. I saw her mouth form the word "Johnny", and as we left St. Peter's Basilica, the air was filled with the scent of lilacs!

Three mothers were there that day. My mother was there, my natural mother who had seen me in the pits of drug addiction and sin. My holy mother the Catholic Church was there that day to confer upon me the eternal priesthood of Jesus Christ. And Our Blessed Mother, our spiritual mother, I know she was there, too. I know that God's mercy has no bounds.

> "Lo, all things fly thee, for Thou fliest Me!
>   Strange, piteous futile thing,
> Wherefore should any set thee love apart?
> Seeing none but I make much of naught" (He said),
> "And human love needs human meriting:
>   How hast thou merited —
> Of all man's clotted clay the dingiest clot?
>   Alack, thou knowest not
> How little worthy of any love thou art!

Whom wilt thou find to love ignoble thee,
  Save Me, save only Me?
All which I took from thee I did but take,
  Not for thy harms,
But just that thou might'st seek it in My arms.
  All which thy child's mistake
Fancies as lost, I have stored for thee at home."

And so the Lord spoke to my heart:

"Rise, clasp My hand, and come."
  Halts by me that footfall;
  Is my gloom, after all,
Shade of His hand, outstretched caressingly?
  "Ah, fondest, blindest, weakest,
  I am He Whom thou seekest!"

When you find Him, when Jesus becomes everything in your life, darkness is dispersed. Light fills you, and there is nothing you cannot do. "I can do all things in Him who strengthens me."

So, my friend, in a day where despair is taking over many hearts, I am here to tell you that there is a God and that the Lord is God indeed. No matter how dark the darkness gets, remember this: the stars of heaven will shine all the more brightly, and you are those stars.

So, give glory to God, for His mercy endures forever. God love you!

I Found My "Catholic Answers"

Jesse Romero

I was raised in a solid, traditional, Catholic family. I went to Catholic schools, and we went to Mass every Sunday as a family. My parents were president and vice president of the Legion of Mary, San Fernando Valley chapter. My father had a conversion experience through a Cursillo retreat, and he left the life of a functional alcoholic for the life of a sober man of God. My mother was born with the gift of deep abiding faith. I saw many nights when my mother prayed rosaries and litanies for my father, who was at the local bar drinking and gambling until the late morning hours.

In my formative years I was clearly sheltered in a Catholic culture, and as a kid I thought the whole world was Catholic. As a youngster (about the age of twelve), the one event that clearly stands out in my mind is a retreat I attended. It was at Our Lady Queen of Angels Seminary in Mission Hills, California. I don't recall any of the talks or workshops, but I do clearly recall a song that was sung at the closing Mass on Sunday. The choir sang, "I am the resurrection and the life. He who believes in Me shall never die."

I was fascinated by those words the choir sang. I said to myself, in the deep recesses of my soul, "I hope those words are true, I hope those words are true." For me that was a moment of grace; those words of Jesus struck me like a lightning bolt. I kept those words in my heart.

Shortly after this retreat in my early teen years, I became addicted to the martial arts and the Chicano civil rights movement that permeated the barrios in the 1970s. These two influences almost destroyed all the Catholic Christian ethos that had been instilled in me. The crisis of faith that I experienced is but a microcosm of the typical Southern California Latino youth. I became a pragmatic atheist in my teens; I had a Catholic heart but a secular mind. Secularism grabbed hold of me, and I started to become brainwashed by the Dr. Ruths of this world, instead of laying hold of Jesus, who is Dr. Truth. Occasionally during my teen years that song, "I am the resurrection and the life", would run through my mind. But I had clearly descended from "cultural Catholicism" to "cafeteria Catholicism". Being in this condition is like stumbling along in the dark, not even aware that it is dark. I lived in this comatose spiritual condition for many years, although I still attended Mass, more out of trying to keep peace with my parents than out of conviction. My faith was not lively because I hardly knew it, and that meant my love for God was far weaker than it should have been.

I never questioned the Catholic Faith as I was growing up because I was indifferent and apathetic toward religion.

From the age of thirteen to eighteen I became a slave to the martial arts. There is no doubt that the martial arts harnessed my energy in the right direction and kept me from a life of juvenile delinquency. There were a myriad of martial arts superstars that I idolized, with Bruce Lee at the top of the list. I was awarded my black belt at the age of eighteen in Tang Soo Do Korean karate. I became a second generation Chuck Norris black belt. I began teaching karate, I worked at a supermarket, and I went to junior college. At that stage in my life I was a total worldling, thinking about God only on occasions, particularly at funerals and weddings. The things of God just didn't factor into my life.

At the age of twenty-one, I joined the Los Angeles Sheriff's Department and also married my wife, Anita. My parents were quite happy. They had always admonished me to marry somebody from my own religion and culture; they said marriage was tough, but the same faith-walk would be a strong binding agent. I started going to Mass on Sundays with my wife. She was a cultural Catholic who, albeit as uninstructed as I was, was devoted to her religion.

Being a deputy sheriff at the age of twenty-one, with all the authority vested in me by the State of California, made me a bit arrogant, prideful, and self-righteous. I became the embodiment of the deadly sins listed in chapter six of Proverbs. While I was going through the Academy, I was respected for my physical fitness and my martial arts background. I hung out with all the other "jocks" (physically fit cadets), and we would haze the less physically fit, more bookish cadets. There was one cadet in my platoon whom I liked to haze because I saw him as a "softie". I acted "macho" because I was brainwashed with worldly philosophies that told me that "might makes right" and "only the strong survive". I was also carrying a lot of Chicano power residue with such philosophies that I fully embraced, such as "I would rather die on my feet than continue living on my knees." I trained myself mentally and physically to have a fighting spirit.

Upon graduation from the Academy, the cadet whom I considered a "softie" and used to haze gave me a wrapped gift. He wished me well; he said that he had enjoyed our friendship; and then he concluded by saying, "God Bless You." I was stunned. Here was a guy who had every reason in the world to dislike me, yet he gave me a gift and he blessed me. This type of overt Christian behavior had an effect on my secular mind. It was a moment of grace. I went home, opened the gift and, lo and behold, it was a Catholic Living Bible. I asked myself, "What kind of person would do something like this after having been treated so badly?"

I put the Bible on the coffee table, and I promised myself that I would read it daily, because I was genuinely curious to read all it had to say. Well, as in the parable of the sower who scatters seed among thorns, I was one who heard the word, but then worldly anxiety and the lure of riches choked the word and it bore no fruit. My Bible remained on the coffee table for the next couple of years. It stood there lifeless, pages stuck together, spine intact.

My version of "Bible-thumping" was on Fridays, when I would dust the furniture and dust off my Bible.

The job was really changing me for the worse; I was the prime example of the macho worldly husband. At that point my priorities were my career, sport karate, and another newly discovered passion, competitive amateur boxing.

In the midst of the aggressive, competitive, secular world that I found myself in, the Lord sent me a breath of fresh air. I met another deputy sheriff, Paul Clay, at my unit of assignment, who definitely marched to a different drum beat. He had a genuine love for people, and there was a peace about him that surpassed my human understanding. I used to tell Paul that once he put on the uniform he needed to get rid of that happy-go-lucky attitude. He would just chuckle. I am sure he pitied my secular way of thinking.

We developed a very deep friendship. We would work out every day together, running and lifting weights, all the while talking about Jesus Christ. He quoted Scripture with such familiarity that I was mesmerized by the beauty of his exhortations and explanations. His behavior, his vocabulary, his family life were also consistent with his love for God. Paul would ask me questions about my Catholic Faith, but I had no answers. He would ask me if I had accepted the Lord. Where would I spend eternity if I died tonight? Was I saved? Was I born again? Did I have an assurance of my salvation? These questions seemed a little strange to me. I didn't remember such questions from my *Baltimore Catechism* days.

I started taking a spiritual inventory of my life. I came to the honest conclusion that I knew of Jesus, I had heard stories of Jesus, but I didn't know Him as the Lord of my life. I had never appropriated the faith of my childhood; I had never made a personal, sincere declaration of faith in Jesus of my own volition. Up to this point in my life there had been a lot of lip service — I fell under the condemnation of Isaiah the prophet, "These people honor me with their lips, but their hearts are far from me." Here I was, twenty-six years old, having uttered the name of Jesus a thousand times but never really having let Jesus penetrate my heart and invade my world. I came to the startling conclusion that I was spiritually bankrupt.

I was a perfectionist in everything I endeavored to do, whether it be sports, school, or career. I always wanted to be at the top of my game, and I came to realize that I was not prepared for the last four things at the end of my earthly existence: death, judgment, heaven, and hell. My conscience spoke loudly to me, Knowing Jesus is a matter of life and death. In this area I knew I was failing miserably. The words of Scripture came into my heart like a bolt of lightning: "What does it profit a man if he gains the whole world and loses his soul?" I read a tract Paul gave me that said that if you are not moving forward spiritually you are probably moving backward. The worldlings had taught me that he who dies with the most toys wins, but this tract said that he who dies with forgiveness of sins wins (which made sense).

Paul and I had been engaging in spiritual dialogue for a couple of months. He had given me many non-Catholic Christian books, tapes, and tracts for my spiritual growth.

One evening after work, as we walked to our cars, Paul asked me, "Have you ever made a personal commitment to Jesus?" He told me that I could not be saved through the faith of my parents or priest; I had to take that step of faith and invite the Lord into my heart and life personally. I answered him honestly that I had not made that personal commitment. He told me that was what was missing in my life. It made sense to me. Paul told me something I will never forget: "Most people will miss heaven by about twelve inches." I asked him, "How so?" He said the distance between the head and the heart is about twelve inches; saving faith needs to travel from the head to the heart. That analogy hit me like a ton of bricks.

As I drove home after that conversation with Paul, I realized that I had a fair amount of head knowledge about Jesus, but my heart was empty; Jesus was not seated on the throne of my interior castle. I began crying as I drove down the freeway from L.A. to San Fernando. I had let my heart become enamored by worldly things that really didn't matter in the grand scheme of life. I felt like the ultimate scoundrel, realizing that I had let go of God, my first childhood love. The name of Jesus had been a melody to my ears and a song in my heart as a child.

When I arrived home, I knelt down in my living room, and I looked at a picture of the Sacred Heart of Jesus. I felt the unspeakably warm presence of Jesus in such a powerful way that night. I remember my parents telling me that wherever the Sacred Heart of Jesus is honored, he will bless the household. I pulled out a tract that Paul had given me on the four spiritual laws, and I sincerely prayed the "Sinner's Prayer" on the back of the card. I fell prostrate, and I began singing the song that I had heard as a twelve year old, "I am the resurrection and the life. He who believes in Me shall never die."

That day Jesus Christ became *real* to me. That mystical encounter was a pivotal conversion point in my life. In an instant, the current of my life was altered, and I believed in Jesus with such force and tenacity, with such an upsurge of my whole being, with a conviction so powerful, with a certainty that leaves no sort of doubt. Since then, all the hazards of a constantly shifting world have not been able to change my remembrance of partaking in this profound revelation; that the Babe from Bethlehem became the Christ on Calvary and the Lord of the empty tomb. This conversion to the Lordship of Jesus Christ occurred in 1988. That night I felt as if I had reached back two thousand years, grabbed hold of the Cross, and let the Blood of Jesus drip down and wash me clean. The Bible immediately became to me like a love letter; it became like a window out of this prison world through which I could look at eternity.

I listened to all the tapes and read all the books and pamphlets that Paul had given me. I began reading large sections of the Bible daily. I listened to all the radio preachers he recommended, especially the "Bible Answer Man" radio program. I started attending non-Catholic Christian events and services on my own, because I wanted to find out the truth, the whole truth, and nothing but the truth about the Lord. I promised Him I would follow Him wherever He led me. Through my friendship with Paul I found out that he was a fallen-away Catholic who identified himself as a non-denominational (fundamentalist) Christian. I really looked up to him, and, so far as I was concerned, he was honest and sincere. He seemed very sure of himself when he shared his faith with me, and I took it all in. I wasn't anchored very well to the Catholic Faith, just as many of my co-religionists are not. Needless to say, I saturated myself in the world of evangelical fundamentalism.

Every waking moment I was listening to a different radio preacher and following along with my Bible. I heard significant amounts of anti-Catholic bias, and I began to believe it because I had never heard a Catholic answer to refute those charges in a homily or through all my years of Catholic school. After a good solid year of this indoctrination, I was convinced that the Catholic religion was "unbiblical".

I gave my testimony at a small fundamentalist church that Paul attended. My wife knew of all that was going on in my life spiritually, and she knew that my Catholicism was hanging by a thread. I was confused by what I read and heard because some preachers said that the Catholic Church is a cult while others said that it is Christian but has some problems. The Christian truths I was taught through fundamentalism were the Trinity, the deity of Christ, the Virgin Birth, the bodily Resurrection, the blood atonement, and the inerrancy of Scripture. I shared this with my parents one day, and they were surprised that I thought this was novel. My parents told me that those six fundamental truths are historic Catholic truths.

My wife knew that I was undergoing a spiritual odyssey, and she was pleased and worried at the same time. She was culturally Catholic, and she was content. She knew that I was church-shopping and sitting in on other church services. She sat down with me one day and told me that she liked the positive changes that she saw in me, but she wasn't sure she was going to like the ending. I quickly pointed out to her, with my newly acquired biblical repertoire, "Honey, the Bible says, 'Wives, submit yourselves to your husbands.' " The arrogant manner in which I said this quickly ended that conversation. Of course I hadn't read the entire passage, which also says, "Husbands, love your wives just as Christ loves the Church."

We talked the next day when we were calm, and my wife affirmed the good qualities that she saw starting to show in me. However, she added that if I left the Catholic Church this would disrupt our marriage, because she was not going to leave the Church. I then let the cat out of the bag, and I told her that, based on all the reading I had done, the tapes I had listened to, and the radio preachers who were teaching me "biblical" truth, the Catholic Church taught error.

My wife challenged me down to my toes. She said, "Before you run off to some other church or, worse yet, start your own, why don't you study Catholicism from Catholic sources? You have had your nose studiously in non-Catholic Christian literature for the past year and a half. If you can prove to yourself that Catholicism is wrong from Catholic sources, then I will respect you if you still want to leave, but give it a chance." Being a deputy sheriff, I saw great validity to her argument. Hearsay testimony is inadmissable in a court of law, and all of my anti-Catholic biases were hearsay.

I accepted my wife's challenge, especially since I saw the

prospect of her leaving the Catholic Church with me if I proved its errors to her and myself from Catholic source documents. I told her very confidently, "Honey, this is going to be easy because there are no Catholic answers to my objections." I went on to assure my wife that Catholicism is an aberration of the true Gospel.

My wife told my parents that I was shopping around at non-Catholic churches and that I was on the verge of leaving the Catholic Faith entirely. My parents spoke to me, and they affirmed that they were proud that I had experienced a conversion to the Lordship of Jesus Christ. They understood my feelings (unbeknownst to me they had become involved in the Catholic charismatic renewal). My parents had always been authentic, devoted Catholics, but now they were reading Scripture daily and were heavily involved in Catholic evangelization. They invited me to the "Encuentro Latino" in 1988, and they told me that I would meet other Catholics who love the Scriptures, have a relationship with Jesus Christ, believe in evangelization, and are faithful to the Church. I attended, along with my wife.

The L.A. Sports Arena was packed: twenty thousand or more Catholics, clergy and lay people, praised the Lord in song. We heard powerful, Christ-centered, conversion testimonies and dynamic, biblically-based, evangelistic preaching. We took part in Eucharistic adoration, biblically-based skits, and reverent liturgies. At one point a priest had all twenty thousand of us get on our knees while the Eucharistic Lord was exposed in the monstrance, and he led us in a prayer to dedicate or rededicate our lives to Jesus Christ. That was a moment of grace for me. I felt at home, even though I still had questions about Catholicism. I was overcome by the emotional experience. I felt that this brand of Catholicism was something I could relate to, so I put all my questions on hold for a while as I enjoyed this "honeymoon" with the Lord.

My wife also experienced a great spiritual awakening that weekend, and we became involved with the Catholic charismatic renewal.

We attended conferences, workshops, Life in the Spirit seminars, healing Masses, praise gatherings, prayer meetings, and evangelization retreats. We were totally committed as a couple. We went to Marriage Encounter, and the Lord blessed us with our first child. We named him Paul, after my favorite apostle and after the friend who had converted me to the Lordship of Jesus Christ.

Soon, though, the honeymoon phase of my conversion started to wear out, and I wanted answers to some of my questions about Catholicism. I wanted to know what I believed and why I believed it and whether Catholicism could be reconciled with the Bible. My parents referred me to our parish priest, Father David. At that point I had a Catholic heart but Protestant theology and vocabulary. I met with Father David, we chatted, and he said that I had a lot of good questions. Unfortunately, it would take him several weeks to answer my questions one-by-one, due to time constraints. He told me he was going to surprise me with something better; he would send me to a Catholic Answers conference entitled "Go Forth and Teach". This conference was to be held at the Long Beach Marriott Hotel. I said, "Catholic *who*?" He told me that Catholic Answers is a lay apostolate of Catholic apologists who were experts at answering Protestant objections and misunderstandings.

I attended this conference in March 1990, with two other parishioners, George and Danny (who has gone to be with the Lord). Father David specifically told me to ask all the tough questions I had and thoroughly to pick the speakers' brains. The seminar was three days long, but it seemed like twenty minutes. Up to this point in my Catholic experience I hadn't heard of any of those speakers. (How could I if they weren't on Evangelical radio stations!)

The cadre of speakers was the following: the late Bishop Carl Fisher, Karl Keating, Patrick Madrid, Mark Brumley, Scott Hahn, Gerry Matatics, Steve Wood, Thomas Howard, Deal Hudson, and Fr. Mitch Pacwa. That weekend was like spiritual boot camp, thirty hours of power evangelization and high-octane apologetics. All my Protestant residue came crumbling down like a house of cards. All of my objections, questions, doubts, and insecurities received compelling, cogent, biblical, and historical Catholic answers. That was a moment of grace for me, to be in a conference full of scholars of this magnitude for thirty hours. The Catholic Faith came to life for me — right from the pages of my NIV Protestant Bible!

I asked myself, why wasn't I taught this before? Why didn't I know this? Why wasn't I given good Catholic apologetics in all of my years of Catholic school? I thought about the thousands of Catholics who have left the true Church of Christ for denominational Christianity (like my friend Paul), who never knew what they left, who were never given good biblical *Catholic answers* to their questions. Watered down Catholicism doesn't attract, but unadulterated Catholicism is like a divine magnet. It is addictive.

Attending the conference that weekend was like injecting myself with spiritual steroids. It overhauled my Catholic education *big time*. I was literally "Surprised by Truth". I took out my credit card and loaded up on books and tapes. I started to subscribe to *This Rock* magazine when it was just a newsletter. I got hooked on Dr. Scott Hahn's Bible tape ministry (I became a Hahn-aholic). I felt truly born again after this conference, no more confusion, no more searching. I found the Church built on the *Rock*, the One, Holy, Catholic, and Apostolic Church. That day the Lord put a song in my heart: "Glory, Alleluia, you're the reason why I sing, Glory, Alleluia, for all eternity you're the reason why I sing."

I went home, burst through the front door, and embraced my wife. I cried and repented for having tried to take her out of the Catholic Church. I repented for having slandered and spoken falsely about the true Church of Jesus Christ. We wept in each other's arms. We truly became a Catholic Christian couple on that day. We were now submitted to the Lordship of Jesus Christ and obedient to the Church; we loved the Scriptures and were committed to evangelism. I made a vow to my wife and to the Lord that I would serve the Catholic Church for the rest of my life with the same fighting spirit that had catapulted me to the status of USA national kickboxing champion and three-time World Police Olympic middleweight boxing champion.

As Pope John Paul II says, "It is not enough to discover Christ; we must bring him to others."

We are not in this world to witness for Christ, *we are in Christ to witness to this world.* Jesus left heaven and lived in time that we might leave time and live in eternity. Dear friend, when we stand before the judgment seat of Christ, will we stand empty-handed or with the record of many souls won for Christ? Evangelization is a matter of life and death. If the Holy Spirit has enlightened you with the truth of Jesus Christ and the truth of His Church, you are expected to share these pearls of great price freely with a lost and dying world.

An informed Catholic is a contagious Catholic. I have a dream that one day a worldwide battalion of Catholic Christians will start following the Lord's marching orders and get busy with the primary reason for living: *to win souls for Christ.* Catholics were the original evangelists and the best evangelists throughout the centuries. I am committed to this vision and to leading the charge.

It is my prayer, dear friend, that after you read my story you will give Jesus all the glory. I also pray that you become moved to the depths of your soul and dedicate or rededicate your life to Jesus. We are just a heartbeat from eternity. Today is the day of salvation. Get right with Jesus: run to confession, clean that soul, and then run to Jesus in the most Holy Eucharist. This is soul food, this is the medicine of immortality. Get on your knees before a crucifix (perhaps the one on your Rosary), and promise, not under the pain of sin but simply on your word of honor, the following: "Dear Jesus, my crucified Lord and Savior,

I promise that I shall heed Your invitation to seek and to win for You the precious souls for whom You died on Calvary's cross. I shall try earnestly and zealously to win souls for You through a life of virtue and holiness, by setting an example of charity toward all men, and by sharing with people the truth of the Catholic Faith. I shall do my utmost to win at least one soul for You, dear Jesus, every year of my life, so help me God."

Then, kiss the crucifix and seal your promise with the sign of the Cross, saying slowly, deliberately, "In the name of the Father, and of the Son, and of the Holy Spirit, Amen."

There is a world to be won for Jesus. It is time that those who bear the name of Catholic Christian get on with the task. Here ends the reading of my story; now is the time for living it.

Welcome Home

Victor Claveau

My story begins in 1974, but it may be helpful if I relate a bit of my background and early years in order to make clear what brought me into Roman Catholic apologetics.

The youngest of three sons, I was born to Joseph and Corinne Claveau in St. Peter's hospital in Lowell, Massachusetts, on June 21, 1942. My father emigrated from Canada and made his living working as a plumber, while my mother worked in one of the numerous textile mills in the Lowell area.

We lived in one of the many tenements on Chapel Street, a poor multi-ethnic neighborhood. We could not afford the luxury of an automobile, so it was important to live close to church and school. I have a vivid recollection of what seemed to be long walks to church on Sunday mornings, with the family dressed in our best clothes and in shined shoes. In actuality, it was only a few blocks to the church, but since my legs were short it seemed like miles.

I passed my first three years in school at St. Peter's

Catholic school. My best friends were the sons of immigrants from Portugal and Russia. It was a good time in my life. All the families in the neighborhood were on the same economic level, and this made for strong bonds of friendship. Everything was going along just fine until my father decided to put a hot-water tank and shower in our apartment. No longer would we have to bathe in a tub in the middle of the kitchen floor. Unfortunately, everyone in the neighborhood began talking about our luxury. The landlord found out and doubled our rent. By this time my father had started his own plumbing company and was beginning to do better financially. Rather than pay the increased rent, he decided that we could afford to move to a better part of town. That was the last I saw of my friends.

My father was a hardworking man whose responsibilities as a husband and father weighed heavily. In spite of a lot of effort on his part, his business failed in 1955, and, like so many others before us, we migrated to California in search of a new start in life.

My parents were what I would consider good Catholics, typical of that time and place. As a family, we never missed Mass on Sunday. We watched Bishop Fulton J. Sheen on television, prayed a weekly Rosary, and ate fish on Fridays. Whenever there was a family difficulty, you would find my mother at church praying a novena to St. Jude. She spent many hours on her knees in prayer while trying to raise her three sons. My parents made certain that each of their sons received the sacraments of the Church. According to church records, my baptism took place on the day I was born. Although I have an old photograph showing me dressed in a white suit with short pants on the day of my First Holy Communion, I have no recollection of the event. My confirmation took place in St. Peter's Church when I was twelve years old; again I don't remember the experience. In fact, I cannot remember being taught anything about the Church's teachings except by the example of my mother's living a prayerful life. Unfortunately, neither parent shared the Faith with me or spoke about the importance of living a holy life in submission to God. I did not find out until after his death that my father prayed on his knees each night. I regret that he never shared this side of his spirituality.

I was never really a rebellious kid at home, but I did my share of misdeeds. Right from wrong was not really taught in my father's house, and the subject of sex was absolutely taboo. I remember one incident that took place just after I entered high school. I was taking a class in animal husbandry. I asked my mother a question about artificial insemination; she was so embarrassed by the subject that she could not look me in the eye for quite some time. It was as if we were supposed to know how to live a moral life by osmosis, rather than direct instruction. As a result, I got involved with some friends who considered that a thing was right if we could get away with it and if no one got hurt. Fortunately, this stage of my life did not last long, and I didn't wind up in serious trouble.

My mother passed away when I was sixteen years old. She went into the hospital for surgery to remove a tumor on an adrenal gland and hemorrhaged the following day. Since this was on a weekend and the doctors were away, there was no one available to help her, and she bled to death. Her death was totally unexpected, and our family was devastated. There was so much left unsaid. I didn't understand why God took her home, and I was in a sort of daze for weeks. There was no bitterness, only confusion and emptiness. With my mother's death the possibility of proper religious guidance ended.

After I graduated from high school, I began attending the local junior college. I overloaded myself with classes and soon found I couldn't keep up. Rather than fail any class, I just dropped out. I had enlisted in the U.S. Navy Reserve while still in high school, and I had a two-year active duty obligation. I requested active duty and was assigned to Midway Island in the middle of the Pacific Ocean.

Since my religious roots were shallow, it did not take very long for me to drift away from the Church. I stopped going to Mass and confession. The chaplain on Midway was a heavy drinker and didn't set much of an example; this was just the excuse I needed to drift away from the Church. In retrospect, if it hadn't been the priest, it would have been something else. My dog tags proclaimed that I was a Catholic, but my life was devoid of any prayer or Catholic activity. During the next few years, however, I occasionally went to Mass, looking for something to fill the emptiness inside me.

After my two-year Navy obligation was completed, I returned home and managed to get a job as a bank teller. The only part of the job I liked was meeting people.

One of the banking customers offered me a job working in his Italian restaurant. It was hard but enjoyable work. It was there that I met my wife, Janet, in March 1963.

Her mother worked as the head waitress, and one day Jan came by to visit. We dated for a very short time, and we were married in a civil ceremony the following July.

Although Jan had also been baptized Catholic, she had been raised in somewhat of an anti-Catholic environment and had little knowledge of the Church's teachings. When our daughter, Michelle, was born a year later, Jan agreed to have her baptized as a Catholic.

During our third year of marriage, we began attending a fundamentalist church. I was not comfortable going to a church that didn't have a liturgy, but we felt we needed something. This church was typical of so many small fundamentalist churches. The pastor was young, enthusiastic, and basically ignorant of anything other than the New Testament. He simply taught his personal interpretations of Sacred Scripture. I had the feeling that we didn't belong there, but we didn't know where else to go. All this came to an end during an evening service, when the pastor asked the congregation for a few personal testimonies. People stood and related how the Lord had changed their lives. It was all very moving until a young, mentally retarded man stood and proclaimed his love for Jesus. The pastor looked at him and said, "Will you sit down!" I was shocked and saddened for the young man. I had been touched by his simple declaration of faith and was upset about the pastor's retort. It seemed to me that the young man was closer to the Lord than was the pastor. Jan and I left that church, never to return.

In 1969, my Catholic roots began to show. We had our marriage blessed in the Church and had our sons, Chad and Victor, Jr., baptized. The ceremonies were simple but eloquent. Shortly thereafter, I decided that the Church deserved another chance. We began attending an adult education class, taught by the same priest who had blessed our marriage. During the instruction, he brought up the subject of the "limbo of Infants". He explained that limbo was a state of existence after death for infants who had not been baptized and whose souls would never see God face-to-face. I could not believe that the loving Lord Jesus would relegate innocent souls to an infinite existence without him because of the neglect of their parents. At the time, I didn't know that this was simply a theory put forth by St. Augustine. We were told that this was Catholic dogma and that if we didn't believe it we couldn't be Catholic. I left the class a bit bewildered.

The first five years of our marriage were financially difficult.

I worked at the restaurant until it was sold, and then I ended up in an aircraft factory, pushing rivets into Boeing 707s. After I mastered my job, it became routine. I began to believe that if I stayed there I would be stuck without a future. While visiting my brother one day, I shared my frustrations with him and one of his neighbors. The neighbor turned out to be a Navy recruiter. He offered me a career in electronics. It seemed reasonable that, if I re-enlisted for a few years, I could get a solid education in a growing field and would finally have a worthwhile career. At first, Jan was against the idea. At the time, the war in Vietnam was hot and heavy. After a few months of my trying to convince her that my re-enlistment would be good for us, she agreed. A week later we were on our way to the Navy's Aviation Fire Control School in Millington,

Tennessee. After completion of school, I was transferred to a squadron at the Naval Air Station in Miramar, California. We knew that my squadron would shortly have to leave for Vietnam, so we found a house in Riverside, California. It was important that Jan and the kids be near our families for support.

It wasn't until 1974 that things began to change. I had reached a period of my life when I was beginning to recognize that I wasn't God. At the time, I didn't really understand what was going on, but looking back, I realize that for many Catholics this is a normal pattern. I had a wife I adored, three wonderful children, a satisfying career, and good friends. What else could a person want? Yet there was emptiness in my soul. Now in my early thirties, I began to realize that my life was not complete.

Jan and I had been married for about eleven years when a work associate, Ray Cote, experienced a Marriage Encounter weekend with his wife, Judy. Ray bugged me for almost nine months until I agreed to talk to Jan about going on a Marriage Encounter. I didn't really want to go, and I was certain that Jan would not want to attend when she found out that it was a Catholic experience. To my surprise, Jan did agree to go. Our Marriage Encounter weekend was held at the Mission in Santa Barbara, California. We were fortunate to have an especially wonderful priest, named Fr. Paddy Colloran. Shortly after our return from the weekend, Jan announced that she wanted to become a Roman Catholic. I was overjoyed when she began instructions with our Navy chaplain, Fr. James Boyd. Father Jim is a wonderful pastoral priest, and he spent many hours instructing Jan on the tenets of the Faith. She received the Holy Eucharist for the first time during a Mass celebrated by Fr. Jim in our home in the company of our new Catholic friends. A few months later, Timothy Cardinal Manning confirmed Jan.

Jan developed a hunger for learning that has not ceased. It is a rare day that passes when she does not spend time in the study of God's Holy Word and the teachings of His Church or in the instruction of others. She has been an inspiration to me and to many others.

Jan's conversion was the impetus I needed to return to the Church. For me, returning to the fold simply meant making a sincere confession of my sins to a priest. Through the Marriage Encounter community, we met many wonderful people, and, early on, I sought out a priest to hear my confession. I remember being extremely nervous as I began my confession. It had been many years since I had searched for a priest to cleanse my soul. When I completed my confession, I embraced the priest, and tears of relief ran down my cheeks; a heavy burden had been lifted. My confessor simply said, "Welcome home."

Jan and I began attending the base chapel each Sunday. It didn't take long for us to be absorbed into the Catholic community. After Mass, it was the custom for a number of us from the Catholic community to go to the naval base galley for brunch and conversation. One Sunday, I shared with a good friend, Sid Durham, that I felt something was missing in my life, but I just couldn't put my finger on it. Even though I had returned to the Church and was seeking to rediscover my Christian faith, there was still emptiness within. I had begun to be open to God, though I did not as yet have true faith. I tried to believe with my reason, without praying, or by praying very little.

Sid suggested that I attend a Cursillo weekend, which he described as a mini-course in Catholicism. I trusted him, so I agreed to attend. The only problem was that there was an eighteen-month waiting list. Sid said that he could put my name on a standby list, and, if the Holy Spirit wanted me to go, He would make it happen. The following Thursday morning Sid telephoned and said that there was an opening for the upcoming weekend. The Cursillo experience is a three-day process, beginning on Thursday evening and continuing until Sunday afternoon. I arranged for the time off from my work and I was on my way, not knowing what to expect.

I had been brought up to be self-reliant and independent. My grandfather abandoned my father and his older brother on a railroad station platform in Canada when they were three and six years old, respectively. Their mother placed the boys in an orphanage because she could not afford to care for them. After three years, my father's brother was taken home from the orphanage; my father was left behind. At age twelve, he ran away, and he had been on his own ever since. Because of these early experiences of abandonment, he became self-reliant, and he raised me to be the same. He taught me that if I were to get anywhere in life it would be by my own initiative and that I could not depend on anyone else. It was imperative that I always be in control. It was drilled into me that I alone was responsible for my family's welfare.

Ten years of military life had added to my belief that I was self-sufficient. I felt that the only person I could truly trust and depend on was Jan.

I was always trying to prove myself to my father and the world. At that time, I was serving as a Navy recruiter and earning numerous awards for outstanding achievement. My peers would telephone me regularly to find out how I accomplished my recruiting goals. I had to keep up the pace to meet or to exceed previous accomplishments. I needed praise as much as I needed breath, and I was driven to succeed because I was so afraid of failure. It was as though I were on a treadmill going too fast to get off. I felt alone, and I didn't understand how God could help. Then came my Cursillo experience.

During a Cursillo weekend, there are thirteen presentations, nine given by laymen on various topics and four given by a priest or a deacon on the sacraments. Men attend the first weekend and women the next. My Cursillo weekend turned out to be the most extraordinary and significant experience of my life.

During one of the presentations on the sacraments, a newborn baby was baptized. Father explained the sacrament in such a way that we were in awe of this new infant saint, cradled in his mother's arms. Before us was a pure soul in perfect unity with God. It was almost comical as we lined up hesitantly to touch the baby. Many, including myself, understood the sacrament in an entirely new perspective, realizing for the first time that we were in the presence of holiness.

As a child, I had been raised to hold clergy and other religious in the highest regard because they are called by

God to be holy people, to live consecrated lives. I did not realize at the time that God calls each one of us to holiness. The Cursillo opened my eyes.

The philosopher Nietzsche said: "I will believe in their Savior when men act as if they have been saved." For the first time in my life I was confronted with men who truly believed and loved the Lord Jesus and His Church, who were not afraid to express their feelings about what His gift of salvation meant in their lives. I desperately wanted what these men had, yet everything in my life prevented me from self-surrender to Christ. I had to maintain control. The Cursillo team shared what being a Christian was really all about. I was struck by the fact that these were men in the full sense of the word, yet they were in submission. It seemed like such a contradiction. Little by little their words began to seep into my consciousness. I felt that Christ was waiting for me with His arms outstretched, calling my name, desiring to envelop me in His love. But still I resisted. By Saturday evening I was in complete turmoil. God was calling, and I was holding back with all my being. I had no understanding of the love God holds for us or the depth of His compassion. I could not and would not surrender. Surrender is not a means but an end, and my refusal came from a lack of humility.

After the last presentation on Saturday, we were sent off to bed. It had been an exhausting day. I couldn't sleep, so I went to the chapel and sat in the back on a small bench, thinking about what I had experienced in the past two days. After a few minutes, the Cursillo team came in and gathered around the altar to pray. I was in the darkness, and no one knew that I was there. As I listened to their prayers, I realized that they were praying for me and all the men the Holy Spirit had brought together on that weekend. After ten minutes or so, the team left the chapel — all but one. He stayed behind to pray the Rosary on his knees, with his arms outstretched, before the Blessed Sacrament.

As I listened to his prayers, I realized the cultural difference between us. He was a Mexican-American, with tattoos on his hands and arms. If I had met him on the street, I would have probably assumed that he was a gang member, and I would have avoided him. Yet here he was, praying for the others and me. When he completed the Rosary he began making the Stations of the Cross, while remaining on his knees. At each station he spoke to Jesus as though he knew Him personally, pouring out his heart and his love. I wanted so much to have the same relationship with Christ, but everything in my being held me back. I was afraid that, if I surrendered to Him, I would somehow lose my identity. I sat listening, not daring to breathe, overwhelmed by the exhibition of piety before me. Little by little, this man's example began to penetrate my heart. It is no exaggeration to say that I was actually frightened. My heart was pounding as I too got down on my knees before the Lord. I began to pray that He would be with me. Finally, I somehow found the courage to prostrate myself before Him and totally surrender my life. As I lay on the floor, all the fear and anxiety drained from me, and I felt a peace that was absolute. Mere words cannot begin to describe the overwhelming sense of melting into the love of Christ. I lay there for a long time, not wanting to move, lest I shatter the moment. Once I became completely detached from myself, a torrent of grace sprang up in my heart, and inexpressible joy and peace were given to me. Without the cross there can be no salvation. I understood what is meant by "the peace of God that passes all understanding" (Phil 4:7). An interior transformation had taken place. This experience marked the beginning of my conversion. Sometime later, I returned to bed, renewed in spirit, with joy flooding my soul.

I never knew the name of the man who helped me by his example, but I will always be indebted to him, and I have remembered him in prayer. That evening marked for me a new beginning, a new life in Christ.

On Sunday afternoon, as the Cursillo was coming to an end, Don, a guy who had played center for the Oakland Raiders football team, came over, grabbed me under my arms, and picked me up as though I were a little child. He said, "I've been watching you all weekend, and I want you to know that I think you're beautiful, and I love you." A few days before, I probably would have punched him in the mouth for saying something like that, even if he was a giant of a man. Now I knew what he meant. For the first time in my life I really felt lovable and worthwhile. I knew that God unequivocally loved me. His love for me was not predicated on my accomplishments. There was a sense of peace and at the same time an exhilaration that I never realized was possible. Don became a good brother in Christ, and I'll never forget him.

Everything changed, and nothing changed. I was still winning awards for my work, but now I had a sense of freedom. I now had a sense of confidence, joy, and peace in my life. The burdens were still there, but now they seemed so much lighter. Someone was sharing the load. He had always been there offering to help, but my pride had been in the way. Now, I truly felt as if I had received a new life.

Jan and I met some wonderful people through the Marriage Encounter community, and she began a weekly Bible study with two friends, one Catholic and one Protestant. They started a couples fellowship group. I'll never forget the first night we met. We men felt uncomfortable and out of place, reluctant to open up. It didn't take long for that small group to grow to about thirty people. Some were single, some married, some Catholic, and some Protestant. Doctrines were not discussed, partly because we did not want to jeopardize friendships, but mostly because none of us really knew how to explain or defend what we believed. We came together as friends in Christ. We laughed together, prayed together, and shared our lives, our hurts, and our joys. We met every Friday evening for three years before we were transferred to our next duty station. We both look back on that time as one of the happiest in our lives. True Christian fellowship is sometimes difficult to find.

I became an extraordinary minister of the Eucharist and was trained to hold Communion services on Father Boyd's day off. Daily Mass was conducted in a small Eucharistic chapel, and I was given the key. With that key, I was able to visit the Blessed Sacrament at any time. What an extraordinary privilege! There were times when I would wake during the middle of the night, dress, and drive to the chapel. Sometimes I talked to Jesus and shared my troubles, hopes, and dreams. Sometimes I just sat, listened, and basked in His presence. It was on one of these occasions when I began to think seriously about my relationship with my father.

Since my mother's death, my father and I had drifted apart. I had always felt as if I was somewhat of a disappointment to him. Of his three sons, I was the only one who hadn't followed in his footsteps and made plumbing my profession. His dream was to have Claveau & Sons Plumbing Company, a dream that went unrealized when I decided to make the Navy my career. Over the years we had become more and more estranged. Each time I visited him he let me know that I just hadn't measured up to his expectations. There was no money in a Navy career, and money meant security to my father. After he ran away from the orphanage as a child, he spent many years struggling for food and shelter. I know now that he just wanted me to be financially successful so that I would never have to go through what he did. But at the time I simply saw his concerns as criticism. The more he criticized, the longer I stayed away.

Now it was time to make things right between us. I made the two-hour drive to see him, determined that I would not argue with him and that I would tell him that I loved him. As usual, as we sat at his kitchen table, he criticized. I just sat there and listened, determined not to argue. When I left, I embraced him and told him that I loved him. He became flustered and just said, "Yah!" A month later, I visited him again, and we went through a similar scene; again I expressed my love, and again he became flustered. It was difficult for him to show any real affection. I was determined that we would completely reconcile, so, about a month later, I again drove to see him. This time our meeting was really different. We actually talked and listened to each other. He asked me about my family and my work. When I left, he followed me to my car. As we stood by the curb, I embraced him and again said, "I love you, Dad." This time he hugged me back and said, "I love you too, Son."

A few days later, the ringing of the telephone by my bedside awakened me at two o'clock in the morning. My father had died of a heart attack an hour before.

As I laid my father to rest, there was deep sadness but not the feeling of self-recrimination that comes with things left unsaid. We had shared all that was necessary by that curbside. I buried my father with peace in my heart, full of gratitude to God.

Jan and I continued to be involved in church activities wherever we went. We taught religious education classes. I served as an extraordinary minister of the Eucharist, usher, fund-raiser. In short, we served our parish community in any way we could. There were times when we had spiritual highs and there were low times when our faith was not the primary focus of our lives. After a while we settled into a routine as somewhat typical Catholics. We never missed Mass but also did not really champion or grow in the Faith.

My retirement from the Navy came in January 1986. During the last four years in the service I had served as an organizational management consultant, and, in addition, I went to school full time. I managed to complete my bachelor's degree and two master's degrees in preparation for my retirement. I fully enjoyed my work and expected to continue in that profession upon retirement. As the time grew near to our separation from the Navy, Jan and I began to discuss where we would finally settle down. After so many transfers that had meant sacrificing family relationships, Jan and I wanted to live in an area close to family. Eventually, we moved to the high desert of California to be close to her sister Margie.

Unfortunately, there was no possibility of employment as a management consultant in the area, so I took a position as a sales manager for an international company. The position paid well, and we began to enjoy the fruits of a good income. We had a new home built, and we became active in our local parish.

My responsibilities in my new position included hiring and training a sales staff. As part of this staff, I had hired two Protestant ministers and a Mormon. Once we became familiar with each other, the employer/employee relationship was set aside, and we became friends. As a result, these men occasionally brought up questions about Catholicism, questions that I could not answer. I felt very uncomfortable and tried to avoid these sessions by saying that as long as we believed in Jesus, that was all that really mattered. I soon had to face the fact that I was an ineffective witness for the Catholic Faith.

Jan was experiencing similar problems. She had come into contact with a Jehovah's Witness and a fundamentalist. They began to ask questions about Catholicism. Our son Chad began to attend a youth-oriented fundamentalist church. These occurrences demonstrated that we did not know how to defend or even properly explain the Faith.

The final straw came when one of my sales representatives came to me and boasted that he had enticed the daughter of a friend of ours into leaving the Catholic Church and joining his denomination. He proclaimed the fact as though he had just scored a point for his side. I became quite angry and told him that she was the last Catholic he would ever get, as long as I had anything to do with it. Jan and I discussed the matter and decided to put out the necessary effort to learn our Faith well enough to champion it to others. But where and how to begin?

The most obvious place was our pastor. He was a wonderful man, nearing retirement. He explained that he had neither the time nor the knowledge of apologetics to help us. I went to the diocesan offices, where I was shown into a little cubbyhole that was described as a library—no help there. Next, I began to make the rounds of the "Christian" stores. I remember going into a Berean bookstore about thirty-five miles from my home. When I asked for books about Catholicism, the manager led me into a back room, opened a cabinet, and showed me their books on Catholicism. The cabinet was full of anti-Catholic material. They would not display these materials on their open shelves for fear of offending their Catholic customers. We had a few words, and I departed, never to return. Even the Catholic stores left much to be desired. There we found books that dealt with spirituality but not fundamental theology. We were beginning to feel frustrated, but then friends told us about an organization that lectured on Catholic apologetics. Our friends promised to find out about it and let us know.

The organization turned out to be Catholic Answers,

based in San Diego. As it happened, representatives from this organization were scheduled to speak for two evenings at a church about fifty miles from our home. Jan and I enthusiastically listened as Karl Keating and Pat Madrid explained ways in which Protestant claims could be easily refuted. Upon the conclusion of the presentations I sought out Karl and told him that I wanted to do what he was doing. I was so exhilarated that, to this day, I can't help wondering if Karl didn't think I was a bit strange. Nevertheless, two days later he telephoned and suggested some reading materials. A few of the books he recommended were *Catholic and Christian*, by Alan Schreck; *Theology for Beginners*, by Frank Sheed; *Fundamentals of Catholic Dogma*, by Ludwig Ott; and Karl's own book *Catholicism and Fundamentalism*. Jan and I began an intense preparation, many times interrupting each other's study to relate some exciting bit of new information. Little by little we began to grow in our faith and in our knowledge of the Church's teachings. I had been lecturing and teaching for most of my adult career, and now it was time to put those skills to work in the service of the Church. Karl Keating suggested that I work up a lecture on the teachings of the Watchtower Society. While reading the section about Jehovah's Witnesses in Walter Martin's *The Kingdom of the Cults*, I realized that the author was an outsider looking in. I have always been critical of people who rail against Catholicism without going to the source of Catholic beliefs. So I promptly put Walter Martin's book aside and called a friend who had been with the Jehovah's Witnesses for most of his adult life. I explained that I was interested in studying the teachings of the Watchtower Society and needed his help. Within a few days I was inundated with Jehovah's Witness materials. I began my research by doing a comparative analysis of the Watchtower's teachings and the teachings of the Church.

A priest at a local retreat house allowed me to advertise my lecture and use his facilities. We filled the small chapel, and, even though the lecture lasted more than two hours, nobody left. The question-and-answer session went on for another hour. I was asked to repeat the lecture and did so two weeks later. The response of the people who attended spurred me on to do more. The most heartening comment came from a young woman who said that, although she probably could not and would not remember all that she had heard, she knew in her heart that the teachings of the Catholic Church were true, and no one would ever convince her otherwise. I began lecturing whenever I could wrest an invitation.

Jan and I invested a few dollars and opened trade accounts with a number of Catholic publishing companies. Little by little, we convinced parish priests to let us set up book fairs in their parishes. The response we received from the laity was overwhelming.

I remember one church in particular. A dear friend, Fr. Henry Johnston of St. Patrick's Church in Angels Camp, California, invited me to lecture. He is the pastor of three churches about fifteen miles apart. Angels Camp is a small community, yet over one hundred people attended the two evening workshops. We had brought a truckload of good books to offer for sale. After each presentation I recommended some of the same books that Karl Keating had recommended to me. Jan described the sales as a feeding frenzy. It was the same almost everywhere we went. Catholics cannot seem to get enough good material that is faithful to the magisterial authority of the Church. Catechesis in our Church has been in such a poor state for so long that many people hunger for the purity of the Church's authentic teaching. Seeing the need, Father Henry opened a parish bookstore to serve his parishioners.

When I began to take books to churches, I did so in a Chevrolet Sprint. At first, I just loaded the books in the back of the car. After a while, I had to take out the passenger's seat to accommodate all the books. People used to shake their heads, laugh, and stare as I drove the Sprint down the freeway, about six inches off the pavement and crammed full to the roof with boxes of books. After about a year and a half, we broke down and bought a small pickup truck with a camper shell. By 1990, we were going out an average of twice a month.

In September of that year, I went to a sales manager's meeting in Las Vegas. I happened to tell the company vice president what Jan and I had been doing. To my surprise, he told me that I had signed an exclusive contract and that I would have to stop this "moonlighting". I had never considered lecturing or taking books to churches on the weekends as moonlighting. We weren't trying to make a profit. The money we made went back into the pot to purchase a wider selection of books.

We were now faced with a very serious decision. If I stayed with the company, I would have to stop evangelizing. I knew that what we were doing was having a positive impact on the lives of many people. I just couldn't quit.

After serious consideration, I resigned my position. Jan called this decision my mid-life crisis. At the time of my resignation I had no idea what I was going to do to make a living. Little by little, the idea of opening a Catholic bookstore began to germinate in my mind. The more I thought about the idea, the more excited I became, common sense notwithstanding.

I looked around for a place to open our Catholic Footsteps Bookstore. We found an eleven-hundred-square-foot store on the main street of Hesperia and opened for business on January 1, 1991. At first we didn't have much of an inventory. I purchased some used bookshelves and display cases from a Catholic store that was going out of business. We opened with about six hundred book titles, a dozen or so rosaries, and six videos that we used as rentals.

By the time we had been open about nine months, we were deeply in debt. My credit cards were charged to the hilt, and our funds were completely depleted. We were fifteen thousand dollars in debt, and I could see no way out. One day a wonderful couple came into the store. Even though they lived about sixty miles away, they visited the store about once a month. When they asked how we were doing, I answered that I was going to have to close at the end of the month. They made their purchase and left. A few minutes later, they returned, made additional purchases, left, and then once again returned. They stood before me and offered to loan me the money I needed. Needless to say, I was stunned. They wrote me a check for an interest-free loan. I paid the bills, and we remained open. The couple said that if we could win just one soul for Christ, then it would be worth the investment.

It has not been easy to keep the store open. We are still many thousands of dollars in the red. A few years ago, we expanded the store to 2,200 square feet and considerably increased the inventory. We now have a full line Catholic store with about three thousand new and six thousand used book titles, all in accord with the teachings of the Holy Father and the Magisterium of the Church. We have more than 550 rental videos, hundreds of rosaries, and just about anything else a Catholic family could want. These have been difficult years, but also most rewarding.

I still travel and teach whenever possible, but my heart is in the store. I spend at least eight to twelve hours a week in teaching and evangelizing. Most of our customers are Catholics—some searching, some fallen away—but most loyal to the Church, with Catholicism a central part of their existence. Occasionally, a non-Catholic will visit to purchase a gift for a Catholic friend, and some come in to challenge the Faith. I've even had a couple of Protestant ministers try to convert me. These occasions are wonderful opportunities to share the Church's teachings. I have yet to find anyone critical of Catholicism who has a correct understanding of the Church's doctrines. These people simply don't have all the information they need to make correct decisions.

I am always on the lookout for ways to share the doctrine of the Real Presence of Christ in the Holy Eucharist. Many cannot imagine that Jesus was speaking literally when He said that His flesh is real food and his blood real drink. I explain that there are many mysteries in Christianity. How this action of the Holy Spirit comes about, I can only imagine. I believe it, not only because I have been given the gift of faith, but also because of the avalanche of evidence from the early Church that supports this belief. The Holy Eucharist is a most precious gift, Jesus' legacy to His children. It grieves me that so many of our separated brethren deprive themselves because they have been led astray.

Typically, women manage religious bookstores. I would estimate that as many as forty percent of our customers are men. Men's spirituality is quite different from women's. Having a man behind the counter facilitates open sharing about issues that are particular to men. Sometimes, men will share concerns that they are not comfortable sharing with their wives or even with clergy. One example is birth control. Every man I know who has had a vasectomy or whose wife has had a tubal ligation for birth control purposes has seriously questioned and regretted the decision. These men indicate that the unitive aspect of their lovemaking has been destroyed; the men feel that they can no longer get close enough to their wives. Many couples are practicing birth control with the "pill", without recognizing the pill's abortifacient nature. Most are horrified when they consider for the first time that, by using the pill, they may have unknowingly aborted one of their own children. It is imperative that we as Catholics learn the foundations for Catholic teaching on these and other issues.

Operating a Catholic bookstore is a lot of work. The financial rewards are almost non-existent, but the spiritual rewards are plentiful. The store has brought me into contact with wonderful people on a daily basis. Little by little, over the years, we have grown in our knowledge of the Faith. Jan and I have found that there are solid foundations for each and every one of the teachings of the Roman Catholic Church, and we have shared this knowledge with others. Occasionally, I travel to other areas of the country in order to share the Faith at seminars and conferences. I realize how fortunate I am, and I praise God for all that He has done in my life. It has been twenty-two years since the Lord called me in His mercy. Thanks be to God for His inexpressible gift. Serving Him brings fulfillment to my life. I enjoy what I do, and I just can't imagine doing anything else.

The Twelve Steps Back

Ann E. Krach

I grew up in a Catholic family, the second oldest of ten children. I went to a parochial elementary school and a private secular high school. We attended Mass as a family every Sunday. I went to confession about once a month and attended CCD catechism classes while in high school. My father was a cradle Catholic, very strong in his faith, very knowledgeable in matters of doctrine and history. He knew the Faith well, as Jesuits had taught him in college. As a teenager he participated in the Catholic Evidence Training Guild. Although my parents were knowledgeable Catholics, strong in their faith, they generally failed to communicate this faith to their children. My father is not an easy man to talk to, and my mother is a convert to Catholicism. Our dinner table was a place of discussion and debate about various subjects, but, unfortunately, we never discussed religious matters.

My separation from the Church began when I left home to attend a Catholic college. For a time I lived with my grandmother, a second-generation Italian, who made certain that I went to church on Sundays. When I moved to be closer to the college and work, I stopped going to Mass. I was away from the sacraments for about seventeen years.

It did not bother me to stop going to Mass, and although it was very much a rebellion against anything parental, I did not see it that way at the time. It was also during this time that I not only turned away from the Catholic Church, but I also turned away from Christ and the idea of God Himself.

I left through a wide gate. There was no single step that was abrupt or any sharp deviance, but my path was steadily downward. No step was difficult to take or challenging to my conscience. I was a child of the sexual revolution, and I bought into the myths of that time. I thought that women should be able to have "natural and normal" sexual relations without the natural and normal consequences of those acts, consequences such as pregnancy.

I stayed at the college for two years. During this time I had four or five different majors, changing as often as a new semester rolled around, and at the end of two years I was not very far along in my education. These changes did not help to provide a focus for my studies. After I left college, I moved back to the town where my family lived. I worked for a year and then went to a local community college for a year, taking mostly science courses. At the end of that time I still had no clear idea of what type of degree I wanted, so I quit school again and joined the military service. I was tired of going to school without a clear direction and of working to support the cost of my education as well as myself.

The teaching I received in parochial school and CCD classes left me morally unprepared. During the sexual revolution of the '70s, we were not taught that contraception was morally evil. We were in a doctrinal desert. We were not even taught that, according to Church teaching, procreation is one of the ends of marriage. I entered into marriage without the sanction of the Church, and I entered into the relationship with the idea that we would not have children. There was also the understanding that either of us could change our minds about having children and even that this would probably happen. Neither of us was concerned about the outcome of our marriage one way or the other. I returned to school after the completion of military service and managed finally to finish my degree. I then followed my military husband as he was reassigned to California.

During this time, our marriage became mired in alcoholism. That was the lowest point in my life. One of the few beliefs that I managed to maintain from Church teaching was that marriage was for keeps. As far as I was concerned, there was no excuse for ending a marriage, and this belief left me no way out. I couldn't cope with my husband's alcoholism, and yet I did not see divorce as a possibility. I was so depressed that I wanted to be able to fall asleep and never wake up.

I had no spiritual resources, and my belief in God had been reduced to a vaguely held idea of deism: that there was a Creator but that He had abandoned us. We were left to our own devices. There was no thought of a loving, caring God.

That was when I found AlAnon. AlAnon is a spiritual program for friends and relatives of alcoholics. It was through this Twelve Step program that I was able to reach out spiritually. I started believing in a caring God again. Not because I knew that there actually was a caring God, but more simply because I needed to believe in Him.

I was also helped tremendously by a friend of my mother's, who had been in AlAnon for many years. She told me that the anger I was feeling was justifiable. She explained that anger was a normal reaction to the situation I was in and that I should try to understand my feelings and not feel guilty about them. She also told me that I would come to realize that the anger I was feeling was hurting no one but myself and that eventually I would be able to let it go.

In accordance with the traditions of the AlAnon program, I found a sponsor and started to work the Twelve Steps of the program. I attended as many as five meetings per week. I also went to Alcoholics Anonymous and Alcoholics Anonymous speaker meetings. It was at these that I learned to have compassion for the alcoholic and yet not get wrapped up in the problems that his drinking was creating. In program language this was called detachment; in Christian parlance, to love the sinner but hate the sin.

I mentioned to my sponsor that I didn't seem to be growing spiritually. My sponsor asked if I had gone to church as a child. When I told her that I had, she suggested that I still had to make amends. She said that if my religion had given something to me as a child, I should think about returning to church. Because of my belief in the AlAnon program, I always took her suggestions as commands, even though she never put them in those terms.

I did not return to the Catholic Church right away. The impetus for that was provided by finding out I was pregnant. I returned to the sacraments of Confession and Communion because I believed that my child would need to be baptized. Because of my doctrinal ignorance, I was not aware that my marriage needed to be sacramentalized.

I do not mean to say that I had any deep emotional, religious, or conversion experience. My road back to the Church was similar to my road away in that there were few markers. I simply wanted my son to receive the benefits of a religious upbringing. I went back to church, made a general confession, and started receiving Holy Communion and preparing for the birth and baptism of my son.

There was still a deep, wide gap between the God of my AlAnon program and the God I saw in church. This difference between the two was slowly reconciled. Over a period of years the God who supported me in the alcoholic marriage became the same God I found in the Eucharist. The completion of this transformation probably did not happen until my son was preparing for his First Holy Communion.

It was shortly after the birth of my son that I wanted and needed my husband to make at least a partial commitment to his family. I told him that, since I had stayed with him through eleven years of his drinking, he should now give our son and me eleven years of sobriety. He agreed, but sometime later he started drinking again, this time secretly.

He then volunteered for a tour of duty overseas, where he could not take his family. I was not consulted about his decision to volunteer for a remote assignment overseas, and I knew that this was a signal that there would not be any commitment to staying together.

I was given the understanding that sometimes you are given an insight into your life that radically alters your viewpoint. Such had been given to me early on in the AlAnon program. I had come to understand that my husband was not going to find a reason for sobriety in our marriage. I had hoped that our child might move him to at least a temporary sobriety. I did not want my husband to miss our son's childhood. But my hope proved to be in vain.

During the three years we were apart, my husband's drinking continued. We had been separated not only physically but also emotionally. I would not discuss reconciliation unless he agreed to sobriety and involvement in an active AA program. There seemed to be no effort on his part even to try. It was an agonizing time; I was always hoping that somehow a change would take place. I had long ago put my husband under God's protection, and I continually thanked God for that protection. But in the end, in order to protect my son and myself emotionally, I filed for divorce.

I had been living in the east, near my family, so that I could return to school. I was there for about a year and a half, and then I returned to work in California. I settled in a small town that had a good school for my son, a four-page section in the phone book, a minuscule country store, no gas station, and a twenty-five-mile drive to the nearest supermarket, but it was only twenty minutes away from where I worked.

Anne, a woman who lived across the street from the house I rented, was a devout evangelical Christian of a fundamentalist sort. I hired her to care for my son after his return each day from kindergarten, and she provided full-time care during the summer. Anne and her husband had decided for various reasons to home school their two daughters. This proved to be a good decision, since the school was closed the following year. My son was bused to a public school, which was not satisfactory. In California, a notice is sent out to parents at the beginning of the year, stating various school policies and rules and anything else that was mandated by legislation. I learned that if a child wanted to go to the public health office in order to be tested for pregnancy or a sexually transmitted disease or to receive information on contraception or abortion, for the purpose of that visit the child was to be considered an adult. This meant that parental notification of the child's being absent from school grounds was not required. I could scarcely blame the school, for the legislation was beyond their control, but the notice disturbed me deeply. I was also unhappy with the school's reading program.

The final disturbing incident that caused me to change my son's school was a notice I received concerning school dances held for second- to sixth-graders. These dances were sponsored by the parents' association as a means of fundraising. It seemed to me that there might be a correlation between the fact that the town had a very high rate of teen pregnancy and the fact that dances in the school started at an inappropriate age. Changing schools would mean moving much farther away from work and a correspondingly longer commute. Moving to another town would necessitate making new arrangements for babysitting and emergency care. The upshot was that Anne and I agreed that, if it could be done within the legal limits imposed by the state, she would also home school my son for the second grade. This was managed by enrolling my son in the umbrella school maintained by Anne's church to support home schooling families. It was open to anyone who wanted to home school and would become a member of the Home School Legal Defense Association. The school kept records that were submitted by parents and sponsored events for the group as a whole. I was very grateful for the church's willingness to consider an unusual arrangement to help out a single parent.

One of the group's requirements was mandatory Bible study as part of the curriculum. This did not bother me because very little doctrine was introduced, and I felt that my son would probably benefit and become one of the few Catholics who knew Scripture.

However, since my son was preparing for his First Holy Communion in CCD, some doctrinal discussion occurred between Anne and me. Although she had been to Mass before, she in no way knew or understood the Catholic belief that Jesus Christ is really and truly present in the Eucharist—Body, Blood, Soul, and Divinity. She then asked how Christ could be re-sacrificed on the altar at every

Mass. I told her that He was not re-sacrificed, but that the sacrifice at Calvary became present at Mass during the moment of Consecration. To say that Christ was dying again was in fact unscriptural. She then asked me how it could be that the same sacrifice on Calvary could be present at the altar. I'm afraid I did not cover myself in glory by my explanation. I was startled into crying out, "You want me to explain a *mystery*?" Nevertheless, our talks continued.

It was during one of those talks that I was given a wake-up call. That conversation has driven my studies and readings ever since. We were talking about Purgatory, and Anne told me quite plainly that the doctrine of Purgatory was an invention of the Catholic Church. She quickly modified her statement and then said that Purgatory was a "tradition of men". The statements to me were equivalent. I was shocked, truly shocked, that this woman, whom I considered to be very tolerant and willing to try her best to accommodate our differences, could believe that somehow the Church had invented this doctrine. I was not angry, just amazed.

It was also amazing to me that of all the doctrines Anne could have questioned me about, the doctrine of Purgatory was the one doctrine that I knew something about. So, in response to her statement, I asked a question, a question whose answer I did not know at the time but have since found. I asked her how long the Jews have been saying Kaddish.

I knew that the Jews pray for their dead just as the Catholic Church has done from her beginning. I knew the section from Maccabees that described praying for the dead as a "holy and pious thought" (2 Mac 12:45) in order that the dead be released from their sins. I asked her why the Jews pray for their dead if there is no way that the dead could benefit. Anne, of course, did not know that Jews and Catholics alike share belief in prayer for the dead.

Her statement that the Catholic Church had invented its doctrines caused me to begin a course of reading and study in order to show, at least to myself, that the Church as it was in early times was the same Church to which I now belonged. I remember, early in my reading, being surprised by a quote by John Henry Newman in which he said that the Catholic Church was either diabolical or she was right. As I continued to read, however, I began to see what Newman meant. I still could not come to word my belief as strongly as Newman had, but I understood that either the Catholic Church was opinionated, stubborn, totalitarian, stiffnecked, dictatorial, and bigoted, or she was right. Much later, as I was studying the many miracles throughout Church history, I came to understand why Newman had used the word diabolical.

I started with Eusebius' *Ecclesiastical History*, which I found in the bookstore of Anne's church. I thought it odd that it would carry such a book, but I was grateful that my study could begin with the earliest period of Church history. I was in Anne's church for a meeting of the home schooling group when one of the other home schooling mothers, a former Catholic, stopped by my chair to look at what I was reading. She looked at the book by Eusebius and declared, "This is Catholic!" I understood her meaning. Of course early Church history would have to be a history of the Catholic Church, but the way she said it sounded like an accusation. I told her that I understood that it was Catholic, but I had bought the book from her church's bookstore. If the bookstore at her church was going to carry a history of the Catholic Church, I could hardly be to blame.

I remember reading about the Emperor Constantine, when he stood up during discussions about Christ. I felt a thrill as I realized that this might be the source of the tradition of standing during the reading of the Gospel during Mass. Reading the Church's history also gave me a sense of how important the unbroken line of apostolic succession was to the early fourth-century Church. The book seemed to have been written in order to record the successors for the major churches of the time.

The assistant pastor of Anne's church, who sold me Eusebius' history, also remarked on the book, and I told him that it was amazing to me to see the roots of my religion come out of the pages of a book written in the early fourth century. He must have later read at least some part the book, because he told me that he considered the book biased. I'm not certain what he meant, and I am still puzzled by his apparent attitude that the history of the early *Christian* Church should be something other than the history of the *Catholic* Church.

It soon became clear to me that the evangelical and fundamentalist church worship services were not in line with the worship practices of the early Christians. Justin Martyr wrote one of the first descriptions of Christian worship. He described the reading of sacred writings, a talk on the readings, and then the breaking of bread as commanded by Jesus at the Last Supper and the presentation of gifts. Any Catholic or, for that matter, any non-Catholic with a liturgical tradition such as Anglican, Episcopalian, Lutheran, or Orthodox will recognize in Justin Martyr's description the outlines of the Mass.

I also read the early Church Fathers, works by Ignatius of Antioch, Irenaeus, Augustine, Cyprian, Cyril of Jerusalem, Athanasius, and others, as well as Justin Martyr. Along with this reading, I was introduced to writings by converts to Catholicism that explained Catholic doctrines from Scripture, writers such as Scott Hahn, Thomas Howard, Peter Kreeft, and James Akin, as well as publications from the apologetic apostolate Catholic Answers.

Another quote from Cardinal Newman struck me during my studies. He said that "to be steeped in history is to cease to be Protestant", and, conversely, to be ignorant of history is to become Protestant. It is very clear to me that Newman knew what he was talking about and that those people today who leave the Catholic Church do not know that they are leaving the one, true Church of Christ.

I had other conversations with Anne concerning, in particular, Church history. She wanted to cover a broad expanse of time with the children during the next school year. This was to be a unit study approach where her older daughter and the two younger children would cover creation and early man and proceed through Egypt, Israel, Greece, Rome, and the early Church through the Middle Ages.

While we had some differences between the creation story and a six-day or six-thousand-year creation versus a 4.2-billion-year-old earth, those differences were minor compared to the differences between our ideas on the structure and practices of the early Church. I was not sure that the friendship and trust we had worked so hard to develop and maintain would survive our different views on that period of Church history.

Anne was not aware that the early Church practiced infant baptism. On the other hand, I was not aware that some adults in the early Church — Constantine, for example — foolishly delayed baptism for as long as possible. Of course, it is easy to see doctrinally why baptism was delayed. Since baptism washes away all stain of sin and remits temporal punishment for any sin committed, some people risked the delay so that they could receive the sacrament as close to death as possible. That was the reason for a papal proclamation that condemned the practice of delaying baptism and encouraged people to baptize their babies.

Another area of contention was the use of the title "saint". I knew that in the New Testament Paul used "saint" to refer to those living and in the Church. The title was used by Paul in anticipation of the final outcome. I told Anne that Catholics had lost the habit of referring to themselves as saints in the general manner of Paul. I also told her that Protestants had lost the reverence for the saints in heaven that had been exhibited by early Christians. I considered this a minor point. I was surprised that my mention of the graffiti on the catacomb walls saying "St. Peter, pray for us", and "St. Paul, pray for us" was comfortable to her only if these had been placed there while the apostles were living. She could not concede that the early Christians referred to the dead as saints in the same manner that Catholics use the term today.

Peter of Alexandria became archbishop of Alexandria in 285 A.D. He was the last martyr of Egypt under Constantinus Major in 311, before the Edict of Milan went into effect. In the *Life of St. Peter of Alexandria*, by Anastasius the Librarian, we read that Peter, to prepare for his martyrdom, asks permission of his captors to go before the tomb of St. Mark in order to commend himself to his patronage. The prayer of Peter of Alexandria before the tomb of St. Mark is given by Anastasius. In this prayer, Peter asks St. Mark to pray for him that he "may be meet to reach the goal of his agony with a stout heart and ready faith".

Our different views of early Christian beliefs and practices seemed to have provoked something of an impasse between us. I asked Anne why she was so sure that tradition supported her view of the early Church, when I was the one who took tradition as a rule of faith. If I was the one who looked to tradition as authoritative, why was she so sure that tradition supported her, who did not recognize it as authoritative? This did give her reason to pause, and after that problems were easier to resolve.

At some point Anne and her husband must have had reason to pause, thinking about our discussions, because she told me that they had talked about the Reformation and had concluded that God would not have allowed the Reformation to happen if it had been wrong. I did not tell her that at the same time five million people in Europe were leaving Catholicism for Protestantism, there were more than six million converts to Catholicism in Mexico due to the appearances of Our Lady of Guadalupe. God sometimes lets us have our way even when it will not bring us good. He does this as a father might, to teach us a lesson. This can be seen in the Old Testament, when the Hebrews asked God for a king.

My son has also had to learn to defend his Faith. He came home one day after playing with the two sons of the pastor at Anne's church. He told me that they had called him a cannibal for eating the flesh and drinking the blood of Christ. I asked him what he said to them in reply. He said that he had told them, "But God said: 'Unless you eat the flesh of the Son of Man and drink his blood, you have no life in you; he who eats my flesh and drinks my blood has eternal life, and I will raise him up at the last day' " (Jn 6:53, 54). I took him out to Burger King for dinner.

Since returning to the Church, I have come to realize what I had given up during those years while I was away from God and His Church. It is because of this that I do not want any minimizing or dilution of the teaching of Christ. It is all or nothing. I do not want to stray again. I understand that I must accept Christ and His Church totally, because if the Church were wrong on one single matter of faith or morals, then she could be wrong on anything. Having jumped ship once, I do not want to desert the bark of Peter again.

At my parish church I was part of an adult Bible study group that met on Sundays during CCD. The Bible study was floundering without clear direction. I made a proposal to the head of the religious education program that I structure a course for adults that would examine the scriptural support for various doctrines of the Church and then also look at those doctrines from the standpoint of Sacred Tradition by examining the early Christian writings that underpinned them. Because this was exactly what I had been doing in the course of self-study, it seemed reasonable to me to share what I was doing with the rest of the adult class.

Since I was not aware of any text or series available that covered the topics I wanted to study and teach, I gathered material and wrote my own handouts for the class. I wanted to show that Catholic doctrines are rooted in Scripture and that the earliest Christians viewed these doctrines in the same light as we see them in today. I wanted to be able to show the continuity of almost two thousand years of Church teaching, as a counterpoint to Protestant theology, which can only be traced back fewer than five hundred years, to the time of the Reformation. I also wanted to show that it was relatively easy to compare what was taught by the apostles and the Church's teachings that come to us through Sacred Tradition with what the reformers have recently taught. Over and over in the early Christian writings, we find that, when some new and innovative teaching appeared, the Church Fathers would say that that was not what the apostles taught. This is evident in St. Jerome's *Against Helvidius*, in which he refutes Helvidius' claims that Mary did not remain a virgin after Jesus was born but bore other children. Jerome wrote in his essay, "Pray tell me, who, before you appeared, was acquainted with this blasphemy?"

We worked our way through Christ's Real Presence in the Eucharist, through Purgatory, salvation by faith and love, the Bible and Sacred Tradition as authority, and other topics, including the primacy of St. Peter and apostolic succession. Subjects that have been requested and are yet to be covered are divorce, the brethren of the Lord (did Jesus have siblings?), and the rest of the Marian doctrines.

The class is very small, but some bring their older children who are past CCD age. They share my desire to be able to defend the Faith. I am also stronger in my faith because of this study. I will be forever grateful to my friend and neighbor for her remarks, which caused me to want to know more about Catholicism. Anne never intended to hurt me by her anti-Catholic comments. Yet, it was those comments that spurred me to study. Without really knowing it, Anne did me a favor. May God bless her for being God's instrument. May the Holy Spirit lead us both to the Truth.

Spider-Man and the
Return of the
"Radical Conservative"

Mark E. Hingsbergen

The story of my "reversion" is both unique and representative. While I had a great many one-of-a-kind experiences in my journey, I sense that there are thousands of cradle Catholics who, although exposed to so-called Catholic higher education, fall away due to lack of apologetics and a complacent prayer life. And I know that there are millions of Catholics who do not know the grave state of Catholic secondary and higher education in the United States. Still, I do not wish to blame any person or organization for my own choices but, rather, to look upon the events of my life as a reason to give all praise to God for what He has done.

I was born and baptized Catholic in 1963, and I was raised in a devout Catholic home. We never missed Mass without serious reason, and we observed all fasts, abstinences, and holy days. I attended nearby Saint Ann

School, which was run by Franciscan nuns. About one-third of the teachers were sisters when I started second grade (today there is only one nun left). There and at home I was taught my Faith.

I came to realize that I was one of the more gifted students in my class, yet I had always been taught humility, and I attributed my abilities to God or downplayed them. I also began to realize I was among the more pious of my classmates in my refraining from bad language and in my attention during daily Mass. I had also cultivated a devotion to the Rosary, and from age seven to ten or so I recited it almost every night, sometimes as many as five times.

I knew I was different from the other kids in many ways, so I tended to withdraw. I was not the most unpopular child, but I was far from being in the "in" crowd (yes, there was an "in" crowd as early as third grade). I had a few friends at school, but until I was about twelve my only friends outside school were my younger brother and a few cousins. I developed another world in my own mind, filled with action heroes and brilliant scientists. My favorite toys were action figures and comic books. In the mind of a creative, pensive child, make-believe heroes can seem rather important. My favorite hero at this point in my life was Spider-Man, and I had watched the cartoon version before school when I was six. The cartoon was no longer on, however, and as I read my Spider-Man comics, I longed to see the cartoon again. I included in my prayers a fervent supplication that Spider-Man would return to the airwaves. I even invoked the intercession of St. Clare, patroness of television. I checked the *TV Guide* every week for several years, but the program never came back.

Things began to change as I got into sixth and seventh grades, though. I began to notice girls, both on television and in my class. I discovered popular music (Aerosmith, Boston, and Led Zeppelin), and I began to desire more social acceptance. Always on the small side, I couldn't play basketball or football (the two status sports in Catholic schools). I joined a Little League team, and I struggled in order to be an average player, but even that level of acceptance felt good. I also discovered it was not "cool" to be really "religious", so I gradually let my prayer life atrophy and my piety decay.

I had also begun to hang around with a couple of other social outsiders like myself, and in our own little group we found solace. We started getting into mischief at school (mostly low-key things) to amuse ourselves. We found it especially amusing to cut up during daily Mass, and one of my friends even went so far as to entertain us by dismantling kneelers and missalettes so that they would fall apart when the next person used them! (I am happy to report that my friend has put all this behind him and is now one of the finest young Catholic priests that I know!)

Throughout this entire decline, my parents probably did not suspect anything, because I still knew how to behave around them, and I wasn't getting in any serious trouble. So, after eighth grade I continued on to the local Catholic high school. This school was typical of the crop of coeducational "modernist" high schools built in the fervor of the post-Second Vatican Council years by well-meaning parents and local Church leaders. Though the theology being taught in the late '70s was still sound and we had a full calendar of religious events, the school permitted conduct that in retrospect was most unbecoming for Catholic youth. As an adult I see that this is typical, misguided, liberal behavior, to be permissive for fear of alienating others by strict rules. Too many of the teachers wanted to be our "buddies".

Although it was legal only for some seniors to buy beer (Ohio had a 3.2% at 18 law), drinking was commonplace in all four classes. The majority did not consider drugs "cool", and guns were virtually nonexistent, but alcohol was everywhere. An environment of sports enthusiasm and social drinking nurtured this behavior, and football was considered the single most important activity at the school. Many of the parents of athletes relived their own glory days vicariously through their children.

Competing with football for most important activity (and easily winning during basketball season) was dating. As much as all the young men relished sharing classes with dozens of blossoming young girls, I must say now that it was a tremendous distraction. Apart from a junior year morality class, not much was said to us about sexual activity; the school staff assumed that our parents took care of such discussions. Mine did, but I can't say the same for everyone. Most of the kids I knew remained virgins, but behavior on dates was, on average, far in excess of what a caring parent would have allowed.

I made it through these years with my virginity intact and without drugs, but my faith foundation was weakening further. My affinity for rock music had increased, and

I formed a band with some new friends. We played some absolutely atrocious music with no regard for the lyrical content. We revered the stars of the music world, blind to the fact that their lyrics often represented a denial of the truths of Christianity.

Encouraging this attraction to rock music was a priest who taught at the school. My friends and I hung on his every word, and he steered us toward progressive rock artists such as Genesis and Yes. Relatively speaking, this was better than Van Halen and AC/DC. But his own admiration of the members of these bands fostered in us an almost god-like reverence for them, and the surreal lyrics wandered close to New Age notions and occultism. Years later this priest became involved in a sex scandal that received national attention. He had never "approached" my friends or me, but his crude jokes and lack of priestly piety made it difficult to deny that he could have been guilty.

The most damaging years, however, came when I went to college. I had chosen a small Catholic university close to home. It had a respectable engineering program, and I remember part of the appeal was the notion that I would be nurtured in my Faith and prepared for adulthood. Perhaps I had felt the spiritual weakening, and I trusted the Marianist brothers to build me back up. My trust was unfortunately misplaced.

That particular school was (and still is) a classic example of what is wrong with Catholic higher education in America. Almost totally secularized, the politically correct humanist agenda of the faculty and administrators pervaded nearly every aspect of campus life. From the lionization of John F. Kennedy to the playing of R-rated movies in the campus theater, students were taught that behavior doesn't matter because God loves us unconditionally. Consequently, student behavior was deplorable. Drinking was all but mandated at parties, marijuana was very common, and of course, everyone I knew (except me and a few of my friends) was having sex. I knew not to have sex, and I was convinced I could avoid it if the opportunity presented itself, but still I couldn't figure out why I was not getting any dates. In retrospect, the protection of the Blessed Virgin was undeniably present in my life.

The worst and most damaging aspect of my college years, however, came not from the social life but rather the classroom itself. I had always been a philosophical thinker, so I was like a sponge in my religion and philosophy classes (required even for engineering students). I had come to question the childhood images of God that I had been taught by the good Franciscan sisters, so naturally I embraced the notion of God in more intellectual terms. Ironically, it was a freshman introductory course in Thomistic philosophy that was the foundation for the next twelve years of heresy and delusion. This was not the fault of the instructor, a good man and perhaps the only conservative on campus, but rather the later filtering of those ideas through the corrupt lens of feminism as taught by a professor who greatly influenced me during my college years

In my junior year I took a course on the New Testament taught by a radical feminist. She was sweet and soft-spoken, but her words were from hell itself. She taught us "redactionary criticism" of the texts, which is "lib-eralese" for examination of the Scriptures in light of the time, places, and people who wrote them, and it usu-ally amounts to a denial of the inerrancy of that Scrip-ture. This is how feminists get around what they consider "misogynistic" passages in Ephesians, Galatians, and else-where. They maintain that the author was writing in a less enlightened time and encumbered by his own biases, ig-noring the fact that the Holy Spirit prevents the author from adding to, or detracting from, the asserted truth in any way.

The next year was even worse. So much did I like this woman as a teacher that I signed up for her "Male and Fe-male in the Biblical World" course. We didn't talk much about males, though. Instead we were told that the real reason Jesus was executed was that the Pharisees disliked his treatment of women as equals; also, that Jesus may have been "rather androgynous", and that paintings in the catacombs show that there were female priests in the early Church. We also had a number of guest lecturers. One was a female Episcopal pastor who spoke of how wonderful it was that her church ordained women. And, in perhaps one of the darkest moments in the history of Catholic higher education, we had a pagan priest and priestess, members of a coven, perform a "circle" (a wiccan ritual involving a group of people holding hands and waving slowly around a set of lit candles and other mystical objects while chant-ing). Not fully understanding the true Satanic nature of this ordeal, many of us participated (we were encouraged to do so). We chanted "Like a bee my mind is buzzing

round the blue lotus feet of my divine mother" for five
minutes or more. If a wicca spell was cast on me that
night, it lasted nine years!

Totally confused, I lapsed into agnosticism. Much the
way the Protestant Reformation stripped down the deposit
of Faith, I found myself stripping down my theology. I
still believed there was a God, but I saw Him as more
of a force, an uncaused cause with no personality. During this time I became friendly with another professor.
This man taught the campus martial arts class, which I
signed up for in an effort to fulfill my lifelong dream of
"getting tough". He immediately won my respect with his
good nature and near invincibility, both physically and
intellectually. He also taught yoga and philosophy classes,
both of which I eagerly attended. He became a mentor of
sorts for the next eight or nine years, as I strongly identified with his theology (but not his liberal, relativist philosophy). He saw God as an aloof being who set the world
in motion and observed but did not intervene. "How
could a loving father allow war and starvation?" he reasoned, and I couldn't answer that. So, remembering from
my freshman-year Thomistic philosophy class that God's
essence is existence itself, I made the serious mistake of
leaping into pantheism, the notion that God is merely
the sum total of all that exists, in material or thought or
spirit, and that each and every thing was "a little piece of
God". I had become a Hindu! Of course, in my youthful
arrogance I figured that this was rather novel thought and
that the priest at my parish back home had not been so
enlightened. For the time being, at least, it was a way in

which I felt I could participate in the Mass (for my parents' sake) without being a hypocrite.

I saw Jesus (if He actually ever lived) as a man who somehow had all the power of existence concentrated into Him, which was how He worked miracles. Not too far off base, I must admit, but my thinking got worse from there. I theorized that the Real Presence was due to our belief in it, the actualization of the existence of our thoughts. (Interestingly, I never denied the Real Presence, but I did seriously distort its significance.) And, being at a Marianist school, I pondered Mary's role. Was she perhaps divine herself? Did she suffer as much as Jesus and thus "co-save" us? Was she the Holy Spirit incarnate? Was this perhaps the "great secret" of the Catholic Church?

My theology had become a strange mix of New Age notions and classic heresies. Such a theology had serious moral ramifications. I understood the immorality of such evils as abortion, alcoholism, and drugs (which hurt others), but I was blind to the evils of pornography and the wrong kinds of music (which I believed affected only the individual). If one could "handle it", it was OK. And not once in those years did I meet up with someone who could argue for the true Faith. That was proof enough for me that the Church had a lot of excess theological baggage and used childish imagery of fathers and angels to minister to the "common people". Such was my arrogance.

I continued to attend Mass, still wishing that I could return to the innocent faith of my childhood, in which I did not have to deal with such difficult questions. Perhaps I attended out of that desire or out of love for my wise but "common" parents, whose unquestioning faith I envied. If there was one prayer I sent up during this time, it was something like "God, or whoever You are, I wish I could go back and undo all that I've been exposed to in college. I want to believe like a child again."

One day, when I was home from school on a weekend, I flipped on TV to pass the Friday afternoon. Kids' programs were coming on, and I felt my heart jump as I heard the familiar Spider-Man theme song. It had taken more than twelve years, but I could no longer claim that my prayer was unanswered. Still, I reasoned, it could have been just a coincidence, the inevitable resurgence of popularity of Marvel Comic's most notable character. But I remember my initial reaction. And I enjoyed watching the old cartoon!

In May 1985, at the start of my senior year, I met a young lady at a cousin's wedding reception. Tracey and I hit it off right away, and in six months we were engaged. She and I had very compatible theological views (though she had not been "ruined" by college philosophy courses!). We married in November 1985, at St. Ann's Church, where we had both been raised. Our sentimental desire for a traditional Catholic wedding exceeded our understanding of the importance of the sacramental nature of the marriage covenant, but at least the end result was good—we were married in the Church.

Unfortunately, we started off a good marriage on a bad foundation. We did not accept the Church's teaching on contraception (though we were both adamantly against abortion), and we began to miss Mass more and more frequently because we were "just too busy" or "not getting enough out of it". By this time, I was no longer claiming to be a Catholic when asked, preferring the benign label "raised Catholic". We soon were attending Mass only on major feasts and when my musician friends and I were asked to play at a wedding or a Sunday Mass. I often ridiculed Church teaching and made accusations of hypocrisy when the subject came up.

I was searching for the truth all this time. At various points I put my faith in Zen, environmentalism, nutritional extremism, and Rush Limbaugh. (I still like Rush, though I don't revere him as I once did!) At one particularly embarrassing low point of gullibility I nearly got involved in Scientology at the behest of a co-worker who was convinced of its validity. One look at the biography of L. Ron Hubbard ended that little episode, thankfully.

My life to that point could be characterized by the paradoxical phrase "radical conservative". What I mean by this is that I always go to extremes, but I do it very cautiously and with much thought. I have always had an aversion to highly volatile situations, which is why I have lived all my life in a forty-mile radius from the place where I was born and have not sought thrills like skiing and motorcycling. My falling away from the Church occurred very gradually, so it makes sense that my return would happen very gradually. God, in His mercy, chose to guide me home gently rather than violently jerk me back.

In 1990, Tracey became pregnant, but she miscarried after eight weeks. We were devastated that our child had died, but God knew that my self-centered heart was not yet ready to be a father's heart. He used this tragedy to draw me closer. Shortly after the miscarriage I was up late, surfing channels, and I found myself fascinated by the Power Team on the local "holy roller" station. As a black belt myself, I could relate to their strength and discipline. I was still grieving the loss of our child, though, and, when John Jacobs made his appeal to "accept Christ as your personal Lord and Savior", something touched my emotions. I got past that initial urge to ridicule fundamentalists (which I had at one time and which, regrettably, sometimes results from a sense of "Catholic pride"), and for the first time in years I genuinely asked God for help. I did not like the way I felt, and I asked Him if somehow I could have faith again as I had had when I was nine years old. This seemed impossible, because college learning had jaded me, but I asked it anyway. I did not say the "Sinner's Prayer" out loud but echoed it in my mind, figuring I had nothing to lose.

Sometimes I believe the intensity of the reply is proportional to the intensity of the prayer. Mine was a rather reserved prayer, so God's response was so gradual as to be difficult to detect. But make no mistake, it was there.

Three months later my wife and I conceived again, and this time everything went well. Tracey received what she believed to be a sign to indicate that this pregnancy would be healthy. At the peak of her anxiety over the health of the child she was carrying, a single perfect red rose appeared on a bush that should have been finished producing for the season.

Erin was born in March 1991, but the roughest road was still ahead of us. I had recently become obsessed with good nutrition, and everything I read told me that breast-feeding was the only acceptable way to feed a baby. Tracey, having been bottle-fed in a time when that was encouraged by mainstream doctors, never had much affinity for the idea of breast-feeding. But, sensing my enthusiasm, she offered to give it a try. Things went poorly from the start, and soon she was extremely sore. I urged her to continue, since the La Leche book said soreness and even cracking of nipples were common during nursing. Eventually, her nipples became partially detached, her pain became unbearable, and she had to stop. Unfortunately, I did not deal with this very well. My disappointment and embarrassment that my daughter (the daughter of a nutrition expert) was not going to be breast-fed were too much for me to accept. In my selfishness I failed to be supportive of Tracey, and in this I caused her tremendous anguish, to the point where she thought about leaving for a while. This was the low point in our marriage, and I take full responsibility, since it was my behavior that was out of line. In a moment of despair, remembering that in a Church marriage God is the third partner, I sent up a plea for Him to help our marriage. He did indeed help us, and eventually I was able to accept formula-feeding. Ironically, this happened largely because I learned that my karate instructor friend had been bottle-fed, and he was a model of physical health. It is wonderful how God can use even the most unlikely persons to bring about healing. Tracey forgave me for my callousness, and we grew even closer than before.

We felt the need to give thanks to God, so we returned to Mass. Tracey also felt a calling to participate in the local pro-life movement. She began volunteering at a crisis pregnancy center, which brought her in touch with a lot of spiritual and holy women. Meanwhile, God was bringing good men into my life at work. I found myself on projects with several devout Catholic men and one prayerful evangelical. Their influence on me was subtle but profound, and I found myself wanting to imitate aspects of their behavior.

Satan did not like our newfound mustard seed of faith, so he set up a few stumbling blocks. One was a strong tithing push at the parish we had joined, and the other was our inability to quiet our daughter at Mass. We stopped going to Mass again for a while, but in 1992, when we moved to a bigger house, we decided to rejoin the parish where we had grown up, good old St. Ann's. We wanted our children to have a faith background "so they could have something to believe if that was their choice", as we would weakly say, still not rock solid in our own beliefs. We now believed in God's love for us, but we still had problems with the Catholic Church (we continued to use contraceptives). Both our sets of parents had been married in Saint Ann's also, and though they now lived outside the parish boundaries (as did we), they also decided to rejoin St. Ann's around that time. Suddenly we had a whole crew to entertain Erin (grandparents are wonderful), so attending Mass became more bearable.

About this same time my best friend (and drummer in my band) lost his mother to a ten-year battle with cancer. She was only forty and one of the sweetest ladies I had ever met. Jeff dealt with her death courageously, and a renewal of his lifelong Catholic faith began to occur. I watched with interest as he began to defend Church teachings to the best of his ability, and I noticed an almost supernatural increase in his wisdom and maturity. I was intrigued but not convinced.

My wife and I decided to be open to life again that summer, and by fall Tracey was pregnant again. It was my deepest desire for this child to be a son, although I recognized that every child was precious. We had intended to have only two children, three at most, and I didn't want to have another daughter and be thinking "last chance" on the third. Somehow, that didn't seem right. I was reluctant to ask God for a son, however, because I felt that after all I had done I didn't deserve to have one; but the desire was there.

On Christmas Eve we had a crisis. Tracey began bleeding, and we feared for our child's life. We both prayed silently on the way to the hospital. Our wonderful obstetrician left his family gathering to meet us, and he calmed us as he examined Tracey. He prescribed a medication to relax her uterus and scheduled an ultrasound for the day after Christmas. Tracey stopped bleeding, and we thanked God for His mercy toward our child and us. Then the ultrasound not only showed no damage or problem with the pregnancy, but it also quite clearly showed us that the child was a boy! I was overwhelmed at God's generosity to His undeserving servant, and a wave of faith swept over me.

At that time I had started listening to Christian radio in my car. My best friend had gotten me interested, and I liked what I heard. But I was still not comfortable with some of the songs that openly proclaimed the name of Jesus, preferring the ones with a more subtle message. I mention this, not only to illustrate that I had a long way to go, but also for the benefit of those who know someone whose conversion is not yet complete. Sometimes an evangelist's zeal is like a bright light that startles a newly emerged mole. It was through Christian radio, though, that I began to learn more about Scripture, Christian living, and Christian finance. I began to feel that I should someday be tithing, but I was not ready to take that leap just yet.

It was now May 1993, and, two weeks before the birth, the baby turned to a breech presentation. From that time on things got a little chaotic. Several attempts to turn the baby were unsuccessful, and his day of birth finally arrived. The doctor tried one final time to turn the baby during labor, but the water broke midway. We didn't know it at the time, but this is a serious situation in which the cord can become pinched. Tracey ended up in the operating room for the delivery, and the baby's heart rate was dropping to eighty during contractions. The delivery was a vaginal frank breech (a rarity), and all seemed to go well. But little Evan's Agar scores were low, and we thought it strange that they whisked him away so quickly.

I had a band performance scheduled that night, and, just as I was thinking how well things had gone so that I would not miss it, a neonatologist from nearby Children's Hospital came into Tracey's room. We listened as he described Evan's temporary, but serious, condition known as polycythemia. His blood was literally too thick with red cells, and he had to have a partial exchange transfusion of saline solution to thin the blood, allowing better profusion through the lungs. We told him to go ahead, and then we talked about what I should do that night. I was torn between concern for my wife and new son and a sense of obligation to the party that had hired our band, as my absence would spoil the event. I rationalized that it was not a high-risk procedure, I would be nearby, I had a beeper, and I would rush back to the hospital after the last note. Tracey nearly cried as she asked me if I really had to go. Selfishly, I went anyway, neglecting to consider what I was putting my dear wife through. Fortunately, Evan came through the procedure well, but he had to go to special care for a while.

Evan became jaundiced as a result of his condition, and each day when we asked the doctors when we could take him home, they would say "maybe tomorrow". Tracey valiantly tried to breast-feed again, but she had to pump. For the next five days we made two trips a day to the hospital for nursing and bonding. This may not seem like much, but, for exhausted parents, not knowing when it would end, it seemed like an eternity. Each time his blood test came back we were disappointed.

The sixth day came, and we were at the hospital for our evening trip. Tracey was particularly disheartened, and I wished I could help her. While she waited for the blood test results (14.7 was the point at which he could go home) I decided to turn to the Lord in earnest. I went to the chapel, picked up a Bible, and it fell open to the book of Psalms. To this day I cannot find the exact passage on which my eyes first rested, but the words were so relevant and so comforting that I immediately felt a rush of God's power. My eyes welled up with tears as I felt His love poured out to me in an event that defied all reasonable argument of coincidence. I silently asked Him for help and was left with a sense that my prayers had been heard. I went out of the chapel to the nursery, where Tracey was waving and beaming. Evan's bilirubin count was only 14.6.

From that day on I started moving Christ into the center of my life. We now took our little family to Mass every Sunday, and I was beginning to cultivate a more active prayer life. At this point I recall strongly identifying with Jesus Christ but not so much with His Church. We continued to attend St. Ann's more out of familiarity than conviction. I was also somewhat infatuated with evangelical radio and its prominent personalities, and sixteen years of Catholic school education had done nothing to provide me with any apologetics beyond an "unbroken line of successors" from Peter to John Paul II. I knew the "what" of the Catholic Faith but not the "why". I would have been an easy target for a fundamentalist with a good argument.

What happened instead was indeed an example of God's perfect timing. My best friend, Jeff, who had lost his mother a year before, had been growing in his faith by leaps and bounds. One night at band practice he gave me a set of tapes and said, "Mark, listen to these. They will make you glad you were born and raised a Catholic!" I remember a polite "Oh, really!" response, but in my head I thought, "How could anything make me glad about being raised as one type of Christian versus another?" In fact, I saw the Catholic Church, albeit familiar, as rather dull and lifeless. I also saw liberalism creeping in, and I had seen no resistance from within.

The tapes he handed me were Scott Hahn's *Evangeliz-*

ing the Baptized. I think everyone should hear this series. It did not strike me immediately, but after a week or so of reflection I could indeed say that I was glad to be a Catholic. Further, I realized that I was just beginning to learn what the Church is all about. My glaring lack of apologetics training was both embarrassing and enlightening. I began to defend the Faith.

Most of 1994 was spent deepening my faith and learning how to be a Christ-centered Christian. Tracey and I learned to pray together (aloud!) in times of need, and we were learning to humble ourselves and let God take over. We laid out a program of increased donations to our parish that would have us fully tithing by early 1995 (this is known as handing the reins over to the Lord very slowly). We had faith that He would help us out of the financial squeeze we had been in since buying our new house. Gradually our finances came back into balance, a really incredible occurrence, since we were actually adding an expense. We started finding bargains, we consumed less, things broke down less frequently, fewer expensive "surprises" popped up, and people started giving us used clothing and other items (which we gratefully received). We have dozens of little stories now about how God met our needs, and we felt as though we were really making Him Lord of our lives. But there was still something being held back.

While working at the pregnancy center, Tracey happened upon a cassette of Kimberly Hahn's talk, "The Bible and Birth Control". Recognizing the speaker as the wife of a man highly regarded in our house, she brought it home and listened to it. Tracey had been feeling hypocritical about counseling young girls not to use birth control when we ourselves did. And after I chided a friend of mine for selling condoms in his take-out shop, I had a hard time figuring out just what businesses should be involved in retail contraceptive sale. Drugstores? Supermarkets?

Drawing on Scripture and reason, Kimberly Hahn cleared this all up for us by presenting a clear case for the Church's authoritative teaching. Like many Catholics, we had not understood the real difference between Natural Family Planning (NFP) and artificial contraception. Since we could see no difference, we concluded that we could "use our conscience" to judge. After all, we were being open to life and not using any abortifacients. The difference of course, was that NFP takes advantage of God's monthly gift of infertility, whereas contraception destroys the monthly gift of fertility. From the moment we heard the tape we decided "never again". Christ was now indeed the center of our lives.

We learned the value and joy of NFP in the fall of 1994. I then went on to begin the study of apologetics in earnest. I had heard more of Scott Hahn's tapes in the meantime, and I decided I had to be better prepared to defend our Faith. I read Karl Keating's *Catholicism and Fundamentalism* and everything else I could get my hands on. It was around this time that I learned why the Church is authoritative and Holy Scripture is inerrant. I started defending the Faith at work and with old acquaintances. And I began praying weekly before the Eucharist with a group of men at a neighboring parish.

We decided to welcome another child into our home,

and Megan was conceived in January 1995. She would arrive uneventfully (the way we like it!) in the fall and bring us great joy.

Finally Tracey and I felt ready to begin a ministry together. In January 1995, we offered our services to the parish to help prepare engaged couples for marriage. Although we had only recently come fully to accept and understand the Church's teachings on marriage, sexuality, and parenting, we felt that our enthusiasm and conviction would help to make up for a lack of history. And having made so many mistakes ourselves, we could help young couples to avoid them. Most important, though, is that we could not only give them the "what" but also the "why" that we somehow had missed for so long.

My primary apostolate, however, is based on an examination of the talents and skills with which God has seen fit to bless me. I have always been creative, with a love for music. In fact, music is always in my head, and bits and pieces of new songs are being constantly "auditioned" as I go about my day. God has given me the physical ability to play musical instruments well (though not so well as to make a career of performing). God has also given me a technical mind, which led me to a career as an engineer. I have developed a keen sense of polemics and argumentation, which almost led me to a career in law, averted only by my distaste for face-to-face confrontation.

I began to try to fit all these talents and skills to what I perceive as a glaring need in the Church today. My new-found love for contemporary Christian music (as an alternative to mainstream pop) and my recognition of the shortcomings of the music programs at most Catholic parishes has led me to see the need for two distinct types of Catholic music. First is a "contemporary Catholic" style, one that encompasses our rich traditions and supplements the good works some of our separated brethren are producing for casual, recreational listening. Second is a need for contemporary liturgical music that does not in any way detract from the Sacred Liturgy but, rather, stirs the emotions of those present and focuses attention *on* the Eucharist and the Word of God. My reasoning is that good, sacred music is not limited to any one musical instrument, and that, as musical styles, tastes, and instruments themselves change throughout the centuries, people are most easily moved by the sounds they have become familiar with. This has led me to include guitars, piano, percussion, and synthesized orchestral instruments in my arrangements. Such musical forms, in combination with traditional forms such as chant and organ, could provide the variety needed for the myriad of sentiments expressed in the Mass: adoration, thanksgiving, joy, praise, sorrow, humility, and awe, just to name a few. Careful not to create anything irreverent, I looked to Scripture for guidance. I found mention of lyre, reed, timbrel, flute, and cymbals (among others), so I reasoned that today's derivatives of such instruments can indeed be used with reverence and piety.

Thus I have begun a series of projects in my basement recording studio to produce two kinds of contemporary Catholic music, recreational and liturgical. The recreational music I have written contains a significant amount of apologetics (sometimes subtle, sometimes not). The liturgical music consists mostly of the reworking of songs that have come to be favorites in many parishes, as well as some original material from my friends and me. Things are proceeding well but slowly, due to my other duties as husband, father, and engineer.

I have also entered into a performance-based ministry for the liturgical portion. My friends and I are taking this music into neighboring parishes and offering it at weddings and other Masses. So far the response has been quite favorable.

As far as the secular music I have played in bands since my high school days, my current band (together thirteen years) has recently "cleaned up" its song list, removing what we decided was offensive material. We specialize in wedding receptions, and we feel that even this secular activity can be a ministry of sorts by keeping a wedding reception wholesome and decent. I realized this when I heard some of the trash that gets played by disc jockeys at the average reception. And I remember where our Lord started His ministry.

Even more important to me than any evangelical ministry is my role as husband and father. Recent enrollment in St. Joseph's Covenant Keepers has helped me to become more aware of my roles and their importance, and it has provided me with valuable advice that has enabled me to improve in many ways. Most significant to me has been the realization that the father is not only the leader and head of his family but also its servant, as Christ served His Church. I am continually reminded that St. Joseph, as head of the Holy Family, was by no means the "highest ranking" member.

I have found great joy in my return to the Faith of my

childhood. I have a renewed devotion to the Eucharist through our parish's perpetual adoration program, and the scapular and Rosary have become a regular part of my life. Our home is unmistakably Catholic, and I find myself with more and more opportunities to proclaim to the world, "Yes, I am a Roman Catholic." I feel as though the veil of darkness has been lifted from my eyes, and I can now fully accept all the teachings of our Church. And as Satan used modernism and intellectualism to erode the foundation and tear down the structure of my faith, God's grace has reinforced the cornerstone and rebuilt the walls using modern and intellectual means. I believe that God allowed me to fall away so that I could return with a renewed zeal and fervor, and I feel a strong calling to address the issues that led to my betrayal of Jesus Christ and His Church. Many who have left the Church for the same reasons that I did may never return, for lack of strong roots and a mother praying for their safe return. I ask God to use me to help bring them home. Tracey and I are closer than ever, thanks to NFP, the Hahns, and some wonderful people involved with the Couple to Couple League. We are open to the possibility of more children, and we more fully appreciate the three we have now.

How Will I Ever
Know What's Right?

Joseph Ranalli

The story of our return to the Catholic Church, as I look back, is a testimony to God's grace, love, and patience. My wife, Mary, and I had found a home at Calvary Chapel Church, and returning to the Catholic Church we considered unthinkable. God knew we were seeking to know Him more intimately and to have Him transform our lives. It seemed that at Calvary Chapel we had been transported to a time and place where the simplicity and purity of the early Christian Church was practiced. During our time there, God did work in our lives in many positive ways, but, looking back, I now see that He was always reaching out to us, calling us back home to His Church. Ironically, in our search for an ever-deepening relationship with God and knowledge of His will in our lives, we would be led in full circle to where we had begun.

I was born the third of six children into a devout Catholic family. My family attended Mass every Sunday. I attended CCD classes while in public school and entered a Catholic school in the fifth grade. I continued in Catholic schools through high school. Although I had many years of a "Catholic" education, my faith in God was very much external and superficial. Simply going to Mass on Sunday was not enough.

Although I believed in God, and my high school years included a very personal experience with Him while on a retreat, I had little understanding of the Church's teachings. I believed what I had been taught, but I did not know how to explain the foundations for what I believed. If asked why I believed as I did, I would have simply said, "Because the Church says so."

I was accepted into the fire academy while in junior college and began seriously seeking a career position in the field. It was at this time that I met my future wife, Mary. I knew right away that she was the person with whom I wanted to spend the rest of my life. I saw a goodness in her that sincerely impressed me. Although at the time we met neither of us was attending church, God was still important. I admired Mary's openness and trust in God. She also had been raised in a Catholic family, but she stopped attending church after the divorce of her parents. We quickly fell in love and, shortly after I was hired as a fireman in San Diego County, Mary and I were married.

We had a Catholic wedding, and we were quickly blessed with the birth of our first daughter, Britney. Even though we were not attending weekly Mass, Britney was baptized in the Church. Soon after the ceremony, we started talking about attending Mass on a regular basis. We both realized the need to hand on a belief system to our children.

Mary had not received the sacrament of confirmation, so we signed up together for the Rite of Christian Initiation for Adults (RCIA) program. We attended only half of the classes because they became frustrating and unfulfilling. The priest gave us a New Testament that had group discussion questions printed in the margins. They all seemed to ask, "How do you feel about this?" We were attending not to discuss our feelings but to learn about the teachings of the Catholic Church. It didn't seem that we were really learning anything, so we eventually just stopped going.

Shortly thereafter, we were blessed with the birth of our second daughter, Rachel. She, too, was baptized in the Catholic Church.

We relocated and began attending a different parish. Our daughters were young at the time and going to Mass was very difficult. It was hard for us to keep the kids entertained and also pay attention to what was happening during the Mass. Even when I could listen to what was going on, I understood very little about the beauty of the Mass. As I remember, the majority of the homilies weren't very informative or inspiring. It was easy for us to leave.

As I reflect on some of the factors that contributed to our readiness to leave the Catholic Faith, a few things stand out. Although I had many years of Catholic school and CCD classes, the primary factor in our leaving was the lack of a proper Catholic education. My parents sincerely believed that our spiritual formation and needs were being taken care of by sending us to Catholic school. Yet I did not fully understand or know how to explain or defend the teachings of the Catholic Faith. I do not recall being instructed by my parents in the Faith. Most of my siblings were also nominally Catholic. For Mary and me, being Catholic was something we had been born into, but neither of us had really made the Faith our own.

As a father, I wanted my children to grow up with a strong faith in God in order to avoid some of the pitfalls I had experienced. I remembered some of the mistakes I had made, especially in my teen years, and I wasn't sure the Catholic Church could help to provide the necessary moral foundation for our children.

It was during this time that I met a fireman who became a good friend. It was as though I were drawn to him. There was something about him that set him apart from the rest. He always seemed to be able to rise above the gossip, crude joking, and other typical conversations that were part of fire station life. I knew he was a Christian, not only by name, but also in his actions. I often saw him reading the Bible in the evenings, and he knew it well. We eventually began talking, and I told him that I really wanted to have the same kind of relationship with God. He had also grown up as a Catholic. As an adult, he made a decision to follow Christ, but not in the Catholic Church. He explained that he had studied the differences between the teachings of the Catholic Church and his Protestant church, and he believed the Catholic Church had so clouded the simple gospel over the years that it would be difficult to grow as a Christian and still remain a Catholic. He did not say that a person could not be a Catholic Christian, as many Protestants falsely believe, but only that it was difficult to follow Christ if one did not attend a church that taught the Bible. I had developed a respect for him and concluded that, since he had studied the Catholic Church and found so many problems, I would attend his church and compare.

One Sunday, my family and I attended the Vineyard Christian Fellowship with him and his family. It was very different from Catholic worship; everyone seemed joyful and happy to be there. In spite of the enthusiasm, Mary and I were pretty uncomfortable. Rather than continuing to attend at Vineyard, Mary thought we should give the Catholic Church another chance.

Shortly after this, we moved to Orange County to live with Mary's mom while our house was being built. Mary became pregnant with our third child, David; we moved into our new house; and I started looking for another church.

At this time I met a fireman from a neighboring fire department who attended a Calvary Chapel. I told him that I would like to try his church one Sunday. The first time Mary and I went, we really enjoyed the service. The music was upbeat, and the sermon the pastor gave was very practical and well presented. Mary and I both started feeling that we had actually learned something in church for a change. Mary still felt somewhat uncomfortable and wanted to try the Catholic parish, but I really liked Calvary Chapel. I figured we had given the Catholic Church enough opportunities.

After a few months, we started attending Calvary Chapel regularly. Mary started going to a women's Bible study and gradually made friends. We also started making friends with other couples in the church. One of the biggest attractions for me was the pastor. He was only a few years older than I and was also a former Catholic.

What struck me about him was his openness about his own struggles as a Christian. I could really relate to him. He led by example. I liked and admired him.

I was ambivalent about leaving the Catholic Church. I felt that the Church was dead, but I did not feel any real animosity. But, as time went on in our life at Calvary Chapel, I began to develop a resentment against anything that reminded me of Catholicism.

At Calvary Chapel people were challenged to respond to the message of the gospel. They were told that Jesus came and paid for their sins on the Cross; that if they would repent of their sins and ask Jesus to be their Lord and Savior, to let them be "born again", Jesus would then come into their hearts and forgive their sins. I had actually submitted myself to Christ while on a retreat at age sixteen. That retreat was the only occasion on which the message of salvation was presented to me while I was in the Catholic Church. I couldn't understand why this message wasn't proclaimed more often. Why did we not hear this message from a Catholic pulpit? I felt that I had been cheated.

I had no understanding of the Catholic view of regeneration (how we are "born again") and justification (how we are made "right with God"). It seemed to me that, at Mass, all we did was say the same prayers again and again and do a lot of standing, kneeling, and sitting. At Calvary Chapel we found a church where we had returned to what seemed to be the simplicity of the faith of the early Christians. We felt we did not need all those extra things that the Catholic Church had supposedly added over the last two thousand years. I would later discover how Calvary Chapel is very unlike the early Church.

The next few years were exciting times for our family. We made many new friends through church, and we really started to live our lives with a different focus. We began realizing the importance of having God in all areas of our lives. By becoming friends with committed Christians and through studying the Bible, our lives began to be transformed. We saw how seriously God viewed the training and discipleship of children. This caused us to change the way we were doing some things in our family.

We began to see that there were biblical principles regarding the roles of the husband and wife in marriage. When we were first married, Mary was the stronger personality. I had always been more of a follower. Those traits started playing out in our marriage, and she ended up leading our family by default. After coming to understand the roles that God has for the husband to be the servant and leader of the household, things began to change. I became willing to lead, and Mary was happy to step back.

We also began to home school our children. It was a wonderful time for us. By following the principles of God as laid out in Holy Scripture, every area of our family life began to improve and function as we believed God intended.

We were so happy to have found a church where we were growing and learning, and we soon felt a desire to share what we had found with others. The one problem for us was that most of our friends and family were Catholic. We believed that we had found something better, but

we weren't sure what to do about our families. We had
been fed so much misinformation about Catholicism. We
had been told that a person could not be Catholic and still
follow Christ. We had been taught that Catholics believe
that a person has to do good works in order to achieve
salvation. As Protestants, we believed that good works, although a fruit evidence, do not play a part in our salvation, because we cannot add to the finished work of
Christ. Therefore, the Catholic Church erred by saying
that good works are necessary in order to be saved. This
confusion on our part about Catholic doctrine was one
of the prime factors that caused me later to study the differences between Catholic and Protestant beliefs.

Somewhere in the midst of all this, a few things happened that would later play a major role in our returning
to the Catholic Church. First, a couple named John and
Cheryl moved in down the street. They had children who
were very close in age to our children. It seemed natural
that we would become friends.

When I first met Cheryl, I noticed a cross on her neck-
lace. I thought "great, another Christian in our neighborhood". That was until I noticed it was a crucifix and realized she was Catholic. I was astonished when I learned
that Cheryl had attended Calvary Chapel of Costa Mesa,
California, before converting to Catholicism. After my
experience in the Catholic Church and then at Calvary
Chapel, I could not even imagine how such a turnabout
could have happened. How could someone start out at
Calvary Chapel and end up Catholic? It seemed surprising, especially since the Costa Mesa Calvary Chapel had
been started by the founder of Calvary Chapel, Chuck

Smith. In spite of this, Mary was very happy to have a neighbor who was so friendly.

The second major event occurred when I came into contact with an old friend, Pat Bump. We had been best friends for years, but I had not seen him since high school. After I started my career and married, we didn't see much of each other. One day my mom telephoned and said that she had seen Pat's mother in a store and found out that Pat was living very close to where I worked. I got his phone number and gave him a call. I was really excited to share all the wonderful things that had been happening with us since going to Calvary Chapel. I had no idea what I was in for when I called. We spent the first few minutes on the phone catching up on each other's lives. I then brought up the fact that we had left the Catholic Church and had found a church where we were really getting to know Jesus and the Bible. I mentioned this to Pat, hoping to spark some interest. I wanted him to experience "Biblical Christianity". His response caught me off guard. Not only was Pat still a practicing Catholic, he was working for Catholic Answers. Pat explained that it was a San Diego-based Catholic apologetics group founded by Karl Keating. He told me that he had learned a lot about his Catholic Faith in the past few years. We were probably both thinking to ourselves, "How the heck did *he* end up *there*?"

I was surprised and also confused by our telephone conversation. Pat told me about an ex-Protestant minister named Dr. Scott Hahn, who had converted to Catholicism. He said that Professor Hahn had recorded some great audiotapes and that these tapes had helped him to grow in his faith. I figured that this ex-Protestant minister must have been a liberal, mainline Protestant who became disillusioned because he was in a dead church and had decided to try something different.

Pat and I had many conversations over the next few years about my problems with Catholicism. I appreciated the fact that he was always charitable during these discussions, and he never tried to dismiss things that I saw as being problems in the Church. He always took the time to explain the Catholic answer to each question.

On one occasion, I brought up the fact that there had been some very immoral popes at different times in history. How could the Catholic Church claim papal infallibility in light of this history? He explained that infallible meant only that God protected the popes from teaching error in the areas of faith and morals and that the infallibility of the Church's teachings was based on God's faithfulness, not the faithfulness of these men. Fortunately for the Church, God prevented these unfaithful popes from improper teaching. He also explained that not every word that the pope utters is protected under this gift of infallibility, that the pope has to intend to teach *ex cathedra* or "from the chair of Peter". Jesus even told His disciples, "The scribes and the Pharisees sit on Moses' seat; so practice and observe whatever they tell you, but not what they do; for they preach, but do not practice" (Mt 23:2–3). Following this statement Jesus went on to rebuke the scribes and Pharisees for their hypocrisy, but He still held His disciples accountable to submit to their legitimate authority. This sure seemed to shoot holes through my arguments against the papacy on the grounds of certain popes living unholy lives. I had understood the idea of infallibility to mean that anything the pope said was automatically true and that the pope could not sin (impeccability). Pat was very patient and gentle in correcting my many misunderstandings.

Another event occurred that challenged us. We had invited my family to go to the Harvest Crusade. (The crusade is similar to Billy Graham's crusades. People are challenged with the gospel message and are given the opportunity to ask Jesus into their lives.) My parents and youngest sister agreed to go. After the crusade, we went out to eat, and I shared my concerns about Catholicism with my parents and told them about all the great things that we were learning, now that we went to a church that was "based on the Bible". A few weeks later, my dad gave us a book to read called *Answering a Fundamentalist*, by Fr. Albert J. Nevins, M.M. It was my dad's way of helping us see the Catholic side without getting into a confrontation. The book began by explaining what a fundamentalist is (I had never heard the term used before), and how the phenomenon of fundamentalism had begun. All the common objections that I had heard and read about were listed, and then the Catholic position was explained and defended. I did not realize that the Church actually had a biblical basis for most of its teachings, and, as I read, I began to feel very troubled. I finished the book very quickly. The smallest doubt began to creep into my mind that maybe, just maybe, the Catholic Church could be right in a few areas of concern to me. This was a very scary prospect. I had been convinced that the Catholic Church was wrong on all crucial issues. In Calvary Chapel, we had returned to the simplicity of the apostolic faith of the early Church, or so we thought. Mary and I talked about these issues. I had a lot of questions that needed answers. We decided that the best thing to do would be to talk to our pastor. Since he had been brought up in the Catholic Church, we were sure he could help us find the flaws in this book.

Soon after reading *Answering a Fundamentalist*, we went to our church's Family Camp. I decided to bring the book to discuss its points with our pastor. I spoke to him at the first opportunity; I asked him to read the book and give me his opinion. A few days later he returned the book. He said that he had read parts of it, but because there were so many things going on during the week, he had been unable to read it entirely. He did write some comments on different sections of the book on little notes. He said that, since I was sincerely interested, he had a book back at church that I could read. I went to see him the following week. We spoke of our upbringing, and I found that his story was similar. He was born Catholic and went to Catholic schools, but his faith never really made much of a difference in how he lived. It wasn't until he had started dating his future wife and going to a Protestant church that he really gave his life to the Lord and started living his life for God. I asked him if he had ever really studied the differences between Catholic and Protestant beliefs. He said that he had read some but he had not really made an in-depth study. He lent me a book called *Roman Catholicism*, by Lorraine Boettner. He said it was one of the books he had read after leaving the Church.

I took the book home and read it in a few days. The book covered just about every subject imaginable and claimed that many of the Catholic Church's teachings had been invented hundreds of years after the time of Christ.

The impression I received from the book was that the Catholic Church set itself on a par with Scripture, therefore it could just "invent" doctrines whenever it desired.

For example, Boettner claimed that the doctrine of Transubstantiation was invented in 1215. In fact, as I later found out through reading the early Church Fathers, the term "transubstantiation" was first used about 1079 but not formally adopted until the Fourth General Council of the Lateran in 1215, under Pope Innocent III. This was done in response to the heresies of the Albigensians, pantheists, and others. It became abundantly clear to me that the doctrine of the Real Presence of Christ in the Holy Eucharist was believed and unanimously taught by the apostles and the Apostolic Church.

One example of patristic evidence comes to us from St. Ignatius, bishop of Antioch, Syria. Ignatius wrote to the church at Smyrna around 107, concerning those who held heretical opinions: "They abstain from Eucharist and from prayer, because they do not confess that the Eucharist is the flesh of our Savior Jesus Christ, flesh which suffered for our sins and which the Father in his goodness raised up again."

There is no evidence that anyone contested the doctrine of the Real Presence of Christ in the Holy Eucharist during the first thousand years of Church history. When so many heresies ran rampant, no one dared to challenge this core belief founded on the words of Christ in the sixth chapter of St. John's Gospel.

Boettner's book brought up many other distinctly Catholic beliefs and gave similar explanations for them. They were either "inventions" of the Catholic Church that were made up hundreds of years after the time of Jesus and the apostles or they were pagan beliefs and rituals adopted by the Church to make Christianity easier to accept for pagan converts. After reading the book, I felt a lot more at peace about having left the Church, and I was hoping to enlighten my Catholic friends and family about the many errors of Catholicism.

The issue of Catholicism seemed to be just like a gnat, buzzing around us and not leaving us alone. Mary and I would get to the point where we were feeling comfortable, believing that we were in the right place and doing the right thing, and then something would happen to cause confusion once again.

Cheryl had become a source of continued questions for Mary. Since we lived only two houses apart, Mary and Cheryl spent a lot of time together. Invariably when the subject of religion came up they would start to have disagreements. These conversations became very frustrating for Mary. She and Cheryl saw eye to eye on practically everything except religion.

On one occasion, I remember Mary telling me about some problem that Cheryl was facing. When they were talking about it on the phone, Cheryl mentioned that she felt she needed to pray to Mary, Jesus' Mother, about the problem. After they hung up, Mary told me that she didn't know what to say to Cheryl. She wanted to be supportive, but when Cheryl said things like "praying to Mary", Mary was at a loss. I remember talking to Cheryl about praying to the Blessed Mother, and I asked, "Why don't you just pray directly to God instead of Mary?" She answered that she was asking Mary to pray for her just as I would ask another Christian brother or sister to pray for me. Her answer took the wind out of my sails a little, but then I came back with, "Well, the Bible tells us to pray for one another, but where in Scripture does it say to pray to Mary?" Her response was, "Where does the Bible say *not* to pray to her?" I came away from the conversation feeling sure that I was right, but I felt frustrated because of my inability to convince Cheryl that she was wrong.

Another conversation between Cheryl and Mary made a big impact on us. I don't recall the subject that was being discussed, but Cheryl asked Mary, "Where does the Bible teach that it is the sum total of God's revelation, in other words, the Bible and the Bible alone?" Mary came to me with that question, and I set out to find scriptural proof of this fundamental Protestant doctrine. Up until this point, I had never questioned my belief in *sola scriptura* (Latin for "Scripture alone"). This belief was one of two primary reasons given by the Protestant reformers to justify their breaking away from the Church of Rome. I set out to find the verse in the Bible that would support this belief. I thought I had found it in 2 Timothy 3:16–17 which says, "All scripture is inspired by God and profitable for teaching, for reproof, for correction, and for training in righteousness, that the man of God may be complete, equipped for every good work." But as I read the verse more carefully I discovered that it did not say to use only Scripture. It said all Scripture is "inspired by God", and that Scripture is "profitable". It did not say anywhere that it is sufficient or complete in itself. I began searching for other Scripture verses. In Matthew 15:3, Jesus rebuked the

Pharisees: "Why do you transgress the commandment of God for the sake of your tradition?" I believed that the Catholic Church held tradition to be on equal footing with Scripture, thereby obviously violating Jesus' teaching. When Mary explained this to Cheryl, she came back with 2 Thessalonians 2:15, where St. Paul tells the Thessalonians, "So then, brethren, stand firm and hold to the traditions which you were taught by us, either by word of mouth or by letter." So, we found that Holy Scripture did not condemn all tradition. Jesus condemned only corrupt human tradition that tried to circumvent God's commandments. I was beginning to feel like a soldier in battle who was rapidly running out of ammunition.

We didn't realize at the time that even our definition of "tradition" was in error. We now understand that when the Catholic Church speaks of "Tradition" she is speaking of God's revelation, passed down from Jesus and the apostles. Tradition with a small "t" designates something changeable, such as a custom.

Mary told me that Cheryl had a copy of Scott Hahn's conversion story on audiotape. I had known of the tape for quite some time, but up until then I had no desire to listen to it. My curiosity was starting to get the better of me as I heard arguments for Catholic teachings that began to sound as though they made sense. Mary borrowed the tape from Cheryl, and I decided to listen to it while driving to work. I prayed before listening and asked God to help me to see all the flaws in Scott Hahn's reasoning. I just wanted to put these arguments aside in order that Mary and I could get on with our lives.

As I listened to the tape, a couple of things struck me

pretty hard. First, I realized that Scott had been a student at a conservative evangelical seminary and a Presbyterian pastor. I had expected him to be from some liberal denomination, so watered down in theology that even the Catholic Church would seem like a better alternative. When I heard his conservative views on Scripture and of the professors and theologians with whom he had been associated, I knew differently. Many of the names he mentioned were people I looked up to as being conservative and orthodox.

He shared with his audience that he had been extremely anti-Catholic since being "saved" as a teenager. He spoke about his seminary education and what he found in Holy Scripture that started him on his journey to the Catholic Church. At the time, I was so prejudiced against the Catholic Church that I could not imagine how anyone studying the Bible could come to the conclusion that the Catholic Church could be right about anything. After all my anti-Catholic reading and indoctrination, I didn't believe the Catholic Church could, even remotely, give a biblical justification for her beliefs. But, as I listened to the tape, I started to feel sick to my stomach. Professor Hahn told the story of one of his students asking, "Where does the Bible teach *sola scriptura?*" and of how he was unable to find the answer after searching the Scriptures and questioning his peers. I knew that if he could not find a satisfactory answer, the odds of my finding one were not very good.

I don't think I heard half the information on the tape. My head was spinning from the thought that there was even the remotest possibility that the Catholic Church could be the true Church. I remember thinking that either Scott Hahn is right about the Church, or he's got to be the antichrist. I knew it couldn't be that he was ignorant of the "true Gospel" that I had come to know at Calvary Chapel. He was either willfully deceiving people, or he was right.

The next day, Mary and I listened to the tape together. We were sitting on the floor of the bedroom, and, as I watched Mary, I saw the expression on her face change to confusion and then to despair. After the tape ended, we sat silently for a long time. Mary finally said, "Does this mean we have to become Catholic?" I didn't know what to say. For us, leaving Calvary Chapel to return to the Catholic Church was unthinkable. We loved our church. We enjoyed our life. If we could have planned it out, we wouldn't have changed a thing. Everything was built around our beliefs and our life at Calvary Chapel. We also remembered our depressing existence in the Catholic Church.

From our previous experience, we felt that the Catholic Church was empty and the people were, for the most part, dead in their spiritual lives. The thought of going back seemed totally discouraging. We could not imagine that God would want us to leave Calvary Chapel. It had become a home; we had grown and learned so much.

The next significant event for Mary and me came a few months later. Cheryl had some friends, Theresa and Renée, who were like a second family to her. They had grown up together as children. It was this family that had introduced her to the Catholic Church. The parents, Bob and Marcie Fassbender, had been like parents to Cheryl.

The Fassbenders and some of their children and grandchildren lived a few hours away. Cheryl had mentioned them many times before and said that they were a fine family. She also said that they had horses and that the place they lived was really beautiful. It sounded idyllic. John and Cheryl were planning to visit them for the weekend, and they invited us to go along. Mary brought up the idea of going with them and asked what I thought. I didn't like it at all. I had heard that they were all pretty radical Catholics, and the thought of being around a bunch of militants wasn't my idea of a fun weekend. Mary and I discussed it, and, after thinking about it, I reluctantly agreed to go. What really surprised me was that Mary wanted to go. She felt the same way about the Catholic Church as I did, so it seemed strange that she wanted to spend the weekend with those people. Looking back, we can see how the Holy Spirit was beginning to open Mary's heart.

After a long car ride, we finally arrived at Bob and Marcie's. When we walked into the house, I noticed crucifixes and statues. Then, when we met Bob, I noticed a big cross hanging around his neck. I could see we were in for an interesting weekend. We met Bob and Marcie's children and grandchildren. They were all very friendly but also very, very Catholic. We ate dinner with them, and afterward we all sat around the living room and talked. The discussion made me feel very uncomfortable. They were saying, "The Holy Father said this", and "The Holy Father said that." All I could think about was wishing I were somewhere else.

One big decision we had to make was where we would go to church in the morning. We thought about finding a Calvary Chapel, but we didn't want to put the children in a Sunday school class where they wouldn't know anyone. Mary brought up the idea of going to Mass, but I couldn't see the point. I had been to plenty of Masses in my lifetime. I didn't see how this one Mass could be any different. She brought up the fact that we are all Christians, and she didn't see why we couldn't go to Mass with our hosts, just this one time. She also said that the verse "Let the children come to me, and do not hinder them; for to such belongs the kingdom of heaven" (Mt 19:14) kept coming into her mind. She felt it was wrong for us not to take our kids to church because of our hang-ups. She said that we were not supposed to have all these divisions among Christians and that if we didn't go to Mass, we would be adding to the problem. I didn't really know what to say, so I didn't say anything. She asked me if I wanted to pray about it. I said, "No." For me to say "no" to praying about something was a big signal that something was wrong. I can't remember ever saying I didn't want to pray with her. Mary could tell I was really agonizing about it, so she just said that she would support me whatever I decided. It took a long time for me to get to sleep that night.

I woke up the next morning and heard everyone getting ready for church. I started thinking that maybe Mary was right—we should go to church somewhere. I woke up Mary and said, "Do you want to go to Mass?" She almost fell out of the bed. We started getting ready, and Mary went out and told Cheryl that we were going to go to Mass. Everyone was surprised but happy to see us going along.

Mass was just about the same as I had always remembered it. Very few of the people sang; the homily seemed totally irrelevant to reality or to the readings of the day; we said the same old prayers and did the same old things. The only thing that was noticeably different was Bob and Marcie and their family. They really participated in the liturgy. They sang aloud, said the prayers, and, at Communion time, they received the Eucharist with reverence and awe. They all knelt before receiving Communion. I could tell they really believed that Jesus was present under the appearances of bread and wine. I had never seen anyone receive Communion with such reverence, especially since people had started receiving Communion in the hand. I was really impressed.

After Mass, we went out to brunch with the other adults, while one of the older grandchildren watched the children. Bob and Marcie's daughters, Theresa and Renée, both home schooled their children. I was surprised to find Catholics serious about teaching their Faith to their children and raising them to be God-loving people. After breakfast we went to Renée and her husband Brian's house. Our children played with their children, and we began talking about some of the differences between Catholicism and Protestantism. They were trying to understand why we had left the Catholic Church, and I was trying to explain. We talked for quite a long time, and Renée gave me a few books to take home to read. One was a booklet called *Beginning Apologetics*, published by San Juan Seminars. It is thirty-nine pages long and gives a brief but satisfactory explanation and defense of basic Catholic beliefs.

After spending the weekend with people who were such

committed Catholics, believing also that they were truly Christians, I knew something inside me had changed. I felt that I was finally ready to examine honestly the differences between the Catholic and Protestant beliefs. I knew I had to come to terms with Catholicism once and for all, in order for Mary and me to get on with our lives. I also believe that the Holy Spirit guided us in our prayer that day. I knew that He would lead us to the truth, no matter where the journey might end — even if that journey would end with our returning to the Catholic Church.

After our return from the weekend with the Fassbenders, I immediately did two things. First, I told my pastor that I was going to be studying these issues in depth. I needed some sort of finality. I told him that I was apprehensive about beginning the study but that I felt compelled. We prayed together, and that helped to give me a sense of peace.

I wanted to begin my study by reading the early documents of the Church. So my second action was to telephone Pat Bump. I asked him to provide all the information he could find concerning the writings of the early Church Fathers. I didn't want a bunch of Catholic Answers propaganda; I just wanted it straight from the Fathers themselves.

I started reading, and I was shocked at what I found. I had expected to find that the Fathers who wrote before 300 would sound very similar to the teachings I received at Calvary Chapel. I knew that Emperor Constantine had legalized Christianity in the early fourth century, and I figured all the pagan beliefs and practices were gradually adopted by the Church after that time. What I found was that the Fathers all sounded disturbingly Catholic in their beliefs. The more I read, the more I saw the same patterns emerge.

Justin Martyr, around 155, was one example of the Church Fathers. He wrote: "We call this food Eucharist; and no one else is permitted to partake of it, except the one who believes our teaching to be true and has been washed in the washing which is for regeneration, and is thereby living as Christ has enjoined. For not as common bread do we receive these; but since Jesus Christ our Savior was made incarnate by the word of God and has both flesh and blood for our salvation, so too, as we have been taught, the food which has been made into the Eucharist by the Eucharistic prayer set down by him, and by the change by which our flesh and blood is nourished, is both the flesh and blood of that incarnated Jesus." In this one passage, St. Justin explained that baptism regenerates us and that, after the Eucharistic prayer, Jesus truly becomes present under the appearances of bread and wine. After reading this and many other passages from the early Fathers, I began to realize that the teachings I heard at Calvary Chapel didn't look much like the beliefs of the early Church. I started wrestling with this dilemma. Either the early Church started becoming polluted and heretical almost immediately after the time of the apostles, or all these distinctively Catholic doctrines were not really "inventions" after all.

After reading a few of the Church Fathers, I decided to concentrate my study on *sola fide* and *sola scriptura*. I reasoned that since these were the two primary reasons given to justify the Protestant Reformation, they would be the logical starting points.

I first started examining the doctrine of faith alone. I bought a book by the same title, written by R. C. Sproul. As I read it, one point seemed to jump out at me. Whenever Sproul brought up a point that he wanted to elaborate, he would quote the work of present-day Reformed theologians. He would give their opinions, then he would go on to say that he thought they were right in this one area but wrong in some other aspect. As I read through the book, I kept wondering to myself, "How does he know that he is right and the other guys are wrong?" I also remembered my reading of the Church Fathers. It would have been far more convincing if Sproul had compared their writings with his present beliefs. But he compared one modern theologian to another, and he seemed to be leaving out large portions of Christian thought written down through the ages. In fairness to Mr. Sproul, he did give an evenhanded comparison of Catholic and Protestant beliefs, and he also quoted heavily from St. Augustine and certain Church councils. Although he relied heavily on St. Augustine's works to support his own views on justification, he left out the fact that Augustine was very Catholic in his beliefs, for example, baptismal regeneration, the Real Presence of Christ in the Eucharist, and the authority of apostolic Tradition. You need only to read Augustine's writings to see for yourself.

The other major issue for me to deal with was authority. I had already examined it previously, but I needed to look into it further. I read a few books from the Protestant perspective, but none seemed to put forth any new arguments. I bought a tape series by Scott Hahn called *The Bible Alone*. After listening to it and reading more on the subject, I became convinced that not only was *sola scriptura* unbiblical; it was also unhistorical and unworkable.

I now knew that the Bible does not teach that it alone is sufficient for faith and belief. I came to discover that the idea of *sola scriptura* was unheard of until the time of the Reformation. Not one of the Church Fathers taught *sola scriptura.*

In addition, I also began to study the origins of Holy Scripture. I began to wonder about the Bible itself. How did the present canon of Scripture come about? How do we know which books belong in the Bible? I found that the New Testament canon of twenty-seven books was not officially decided upon until the end of the fourth century, at several Church councils. It was the bishops of the Catholic Church who decided the canon. How could the reformers have accepted a body of Scripture that had come from a Church that was supposed to have apostatized in 313? Also, by what authority did they reject Old Testament books that had been used by Jesus, the apostles, and the entire Church for more than fifteen hundred years? That just didn't make sense.

Another point struck Mary and me when we read from a book in the library titled the *Handbook of Denominations in the United States*. We never realized that there were more than twenty thousand denominations. That figure did not even take into consideration the non-denominational churches, such as Calvary Chapel. We could not see how God's plan for the Church was for such division. It seemed to us that any time a person disagreed with a particular teaching or doctrine, he would start his own church. If the Bible alone is our only authority and if we all have the right to private interpretation, then this, it seems to me, is a recipe for endless division. If we all sincerely pray to the Holy Spirit to "guide us into all the truth" (Jn 16:13), why do so many people come up with different interpretations? Is there no real recourse to reconcile these differences? Surely these divisions are not the way God wants His Church to function.

The more I read and studied, the more I was being drawn back to the Catholic Church. Occasionally, Mary would ask how things were going, and I would answer that it seemed as if the Catholic Church might actually be right. That wasn't what she wanted to hear. It wasn't really what I wanted to say either, but the evidence kept pointing us in the direction of Rome.

At that point I could see the handwriting on the wall. I just could not envision the Protestant side somehow making a big comeback and suddenly turning things around. I talked to Mary and told her what I thought. She was not at all happy. For Mary, the thought of going back to the Catholic Church was as repugnant as ever. It was an easier transition for me. As I continued my study, I gradually accepted the idea that the Church Jesus established was the Catholic Church.

One night in church at Calvary, the cat sort of forced its way out of the bag. Up until that point, we had told very few people about our studies. That evening, the pastor's wife approached Mary and asked if she would facilitate a small discussion group during the upcoming women's

Bible study. Mary's reply to her was, "I don't think you want me to do that." When asked why, Mary explained that it looked as if we were going to become Catholic once again. The pastor's wife told Mary that she should talk to her husband after the service. The pastor knew about my studies, but he had no idea that we were seriously considering returning to Catholicism. They invited us to come over for dinner the next night.

We arrived at their house the next evening, and, after dinner, we began to discuss our situation. I brought the *Beginning Apologetics* book that I had received from Renée. We started going through the book issue by issue. We discussed the Eucharist and the Eucharistic passages in St. John's Gospel. Our pastor said that it was obvious that Jesus wasn't speaking in the context of Communion. He claimed that the entire passage concerned a belief in Christ. He believed that, when Jesus talked about eating His flesh and drinking His blood, He was really talking symbolically about believing in Him. For me, John's chapter 6 had always been a disturbing passage. It seemed so obvious to me that Jesus wasn't just talking about simple belief in Himself. He was speaking about giving Himself to us totally, under the veil of the Eucharistic Sacrament. This is not symbolic language; His words were then, as they are today, clear and direct.

As I had studied the Eucharistic discourse in depth, I came to realize its literal truth. To begin with, the context of the passage was the Passover (Jn 6:4). Just prior to Jesus' saying that we must eat His flesh and drink His blood, He miraculously fed the five thousand with five loaves and two fish. When Jesus told the disciples to feed the multitudes, Andrew said, "There is a lad here who has five small barley loaves, and two fish; but what are they among so many?" (Jn 6:9). The disciples couldn't see how Jesus would feed all these hungry people. Yet, Jesus performs this great miracle and gives them a meal to sustain them through the day.

The following day, Jesus shows that He was only setting the stage and preparing the people's hearts for the real Bread He wanted to give them. Jesus starts His discussion by telling the people, "Do not labor for food which perishes, but for the food that endures to eternal life, which the Son of man will give to you" (Jn 6:27). He then went on to say, "I am the bread of life; he who comes to me shall not hunger, and he who believes in me shall never thirst" (Jn 6:35). He clarifies His statement by saying, "I am the living bread which came down from heaven; if anyone eats of this bread, he will live forever; and the bread that I will give for the life of the world is my flesh" (Jn 6:51). It was clear that many of His disciples understood Him literally and correctly. They argued sharply among themselves, saying, "How can this man give us his flesh to eat?" (Jn 6:52).

Jesus went on to say, "Truly, truly, I say to you, unless you eat the flesh of the Son of man and drink his blood, you have no life in you; he who eats my flesh and drinks my blood has eternal life, and I will raise him up at the last day. For my flesh is food indeed, and my blood is drink indeed" (Jn 6:53–55). This certainly doesn't sound as though he were speaking symbolically. His disciples also realize this and say to each other, "This is a hard teaching, who can accept it?" (Jn 6:60). Jesus, aware of their grumbling, asks them, "Do you take offense at this?" (Jn 6:61).

He went on to say that the words He has spoken are "spirit and life" (Jn 6:63). Most Protestants will say that Jesus is saying that the words He speaks are to be understood in a symbolic manner. The problem with that idea is that nowhere in Scripture does the word "spirit" mean "symbolic".

After this, Scripture tells us that many of Jesus' disciples turned back and no longer followed Him. If He had been speaking only symbolically, why didn't He explain Himself more clearly, as He had elsewhere in Scripture, for example, John 4:31–34 and Matthew 16:5–12. "After the other disciples left, Jesus asked the twelve, 'Will you also go away?' Simon Peter answered him, 'Lord, to whom shall we go? You have the words of eternal life; and we have believed, and have come to know that you are the Holy One of God' " (Jn 6:67–69). Even though the apostles didn't fully understand how He would give them His flesh to eat and His blood to drink, they believed him. They had learned to see not only with a limited human perspective but with the eyes of faith. They had just been taught that lesson when Jesus fed the five thousand with five loaves and two fish. Philip couldn't see how Jesus would feed so many with so little, but he soon learned not to look at mere appearances. Jesus later rewarded the apostles' faith by showing them how He would give them His flesh to eat and His blood to drink during the institution of the Eucharist at the Last Supper.

We talked about many other issues that night, but we didn't come away with any answers. I told the pastor and his wife that I would either become his resident expert on Catholicism and all of its errors or I would become Catholic.

I kept studying for the next few weeks. The more I read, the more convinced I became that the Catholic Church was all that she claimed to be. Mary and I had long conversations over an extended period and tried to sort out the many implications this would have in our lives.

Our whole life had revolved around Calvary Chapel, most of our close friends were from the church, and we knew only a few people at St. Martha's. There were so many unknowns for us, but we really felt that was where God was leading.

Little by little, the idea of returning to the Catholic Church was becoming easier to accept. I had worked through various Church doctrines and had begun to see the foundations for them in Scripture and Church history. Most of all, I believe that God placed in me a desire to receive Jesus in the Blessed Sacrament. I began to look forward to the day I could partake, once again, in the Eucharistic celebration as a full member of Christ's Church.

For Mary, however, things were different. Although she had read a lot and listened to audiotapes, she had not had the opportunity to study as much as I. She had been busy home schooling our children, keeping our house running smoothly, and being a mom and wife. She trusted me to lead our family to the right decision, and she had been praying for and supporting me as I studied. For Mary, it was a matter of trusting that I had made the right decision. Although I know she trusted me, it was still difficult for her to understand that leaving Calvary Chapel could be God's will. So many good things had happened to us in our time there, and we had grown so little in our previous time in the Catholic Church, it was hard for her to see this move as being a step in the right direction for us. I wasn't totally certain myself.

There finally came the day when I could assent to the truth. I told my pastor of our decision to return to the Catholic Church. He was surprised. Once again, he asked me to do some additional reading. He asked me to read *Roman Catholics and Evangelicals: Agreements and Differences*, by Norman L. Geisler and Ralph E. MacKenzie. He had read the chapter on *sola scriptura* and had it marked with highlighter. I agreed to read the book. I soon found that I was getting confused again. The book seemed to be a good, convincing argument for the Protestants. I started wondering if I would ever come to know the truth.

At that point, I just had to stop reading and pray. I cried out in my heart to God and said, "How will I ever know what's right?" All of a sudden I felt as if God was telling me to step back and look at the big picture. I saw that there were two alternatives. Do I really believe that the Bible is all that God has given us to know Him, to worship Him, and to be our sole authority? I thought of the history of Protestantism from its inception. It began to splinter almost at its beginning, with Luther, Calvin, and Zwingli, and has since been continually dividing.

Although we had benefited greatly from our time in Protestantism, I just couldn't believe that God had intended His Church to function in this way. It seemed to me that when Jesus founded His Church, He also gave that same Church authority to govern in His name and to have final say on issues that would be disputed.

Scott Hahn made a comment on his conversion story tape that also described my situation. He said that a conversion, if it's going to be a true conversion, must have a supernatural aspect; that God's grace would make up for what we lack in understanding. That is what happened to me. I got to the point where I knew that, if I studied the issues for the rest of my life, I still might not be certain that Mary and I were doing the right thing. When I finally threw up my hands and said, "I don't know what to do!" God came in and made up for my deficiencies.

I believe that Mary had a more difficult transition. Although deep in her heart she knew we were doing the right thing, she had to deal with all the questions from people about why we left Calvary. It seemed as if not a day went by that she didn't run into someone from Calvary Chapel. While I was at work, she was facing all our friends and acquaintances, trying to help them understand what we were doing.

The Holy Spirit used Mary to prompt me to study. I would just as soon have ignored the whole thing, but the Lord kept tugging at Mary's heartstrings. She in turn would tug at me to be the leader of our family and to give a good answer for why we believed what we did. Her willingness to submit in love to me as her husband and to Christ as her Lord in coming into the Catholic Church was a great example to me of what it really means to trust in God even when you don't fully understand.

God has so blessed our willingness to follow Him. We

felt many times as if we were losing all the things that were precious to us. Our church, our friends, our life as we knew it, all seemed to be slipping from our grasp. But Mary and I have both learned from experience that when God closes one door, He always opens another, which is the door to the place He really wants to take us. He gives us the choice of trying to keep going through the door that is closing, because it is safe and familiar. But if we continue in that direction, knowing that God is leading elsewhere, we will miss out on the blessing of really walking by faith.

Looking back now, after being back in the Church for a relatively short time, I see that God has already blessed us more than we could have imagined. One of the greatest blessings is being united with our family in the Church. It's been a joyful reunion and also a great awakening for all of us. Mary and I came to appreciate our Faith through studying Scripture and Church history. Now, our families' eyes have opened to the treasure they've had all along but never fully realized. My mom, dad, and youngest sister are each committed to reading through the Bible during the next year. Dad is reading the writings of the Church Fathers, and he and my sister are taking a Catholic apologetics class. We've also had the opportunity to meet some faithful Catholic families who love Christ and His Church and are living out their beliefs. It's wonderful to be around people who, rather than trying to change the Church to fit their idea of what it should be, accept the wisdom and authority of the pope and the Magisterium and follow them faithfully. David was recently baptized (Pat Bump and Cheryl are his godparents), and Britney

received her First Holy Communion. As we now sincerely
appreciate the sacraments, it is gratifying to see our children receive them. The most wonderful blessing that God
has bestowed upon us is the gift of the conception of our
fourth child. We had become convinced that birth control was wrong about a year and a half before leaving Calvary Chapel, but God waited until we came back into the
Church to bless our obedience.

Explaining things to our friends from Calvary Chapel
has been the most difficult part of returning, but it has
given us many opportunities to share with them and has
caused them to examine their beliefs more closely. Mary
and I both felt that, if we were going to return to the
Church, we would have to share with others all we had
learned and come to appreciate about our Catholic Faith.

I had the privilege of teaching a beginning apologetics
course in our parish shortly after our return. The response
in the parish was tremendous. People are so hungry to understand and to be able to explain and defend their faith.
God has also opened many doors for us to share with
other fallen-away Catholics. We try to evangelize as many
of these people as possible. Many friends knew that there
was something profoundly right about the Catholic Faith,
even if they were no longer members. When people hear
that we're back and actually excited about being Catholic,
they want to know what happened. God has really given
us the opportunity to be truly "evangelical" and to help
people see the full truth of the gospel as proclaimed and
taught by the One, Holy, Catholic, and Apostolic Church.

The Wide Arms
of Mother Church

Scott F. Leary

Wonderful, loving parents raised me in a Catholic home. Looking back, I now realize how God was always present in my life, with certain spiritual aspects of my upbringing that I still remember vividly. My family came into the Church when I was five; I can still picture a middle-aged priest looking into my eyes as I was baptized in the name of the Father, and of the Son, and of the Holy Spirit. I was scared to death at my first confession, but Monsignor Clunan helped me through the experience. I read a Scripture reading during the Mass at which I received First Holy Communion, with my family in attendance, cameras in hand. At parochial school I remember a nun whispering "My Lord and my God" as a priest consecrated the Host at Mass. During Confirmation preparation in eighth grade, I struggled intensely with whether to become a priest or a veterinarian; it sounds silly now, but it certainly wasn't at the time. These memories are now etched into my soul — and the following story is about how I forgot them.

During my adolescent years, family devotion consisted primarily of weekly Mass and a meal blessing. I guess my parents believed I received the remainder of my spiritual guidance from Catholic school — but I didn't. It was as if everyone assumed I had been properly processed into the Church, so let's move on to caring for the poor and feeding the sick. At school there were classes on social justice, but no one ever spoke to me about a relationship with Jesus Christ. Church youth group consisted of planning the next car wash or party. There was little if any guidance on formation of the inner life. I went to Mass and received the sacraments, thank God, but no one ever explained why.

My spiritual life in high school evolved into a sort of bargaining relationship with Christ. What do I have to give up to be a Christian? If I get drunk only once a week, is that good enough to get to heaven? If I go to Mass every Sunday, could I play professional football? How could I mesh being a Christian with being a tough guy? I knew that there was more to my faith than status-quo living, but status-quo living was so much easier. Looking back, those gentle convictions were God's call; it just took Him a while to get my attention.

I went to college in 1981, the University of Mississippi ("Ole Miss"), and from a worldly perspective I had an excellent year. I made super grades and partied every weekend. Who could ask for more? I also quit going to Mass and became utterly miserable. I had created an image and by all outwardly appearances seemed to have it all together, but inside there was a confused young man who was very unhappy. I slowly came to the realization that having fun didn't make me happy. There was a void inside that I just couldn't fill. Something had to change, but what?

My roommate was dating a girl whose roommate happened to be Catholic. Her name was Mary, and she was beautiful! I introduced myself to Mary at a fraternity party and made quite a first impression. We had filled a trash can with Hawaiian Punch and vodka. I had the tell-tale red ring around my lips as I staggered up to her and made a fool out of myself. Although she was not impressed, I was. Several weeks later I swallowed a quarter while playing a beer-guzzling game and decided I had better go to Mass and pray for healing — the first time I had been all year. After church I noticed Mary walking back to her dorm room and asked if I could give her a ride. I explained to her why I had decided to go to Mass. She was obviously awed with my lifestyle because when I asked her to lunch she smiled and said, "Thanks, but no thanks", got out of my Jeep, and left. So much for first impressions.

The summer after my freshman year I left home and worked on a construction project. I needed time away to get my head on straight.

I decided that I would go back to Ole Miss, but I set up several parameters to get my life back in order: (1) I would go to Mass every Sunday, (2) I would quit partying so much, and (3) I would ask out Mary. I implemented items one and two, but I needed some help with number three. My opportunity came in late September.

While I was eating lunch with several friends, Mary

walked by, and I commented that she had the best-looking legs on campus. One of my friends, Terry, put five dollars on the picnic table and challenged me to ask her out. Well, it was the motivation I needed. I got up and slowly walked in her direction, but by the time I reached her some other guy had beaten me to the punch. I had to wait in line for ten minutes, and when it was my turn to speak all I could do was ask her to Mass on Sunday, and she said yes. Terry took back his five dollars and said that didn't count for a date, but it did for me.

I asked her to homecoming several weeks later, and she accepted. We never had another date with anyone else. She was the one, but of course I had to convince Mary that I was the one — a little harder sell. I'll never forget dropping off a half dozen roses for Mary at the front desk of her dorm for Valentine's Day. There were lots of other flowers at the front desk, so I thought I would do a little checking. Holy cow! Two other guys had each left her a dozen roses. So as not to be outdone, I raced back to the florist to buy more flowers before she came down. Mary assured me they were just friends — but I still gave her the most flowers.

God truly blessed me with this wonderful Catholic girl, for in Mississippi there are many beautiful ladies but not many Catholics. And Mary was a capital "C" Catholic. She never tried to act "religious"; Mary just had a special "sense of faith", and it attracted me to her like a magnet. She attended daily Mass held in a little room on campus, so I started tagging along — I would go anywhere to be with her. I can remember asking her to go to Protestant Sunday service with a group of friends; she agreed to go only if she could go to Mass that evening. She would not miss the Eucharist. Just being around her changed me. Christ used this wonderful girl to bring me to Him, and in a special way my relationship to God was, and is, tied to my relationship with this Catholic girl from Columbus, Mississippi.

Through Mary I also met a wonderful priest, Fr. Frank Cosgrove. He was the parish priest at the Catholic church just off campus. His Mass was packed with college kids; there was almost no room for all of them. If the congregation didn't participate, Father Cosgrove would remind us where we were. He was also the first, and still one of the few, priests who would spend his homily talking about abortion. I remember seeing tears running down his face one Sunday as he talked about this tragedy. I'm certain he saved numerous unborn lives on the college campus. Father Cosgrove also held retreats every semester, to get the college kids off campus for a few days to reflect on their lives and their faith. After years of not going to confession, I received the sacrament of reconciliation at my first retreat. I felt so clean and free that I stayed up all night rejoicing.

During this time a young man with Campus Crusade for Christ came and spoke to my fraternity. Campus Crusade is a Protestant organization designed to evangelize college-age youth. He spoke candidly of his faith and love for Christ, and his testimony included a word picture that I'll never forget. He said his college days were analogous to a group of kids speeding down a dark highway. The car was packed with friends and beer. Everyone was talking and drinking, the radio was turned up loud, and it was a great time. However, occasionally the car would pass a sign that said, "Wrong Way." No one but him saw the signs. The car kept going faster, the music kept getting louder, but there were always the "Wrong Way" signs. He didn't want to stop the car and end the party, but he was convinced the signs were right—the car was heading for destruction. He said that the signs are from God, that there are several people in the room right now that need to stop the car, and that he was there to help.

Clint was talking to me, and I knew it. At the end of his talk he passed out cards to everyone in the room. The cards asked some benign questions, one of which was "Would you like to have lunch?" If anyone knew that I was talking to this guy I would be ruined—it didn't fit my image. I secretly checked the lunch response and put the card in the basket while outwardly I discounted everything this crusader had just said. I left the meeting and anxiously awaited his call.

During lunch I asked Clint if I had to give up country music, lifting weights, and hunting and fishing in order to be a Christian. He smiled and gently explained that I had missed the point. Christianity was more of a state of being rather than a state of doing. God created me just as I am. The initial inquiry should be whether or not I have given my life to Christ. Jesus will help me out with the peripheral details. The meeting made an impact on my life, not so much by what was said but the fact that the reality of Christ was dealt with in such a direct manner. These guys loved Jesus and weren't afraid to say it. The next week, when I walked into a fraternity Bible study, you could have heard a pin drop. I saw no conflict with my Catholic Faith and Campus Crusade, so I proceeded in both directions.

My relationship with Mary proceeded, and we were married the summer before our senior year. We graduated at Christmastime 1984, moved to New Orleans, and I went to work for an accounting firm. We were twenty-one years old and, for the first time in our lives, on our own.

Immediately after our arrival in New Orleans, one of my superiors asked Mary and me to join a Bible study. He was an ex-Catholic preparing to quit his job to attend a nondenominational Bible seminary. Since we didn't know the difference between nondenominational Christianity and Catholicism, we agreed to go. It seemed as if Protestants were the only people having Bible studies anyway. We met once a week for prayer and study. Never had I been around people who were so vocal about their faith. Our study leader explained that the rapture would occur soon, a time when all Christians would be taken to heaven. Immediately after this rapture there would be a seven-year tribulation period of great torment, followed by a thousand-year period in which Christ would come back to rule the world. Wow! I had never heard such a thing. At the time I didn't know that this type of dispensationalist theology had been in existence only for a little more than a hundred years and was not even accepted by much of Protestantism. All I knew is that these people were sincere and appeared legitimate, and they had a Scripture verse for every proposition.

The study leader gently explained that the reason I had never heard of the rapture and the thousand-year reign was because Catholics didn't believe in the Bible. He also said that most Catholics would be left behind when the rapture occurred. Now, wait a second, "them's fightin' words!" He challenged me to find Purgatory in the Bible and used my dumbfounded expression to prove the point that Catholics were unbiblical. Although I could not respond to his allegations, I could not deny that these folks were sincere and that they were convinced that Catholicism was heresy. We stayed in the Bible study, and through it all our faith in Christ continued to grow.

In 1985 Mary and I moved to Nashville, Tennessee, so that I could enter the real estate field there. We joined the local Catholic church and got involved in the parish youth group. As our participation in Church increased, my desire for a deeper relationship with Christ increased. I began to read the Bible and drop by church to pray on my own. We were invited to join another Bible study, hosted by several Church of Christ couples in our neighborhood. Seeing no conflict in our beliefs, Mary and I decided to go. Nevertheless, our hosts perceived a conflict, because we were dis-invited after several months. It really didn't matter; our faith seemed to inch along, step by baby step.

In 1986, I heard of a children's home in Gadsden, Alabama, founded by John Croyle, an All-American Alabama football player. He sounded like my kind of Christian. Mary and I decided to visit. Big Oaks Boys Ranch is a home that cares for abandoned and abused children, raising them in Christian homes. John Croyle was six foot six, wore jeans and cowboy boots, and talked about Jesus as though Christ were sitting at the table with us. He had started out in the late 1970s caring for three abused kids in a farmhouse, and by 1986 he was raising more than fifty boys. He refused any governmental or United Way assistance because accepting such help would prohibit the proclamation of the gospel, something Croyle would never agree to. Croyle also said that he would open a home for girls in the near future. Tears formed in his eyes as he explained that a judge had recently denied him custody of an abused girl because his home was for boys, and two weeks later the girl was killed by her father. For John, such a situation was unacceptable and had to be dealt with. I was amazed at this man's faith.

Croyle said that the life of Christian service was the most demanding life imaginable, and also the most rewarding. He asked if I had ever considered it. I said I hadn't yet, and I wasn't sure what I should do. He gave me a book to read and told me to write out my testimony and send it to him. I had never seen such an uncompromising form of Christianity. When Mary and I told John we were Catholics, he looked a little puzzled. He explained that he was Baptist because the Baptists were closest to authentic biblical Christianity. I was troubled because this man of faith was uneasy with Catholicism and also because I had never been challenged this way in the Catholic Church. In addition, I knew that, unlike John Croyle, Catholic Charities received money from the government and the United Way; how could they accept the money *and* proclaim the gospel?

One day with John Croyle had a profound effect on my life. I returned to Nashville recommitted to my faith. However, as my Christian journey proceeded, a slight problem developed: my job. My boss patterned himself after Gordon Gecko in the movie *Wall Street*, and I soon found myself very uncomfortable with the greed and quasi-unethical dealings in which I was participating. Life began to speed faster and faster, so Mary and I decided to call "time out", and both of us made the decision to go to law school. If I had been Protestant, I might have gone to a seminary, but since I was a married Catholic, law school sounded reasonable. Certainly God could use our law degrees. We quit our jobs and hit the road. In 1988 we went back to school at Ole Miss.

Upon entering law school, Mary and I again became involved in our local parish, and we had our first child, Forrest. By this time Father Cosgrove had moved on, and the campus church was not the same. Student participation had dwindled; there were no more retreats. Mary and I were lectors at Mass, but again we found ourselves joining Protestant Bible studies, sponsored by members of the Presbyterian Church of America (PCA). There were no opportunities for Bible study at our small parish. I was again presented with a dynamic form of Christianity sponsored by sincere and knowledgeable people. Instead of starting a Catholic Bible study ourselves, Mary and I continued with our Protestant friends. We didn't want to leave.

While in school I also had to commute long distances to work, and I began to listen to Christian radio. The station consisted of programs sponsored by evangelical Protestant preachers and laymen, such as Dr. James Dobson, R. C. Sproul, Dr. James Kennedy, John MacArthur, Steve Brown, Charles Stanley, and Adrian Rogers. They spoke about a dynamic form of Christianity and a personal relationship with Jesus Christ. I knew there was more to my Christian walk than weekly attendance at Mass, and here were people explaining why. It was the kind of enthusiasm I had heard in the voice of John Croyle. But what troubled me was that these speakers occasionally referred to the folly of Catholicism, that the Catholic religion had no real doctrine of salvation, that it abandoned Scripture for ancient tradition unsubstantiated by the Bible. I began to look forward to the drive just to listen to these people preach. I slowly began to evolve into a Protestant, specifically, an evangelical Presbyterian Protestant. I began to be uncomfortable with Catholicism and to contemplate leaving the Church.

We graduated from law school in 1991, had a second child, Mary-Haston, and moved to Jackson, Mississippi. I began work at a local law firm. Mary and I had several close PCA friends, and we were immediately included in their Christian crowd. As our Bible studies continued, we were occasionally presented with questions we could not answer. Why are you Catholic? Why do you worship Mary, pray to the saints, and say that the pope is infallible? Why do you believe information not contained within the Bible? Although I had no answers, my Protestant brothers did, and they began to feed me audiotapes by Protestant theologians who were not in the least bit inhibited in explaining why Catholicism is wrong. In particular, a theological professor named R. C. Sproul explained, in a seemingly analytical and authoritative way, why the Catholic Church was grossly in error and how Christianity had been saved by a group of reformers five hundred years ago. I became addicted to his message.

I also received numerous books from my Protestant friends. While Mary was leery of the volume of information we were receiving, I gobbled it up. During the summer of 1991 I read a book entitled *Born Again,* written by Protestant author Chuck Colson. Colson admitted that the title had become a rather overused evangelical cliché, but he asserted that he could find none better. The book chronicled Colson's life from the power and prestige of general counsel to President Nixon to that of a devoted Christian. The book challenged me to come "out of the closet" and join the fellowship of the unashamed. I started by simply carrying a Bible to work and placing it on my desk for everyone to see. Such a small and seemingly inauthentic gesture was an important step for me. I was soon leading a Bible study at work. To this day I have great admiration for Chuck Colson.

In addition to my Bible study at work, Mary and I began to attend a local PCA church. Its Sunday service was like nothing I had ever experienced. The forceful presentation of Christianity was impressive and, for me, persuasive. My discomfort with Catholicism grew, and I became more vocal about my desire to leave the Church. My wife, however, did not share my views. She agreed that Protestantism was vibrant, but she always insisted that something was missing. The sermons were great, but their service was never over, never complete. There was no Eucharist! Mary argued that there was nothing supernatural about their faith, only great speaking and well argued dogma. I insisted that she was just bound to her Catholic culture and that things would get better. They didn't!

After attending the PCA church for several months, at

my insistence we entered their newcomers' class, which contained more authoritatively presented doctrine and occasional criticism of Catholicism. Sunday became the worst day of the week. We would first attend the PCA church service, then the newcomers' class, and thereafter immediately go to Mass. Mary would cry all the way to the PCA service, and it got to the point that I could no longer sit through Mass.

Nevertheless, my Protestant journey was not without obstacles for me. For instance, I recall the first Sunday Mary and I received the Lord's Supper at the Presbyterian Church. While I was indeed troubled by what had happened, Mary was livid. She was convinced that she had just participated in some uninformed attempt to reinvent the Blessed Sacrament. It was blasphemy. I reasserted that we were both merely reflecting our Catholic upbringing. Besides, I said, Protestants teach that the Catholic doctrine of Transubstantiation was invented in the thirteenth century by Rome. Mary was not persuaded by my explanation.

Mary informed her parents of our struggles, and to say her family was concerned is an understatement. Family tension peaked when my mother-in-law contacted our bishop and parish priest and ordered them to stop us from attending a Protestant church. Mary's aunt was a Benedictine sister, and consequently every nun in Arkansas was praying for us. I, in turn, was praying for them.

By late 1991 I had an established group of Protestant friends, and the backbone of our friendship was our common faith in Christ. With their assistance I became involved in Evangelism Explosion, a Protestant evangelistic program designed to lead people to Christ. The program is based on series of questions designed to determine whether or not the person understands the gospel message, as well as an outline to guide the messenger in the proclamation of the gospel. Evangelism Explosion involved weekly classes and prayer partners, as well as face-to-face evangelism. It is a sincere effort to proclaim the good news according to reformed Protestant theology. I memorized the format.

While involved in Evangelism Explosion, I also became a sponsor in our parish RCIA class, in an undercover capacity, of course. I considered myself a secret agent for Christ. RCIA classes are the process by which non-Catholic adults are initiated into the Catholic Church. In our parish, RCIA classes last for approximately nine months, with initiation and First Holy Communion occurring on Easter Sunday. RCIA provided a perfect format for me to evangelize my uninformed Catholic brothers and sisters. On the night that the Catholic understanding of our Blessed Mother was presented, I attacked with a vengeance. I proclaimed that in the book of Hebrews Scripture teaches that we can come to Christ freely because He is our brother; we don't need Mary as some sort of an intercessor. Of course, I was blind to the fact that if Jesus is our brother, then Mary must be . . . our mother? On another occasion the priest allowed me present a topic to the class, at which time I presented the entire Evangelism Explosion format. My Protestant friends prayed for me in their homes as I proclaimed salvation by faith alone to the entire RCIA class.

I even invited friends to Scripture study in my home,

and I carefully used Galatians and Romans to teach other Catholics the reformed Protestant gospel message: that man is saved by grace through faith alone (*sola fide*). I also incorporated the other pillar of the Reformation into my teaching: that Scripture is a Christian's sole authority (*sola scriptura*). I was convinced that Catholicism had abandoned the fundamental principles of *sola fide* and *sola scriptura* as a result of centuries of corruption and pagan influence. I was happy to accept a Protestant explanation of Catholicism, while never attempting myself to discover what the Catholic Church teaches.

After several years of Protestantism, in early 1992 I finally followed Mary's advice and decided to voice my concerns to a Catholic priest. I had done my homework, and I was convinced that no priest could answer my evangelical objections. Father Cosgrove, my favorite priest from Ole Miss, was then in Jackson, and I drew my Protestant assertions on him like a gun. However, Father Cosgrove would not argue; he only prayed with me and calmly discussed my concerns. I took his refusal to debate as weakness of position and pronounced victory. Father Cosgrove did, however, offer me some tapes by Scott Hahn, a former Protestant minister and theologian who had become Catholic. He had just received the tapes from a Presbyterian seminary professor who taught at Reformed Theological Seminary in Jackson and who was converting to Catholicism. I refused to listen. I knew plenty of Catholics who had become Protestants, and I was not interested in dueling audiotapes. After all, how can anyone defend indefensible positions?

Mary and I also consistently prayed about the issue, asking for God's guidance and will for our lives. It appeared as if we would never make any progress, but then, slowly, I began to make headway with Mary. During the summer of 1992, the dam broke. After numerous meetings with Father Cosgrove, he finally asked me if there were any experiences with the sacraments that I could remember, concerning the Eucharist, or perhaps the sacrament of reconciliation, or any other. I confirmed that there were, but that such memories were not important to this decision. Father Cosgrove, then, to my surprise, informed me that he feared for my soul if I left the Church. This humble priest informed me that I could not leave the Eucharist or force my wife to leave. I asked if he was questioning our salvation. He said he was. Speaking out of love, Father Cosgrove gave us a stern warning, and for that I will be eternally grateful. Nevertheless, at the time I was enraged. I told Mary I would never again attend a Catholic church, and for the first time she agreed. This was not a joyful occasion, simply the culmination of a long process. We called our friends to let them know we had finally made a decision. On that Wednesday afternoon, it was finally all over, or so I thought.

I got to work on Thursday morning ready to get on with my life. It just so happened that a new partner had been hired by my law firm that week, John, from Dallas, Texas. After a meeting at the firm, John approached me about going to lunch. He had heard I was Catholic and was seeking advice on which parish to attend. I agreed and thanked God for providing another Catholic with whom I could share the gospel. John did not know that the day before I had finalized my separation from the Church.

At lunch John told me that he had converted to Catholicism two years earlier. My response was quick and direct, "Why would someone convert to Catholicism?" I questioned John's salvation. John smiled and asked if I wanted the long or the short version. I said I had an hour. He then quietly asked if I had ever heard of a small town in Yugoslavia called Medjugorje. I said yes and braced for a "Mary story", but I must admit I was also curious. John seemed reasonable enough, graduating at the top of his law school class and being a successful lawyer.

He stated that two years earlier he had been struggling with going to the seminary when a friend gave him a book entitled *The Message*, about the Blessed Virgin's alleged appearances in Medjugorje, Yugoslavia, now Bosnia. John read the book only because a Protestant named Wayne Wieble wrote it. But he could not put the book down until he finished reading it. John explained that by virtue of being the Mother of Christ, our first-born Brother, Mary is our own spiritual mother as well, given to us by Jesus at the cross (see Jn 19:26–27). Mary is simply bringing us her Son, just as she had two thousand years ago: "Do whatever he tells you" (Jn 2:8). Her message has always been the same. Medjugorje is Our Lady's call to peace, conversion, and repentance, with an emphasis on prayer, fasting, Bible study, monthly confession, and daily celebration of the Eucharist.

The book spoke to his heart, and John immediately decided to go to Medjugorje. Since at that time he was a partner in a large Dallas law firm, he could afford to take the trip. John reasoned that if it was true, if the Virgin Mary was appearing in a little town in Yugoslavia, then this was something he must see. If it was a hoax, then God would still honor his pilgrimage. John learned how to pray the Rosary, and he began living the messages of Medjugorje. Finally, the big day came. John packed and flew to New York to catch a connecting flight to Yugoslavia.

The plane was a day late, so John had a layover. In the middle of the night before his flight to Yugoslavia, he awoke in his hotel room with an overwhelming urge to pray the Rosary. Hours passed like minutes. John explained that he had never prayed like that before — it was a gift from God. With each decade of the Rosary it was as if he were actually there to witness Jesus' life; the Incarnation of our Lord in Mary's womb, the visitation of Mary to Elizabeth, the birth of Christ, the presentation in the temple, the agony and crucifixion, the Resurrection, the Ascension, Pentecost. When he finished praying the sun was up, and when he turned on the light he saw that his rosary had turned gold. Interesting. I had never heard of such a thing.

The plane ride over consisted primarily of Catholics on pilgrimage to Medjugorje. Nevertheless, when a dumbfounded John showed them his rosary, the passengers were skeptical to say the least. Where did you get it? is it trick metal? why would it do that for you? John said, "Hey, y'all are the Catholics. I thought you folks knew what was going on here." On the ride back the scepticism had been erased, for all but a handful of the passengers had gold rosaries. John went on to describe numerous miracles that occurred while he was in Medjugorje, and he even had a picture of one. Nevertheless, he was careful to point out that this was not a story of miracles. The true miracle of Medjugorje was its fruit, conversion to Christ. People should not go to Medjugorje shopping for miracles; they should only go searching for a deeper relationship with Our Lord. Miracles are just icing, validation of the messages God asked Mary to give us.

While John's sincerity was obvious and moving, his story convinced me of nothing. Nevertheless, the timing of this meeting was bothersome, pushing the "coincidence envelope" so to speak. When I told John of our decision to leave the Church, finalized just the day before, he smiled. Upon his return to Dallas from Medjugorje, John had become Catholic, and, after several years of spreading the messages, he realized that it was time for him to move on. John explained that his move to Jackson, Mississippi, was an act of God. He then quietly thanked Jesus for showing him at least one reason — me — why he moved to Dixie. He looked me square in the eye and said, "God sent me here to tell you that you cannot leave His Church." Nothing John had said before convinced me of anything, but at that moment I was touched by the Holy Spirit. I couldn't speak; I just got up and went back to work.

When I got back to my office, I closed the door and got down on my knees. I could articulate nothing in my prayer; I just knelt down next to Jesus and let His light warm me. I sat there and cried as years of turmoil melted away. At the very height of my arrogance, I was humbled. The Catholic Church was true — and I knew it. At that moment I couldn't explain why, but it didn't matter. I just sat there in joyful awe.

Even today it is difficult to articulate my experience; I

was touched by grace. Any attempt to explain seems only to lessen the reality of what God did for me. And what astounded me most was that I knew the Mother of God existed, not as some female goddess, but as Christ's Mother who had prayed to her Son especially for me. At that moment in my office I knew the Blessed Virgin was present, and it were as if she gently whispered, "Behold, my Son." I was no longer talking to Jesus; I was with Him. I knew my life would never be the same. I called Mary and told her what happened; there was no confusion — only divine grace, acceptance, and agreement. When I got home from work we rejoiced!

I got up Friday morning and went to Mass; the turmoil was truly over. For the first time in years my soul was calm. I had never before just let Jesus hold me, but I did that morning. All the statues and stained-glass windows that depicted Christ's life and the life of His Church, everything that had made me so angry, now comforted me. It was as if I were looking at a photo album of a family I was now part of. And when I went to confession and then received Jesus in the Blessed Sacrament, I believed. I never wanted to leave. Although John witnessed numerous miracles, nothing that happened to him can compare to what happened to me. I was changed, touched by Jesus in the most wonderfully unanticipated way. After years of confusion and consistent prayer, I found out that God was faithful in His love for me. At the very moment I thought I had it all figured out, I was brought to my knees to receive a special grace. Although I still cannot adequately explain the communion of saints, I know that I will be eternally grateful for the prayers of Our Blessed Mother.

Although she faded into the background after that experience, I will always know that she is my constant companion. At the very time I denied her existence, she brought me to her Son and to His Church. "Do whatever he tells you"; the message is still the same.

People may think that John somehow persuaded me to stay in the Church. Not true! I want to make clear that John convinced me of nothing. This mild-mannered business lawyer did not hypnotize me, trick me, or brainwash me. In fact, John is one of the most unassuming people I know. God was just happy to use one of His servants to further His plan.

The next week I was sent out of town on business, and I took those Scott Hahn tapes that I had previously rejected. Praise the Lord! Due to my background, I longed for a biblical appreciation of the Church. Though I had never met the man, Hahn became the teacher I so badly needed— someone who could explain Catholicism with fervor and intellectual honesty. Hahn belonged on those radio shows that I had listened to. Remarkably, almost instantaneously Christ surrounded me with numerous "born again" Catholic friends and teachers of the Faith. I found them at daily Mass.

During my Protestant days I had thought of myself as a pseudo-expert on the errors of Catholicism. However, I had never read a book about Catholicism written by a Catholic author. My knowledge of the Church had come solely from Protestants writing about Catholicism. If I had researched my faith as I research the law, my questions would have been answered much sooner. In addition, by this time in my life I had read and outlined the New Testament several times. But, after my conversion, when I went back and read John 6:48–71, I noticed that I had not even highlighted the text. It was as if I had been reading the Bible with blinders on. Here Christ repeated over and over again, "Unless you eat the flesh of the Son of man and drink his blood, you have no life in you", and I had ignored Him. I remember Scott Hahn saying that after his conversion to Catholicism he went back and read his old Bible, and there between the highlighted portions was the Catholic Church. It was the same for me.

Through my studies I fell in love with Christ's Church. Much to my surprise I discovered that the earliest Christians were the same in faith and practice as the Roman Catholic Church of today. They believed in the Real Presence and baptismal regeneration, and they had a structured hierarchy and liturgical worship. Why, they even called themselves Catholics. My evangelical days had given me a sincere appreciation of Scripture, and I was astonished to see over and over again that Catholicism takes Scripture at face value. Whether it is the Real Presence in John 6:48–71 and 1 Corinthians 10:16–17, 11:23–30; the sacrament of reconciliation in John 20:22, and 1 John 1:9; the papacy in Matthew 16:17–19; baptismal regeneration in John 3:5–8, Titus 3:5, and 1 Peter 3:20–22; the authority of the Church in Matthew 18:18 and 1 Timothy 3:15; Jesus communing with the saints on the Mount of Transfiguration; or the recognition of Mary as blessed from generation to generation, the Church is loyal to the very word of Scripture.

I began to realize that in order to understand Catholicism one must understand family. Through the Catholic

Church, God the Father reestablished mankind into the family of God. This was accomplished by the unmerited gift of our first-born Brother, Jesus Christ, who gives us a participation in His divine Sonship. We participate in Christ's Sonship, and we become members of God's family, initially through baptism, whereby we are adopted as sons and daughters of Our Lord. Suddenly the Catholic term "Holy Mother Church" began to make sense.

The Church is the Bride of Christ, and it is for her that Christ sacrificed Himself to make her holy (Eph 5:25–26). As the Bride of Christ, the Church brings forth new life in Christ through the sacrament of baptism. Through baptism, she gives the Lord the children of whom she is mother. Infants and converts were placed in the waters and emerged "born again of water and the Spirit" (Jn 3:5). Thus, when we are spiritually reborn at baptism, we acquire a new mother, Holy Mother Church. Since the Church is our mother, we are all members of the same great family. "All the saints and angels belong to us," wrote Jesuit theologian Henri de Lubac, "the heroism of the missionary, the inspiration of the Doctors of the Church, the generosity of the martyrs, the genius of the artists, the burning prayer of the contemplative." Mother Church is wide open—not a small group of like-minded individuals; she is truly Catholic. Not an elitist, she has room for every culture, class, education level, and personal temperament. This family is as wide as the world.

I understood Fr. Benedict Groeschel's statement that "Catholics don't go to church with their friends; they go with their family." Through the Mass, the family of God is drawn together to offer praise and thanksgiving and to par-

ticipate in the once-for-all sacrifice of Our Lord through
His sacred family banquet. Because there is one loaf, we
who are many are one body, for we all partake of the
one loaf (1 Cor 10:17). Once I began to understand the
relevance of family and Eucharist, I began to appreciate
the Mass. The value of Sunday service was no longer centered on the sermon and dependent on the personality of
a preacher. Mass is worship, and through the Mass I am
one with millions of fellow believers who partake in the
same loaf all over the world.

This concept was brought home to me several months
after my conversion. One weekday morning, I commented
to a Protestant friend on how special a particular Mass
was. His response was "Really, what did the priest talk
about." And, you know what, I couldn't remember. I had
just had a wonderful experience at church, and I couldn't
even remember what the homily was about. My wife was
right when she had commented that, while Protestant services were inspiring, they were never finished, because
there was no Eucharist. During our time of uncertainty,
I couldn't see that it was the supernatural reality of the
Mass and the Church that she missed.

The Catholic concept of family doesn't end with the
Church; it begins there. The world thinks that the Catholic Church is obsessed with sex and tries to ensure that no
one enjoys sexual expression. In reality, the Church is obsessed with marriage. Being herself a bride, the Church is
forever linked to marriage. The Catholic Church teaches
that marriage is not a chance product of evolution, but
it was established by God to give us some idea of the re-

lationship He wishes to have with us. A husband's love for his wife is to be as Christ's love for His Church (Eph 5:21–33). The Church's concern for marital sexuality arises not from a rigid preoccupation with moral norms, but because sex is the door that seals the marital covenant. Through the Church, I was able to understand that the sexual embrace within a Christian marriage is in reality an act of profound worship. As Scott Hahn says: "Sex isn't good; sex isn't great; sex is HOLY!"

When I realized that what we do with our bodies within the marriage covenant is as much a religious question as is sex outside the marriage covenant, I began to understand the Church's refusal to legitimize divorce, contraception, or sterilization. This realization had a profound and tangible effect within my marriage. Prior to our conversion, Mary and I planned on having only three children, but after our return to the Church, we began to study the Church's explanation for her opposition to contraception. I began to see that the holy and spiritual aspect of sex should not be separated from the gratification of sex; the procreative should not be separated from the unitive. The two dimensions of conjugal union cannot be artificially separated without damaging the deepest truth of the conjugal act itself.

This truth is even borne out by Scripture, specifically the Onan account in Genesis 38:6–10. Here the Lord expressed His displeasure with contraceptive behavior, and Onan was slain for practicing withdrawal. For two thousand years Christians, including Luther, Calvin, and Wesley, recognized this teaching as a condemnation of contraception. It was not until the 1930s that Protestantism broke ranks, beginning with the Anglican Church at the Lambeth Conference.

The Church protected Mary and me from a terrible decision, and by the grace of God we avoided sterilization. Thus, Mary and I have a tangible result of our return to the Catholic Church: His name is Luke. Our fourth child was born six weeks early on July 4, 1995; he stayed in intensive care for two weeks. As I sat beside Luke's incubator, thanking God for my son and praying for his health, my decisions began to make sense. While the Christian walk may be difficult at times, God is always faithful. I have a son to prove it.

By God's grace my faith continues to grow — sometimes in exuberant leaps and sometimes step by painful step. Growing in Christ has occasionally resulted in fear and confusion, as my professional ambition is continually redirected to the cause of Christ. I no longer have a five-step plan for financial security and success, but in the most marvelous way that's OK. My selfish ambition is being replaced by something much more precious: a glimpse of reality. Jesus lives, and my life is but a snapshot of eternity! While I may often be confused as to where I am going, the Holy Spirit will be my faithful guide. I will follow, sometimes complaining and doubting, but by His grace always following.

It may appear that I am now as anti-Protestant as I once was anti-Catholic. That is not true. I have a deep appreciation for the faith of my Protestant brothers and sisters. One of the saddest things in my life is the fact that many of my friendships suffered due to my conversion. This was mostly my fault. I wanted everyone to receive the same gift I had received, to feel what I felt, to understand what I finally understood. In my zeal to explain Catholicism, I alienated many of the people I felt closest to. I never wanted to show a lack of respect for others' beliefs, but perhaps I did. It's just that the Church sorely needs the devotion, enthusiasm, and knowledge of Protestant converts. I hope I can play some role in that endeavor.

Conversion is a form of martyrdom. It involves the surrender of oneself—body, mind, and faith—to Christ. It requires being led to "where you do not want to go" (Jn 21:18–19). Martyrdom does not necessarily mean death, and generally it does not. Martyrdom means walking the way of Christ, and for some it may mean joining the Catholic Church. But martyrdom is also joyful. Christ promised us that:

> Unless a grain of wheat falls into the earth and dies, it remains alone; but if it dies, it bears much fruit. He who loves his life loses it, and he who hates his life in this world will keep it for eternal life. If anyone serves me, he must follow me; and where I am, there shall my servant be also; if anyone serves me, the Father will honor him (Jn 12:24–26).

The Long and Winding
Road . . . Back Home

Sue Sowden

It would be easy to say that my husband and I left the
Catholic Church in 1977 because of some theological disagreement or because of some practice that offended our
sensibilities. It would be easy to say that we strode out
surrounded by a righteous cloud of indignation, tossing
our heads at an obvious spiritual abuse that would have
appalled anyone with any sense. It would be easy to say,
but it just isn't true. Actually, I would have to describe our
exit as a fading out. If our participation in, and love of,
the Church was a bright color photograph in 1967 when
we married, by 1977 it had faded to a frayed brown and
beige print.

Looking back, I think that if someone, anyone, had
come into the cry room — to which we were relegated during Sunday Mass because of our five small children — and
tried to talk us into staying in the Church, we probably
would have. But that didn't happen, and we felt increas-

ingly isolated. One Sunday, after struggles on many levels, and after changing a couple of diapers in the cry room my husband and I looked at each other and sighed, "We can do this more easily at home", and that was that.

Much had happened to transform a pious and fervent couple into two worldly and unbelieving ex-Catholics. Before we met, my husband, Don, was planning on becoming a Jesuit, and I had already been accepted into a convent of semi-contemplative nuns. I was a senior, and Don was a graduate student at San Francisco State University. We met at the Newman Club. The priest who headed the club apparently thought that we were made for each other. One day, when we went to him about my struggle with whether to marry or to become a nun, he spoke strongly against becoming any kind of religious at a time when the Church was in such turmoil and transition. We were both accustomed to submitting to whatever a priest advised, and we were in love.

At the time of our marriage, it seemed that many Catholics were undergoing a subtle but powerful rebellion against authority. Pope Paul's encyclical *Humanae Vitae* had caused a major controversy among our peers. I am sure that there were many Catholic couples who were faithful to the Church's teaching in *Humanae Vitae*, but we knew only one. It was generally assumed that the whole issue was a dinosaur that only quaint old traditionalists took seriously. I guess one could say that we were twenty-something quaint old traditionalists. Those were also heady times for many priests. Several people I knew were advised by their parish priest to violate the Church's teaching regarding contraception. Those people were told that it was simply a matter of time before the Vatican eased up on the restrictions.

Also in the air was a new and intoxicating cynicism. The country was deeply involved in Vietnam, and many people saw American activities there as an abuse of power and authority. "Question authority" became the bumper sticker of the 1970s. That disillusionment with authority spilled over into many Catholics' relationship with the Church. It flooded into the lives of many young priests, who took the new openness of Vatican II as permission to do their own thing. The laity began to hear strange new ideas that the Church had never taught before, and they endured one liturgical change after another in the headlong rush for novelty. The process often ran roughshod over the tender sensibilities of lifelong lay Catholics.

We had very close friends who were the parents of nine children. They were very vocal about their disagreement with just about every change that popped up in the Church. They now had to put up with "banners and broken-necked stick-figures" in the new church art and the increasingly social/humanistic content of Sunday sermons. These friends were a powerful encouragement to us because of their heroic generosity to the poor and their obedience to the spirit of *Humanae Vitae*, and we loved them very much. But we also loved the Church. Even though we agreed with our friends on most of the issues, we began to feel like children who, when they see their parents fighting, would rather back away from both parents than to have to make a choice between them.

I had come into the Catholic Church in the United States at age thirteen, but I had been introduced to the

Church during a four-and-a-half-year stay in Guadalajara, Mexico. My mother had taken my two sisters and me to Mexico to visit friends, but it was clear that the visit was mostly so that she could get away to think clearly about her failing marriage to my father.

I fell in love with Mexico instantly for many reasons, not the least of which was that my parents weren't yelling at each other any longer. In 1955, six months after arriving there, I was stricken with polio and paralyzed from the neck down. I was nine years old. The Salk vaccine had arrived in the U.S., but it had not as yet reached Mexico. After months of therapy, I ended up in a brace and on crutches. My mother allowed me to go to the Catholic school across the street from our house. This was quite a concession, because my mother had strong anti-Catholic sentiments. My sisters attended an American school farther away.

It was at that school that I was introduced to the riches of the Catholic Church and to the kindest and most saintly people I have ever met or am ever likely to meet again. God gave me the Church at the very time that I was beginning to feel the bottom dropping out. I have found that His timing is always exquisite. As a left-handed, nominal Protestant, a grey-eyed blonde with a French last name, I was at first considered a curiosity by my teacher. But this patient and wise nun took me under her wing. I guess one could say I was the teacher's pet, but God used her powerfully to introduce me to Him.

Through that school I also became friends with a girl named Concha and, more important, with her mother. I undoubtedly used Concha's mother to fill the gap where my own mother should have been. My mother was busy enjoying her new-found liberty away from my father, and I remember seeing very little of her. Concha's mother was always home, and I could not get enough of her presence. My hungry little ten-year-old spirit soaked up her love for God, her joy, her elfin sense of humor, and the sparkle in her eyes when she would speak of the miracles Jesus had worked in her life — not the least of which was that she was a diabetic who married at twenty-nine and then proceeded to bear fourteen children. I found out later that she was a descendant of the Ahumada family of Spain, in other words, a relative of St. Teresa of Avila. Concha's mother is to this day my model for what it means to live by a strong and lively faith. Not the kind of faith that some moderns use to try to get God to do what they want, but the kind that prompts one to throw oneself down at Jesus' feet and surrender to whatever He wills. She has always been my model for passionate love and risk, and she is one of the greatest gifts God has ever given me.

Faith was not a struggle for her, whereas for most of us the throne room of God and the whole spirit world are behind a thick, closed door through which we feel we need to yell to be heard and through which we can hear only muffled voices. For Concha's mother, the Lord was right here, right now, as obvious as the next person in the room. As she picked tiny stones out of dried beans at her kitchen table, she would bubble lovingly about how her Precious Lord was doing the same for us — picking the hard places out of the nourishing places in our souls. She did not do one thing with her body and another with her mind; her spirit would soar with the significance of every tiny thing she set her hands to. As she nimbly pulled a needle through linen to create works of art in satin embroidery, we were spellbound by her stories of how her gracious Savior was stitch-by-stitch creating our bridal garments, so that by the end of our lives we could be presented to the Bridegroom dazzling and shimmering with His own creation.

One day I went over to Concha's house and found the whole family sitting on the front porch, dressed for church. They greeted me warmly, and I sat down with them. I looked around at them, gradually becoming aware of the difference between the anxious faces on the children and the playful, even joyful, expression on their mother's face. After years of Jesus coming through for her, you would think (I thought) that her children would have learned at least to trust *her*, if not Jesus. I had no idea this time, however, of the content of her hope. So I asked her.

"My cousin has died", she said. "We're going to his Rosary and funeral downtown." I nodded my head. "Oh." I looked around; I knew they had no car and no phone. I asked, "How . . . are you going to get there?" She smiled and said, "I don't know. We don't even have enough money for the bus right now. I do know that Jesus impressed it upon me that my cousin's soul needs our prayers and that He wants us to be there, so we're waiting for whatever way He will provide for us to get there."

"Oh", I said. For whatever reason, I didn't doubt. We waited about ten more minutes. Concha's brother started whining. "The Rosary starts in twenty minutes! I feel stupid sitting here!"

Just then an old Ford truck pulled up in front of their house, and a lady wearing a hat rolled down the window. "Were you planning on going to the Rosary for Luis? We were on our way and thought you might like a ride."

The angels must have smiled that day, watching that large family crammed into the back of a truck, holding on to their hats. I am grateful that God had me living in a time and place, before the entire world had cars and telephones, in which I could behold His generous attention to detail and His faithful response to a saint for whom the veil between heaven and earth is not thick or even translucent, but transparent.

In April 1976, two months after the birth of our fifth child, Phillip, my doctor discovered that my uterus was covered with fast-growing tumors, and also he found that I was six-weeks pregnant with our sixth child. My doctor recommended that I have an abortion, and quickly. There was absolutely no chance, he said, for the baby to survive to viability, and the prognosis for me was that one day very soon I would stand up and be ankle-deep in blood before I could call an ambulance.

I was accustomed to having doctors shake their heads at me. I had been counseled before marriage not to have any children. I had a very weak back that had undergone two spinal fusions, almost no abdominal muscles, and a brace on my right leg. However, I was also accustomed to shaking my head at doctors. Time and again I had proven their predictions wrong about the things I should not or would not be able to do. When I decided to marry instead of becoming a nun, within that decision was the intent prayerfully to follow the Church's teaching regarding artificial birth control. Don and I believed that God would sustain us, and He did.

The doctor left Don and me alone for a few minutes to consider his recommendation for an abortion. I'll never forget the feeling of loneliness. In spite of the fact that my husband was there holding my hand, saddened and rendered mute himself, I felt dark and abandoned in the depth of my soul.

The recent memory of the events surrounding the delivery of our fifth child earlier that year kept creeping into my mind. A few weeks before Phil was born, I lay in the hospital full of an experimental drug to stop premature labor. My uterus, they told me, was worn out, and I should probably have a tubal ligation during the Caesarian section that would deliver Phil. The doctors said that my life would be in serious danger if I got pregnant again. I knew that sterilization was against the Church's teaching, but I wasn't sure if that held true if my life was at stake.

I called for a priest for advice. About two o'clock one morning an exhausted priest woke me up and gruffly asked me what I needed. I assured him that my problem could wait until he was rested, but he waved his hand and grumbled that we may as well talk, now that he was there. I laid out my problem. His response was curt: "The Church makes rules as guidelines. No rule can fit every circumstance. You have a good case for sterilization. . . . Is there anything else you need?"

I lay awake in the dark with that familiar feeling of falling into an abyss that I had experienced when my mother abandoned us in Mexico to chase after a boyfriend who had jilted her and stolen her jewelry. At that time I was bedridden in a body cast after spinal surgery. Now was the first time I had that sense of abandonment since joining the Catholic Church. I was confused. If the priest had said something like — "Well, this is indeed a challenge to your faith, isn't it? But, God never expects us to break His laws to do what we feel is the right thing. Use this as an opportunity to draw closer to Him in faith and trust" — I would have responded with a wholehearted and joyful surrender to risk. I knew all about risk. But this — this was a whole new way of thinking. Accustomed as I was, however, to obeying a priest, I had my tubes tied.

When I got pregnant again, so soon after the tubal ligation, I was spun into a cloud of spiritual confusion. What was God trying to tell me? Should I not have had the procedure after all? Was this pregnancy His way of communicating to me? I did not have time to consider the possible reasons for this pregnancy. I was being asked to consider ending it before I could even make sense of it. How could a tubal ligation fail so utterly? They cut the tubes, cauterized the ends, and turned them under. What except a miracle could undo that? And if it was a miracle for me to get pregnant, why the threat to my life this pregnancy presented?

Sitting in that little room trying to come up with a proper answer, holding Don's hands in a strained and wordless agony, I found myself moving in a direction I had never moved before. I didn't ask myself what the Church thought; I asked myself what I wanted. I searched my own heart. That is usually a dangerous and misleading place from which to draw. I know that now. But at that time it was the only place I trusted. I was tired of trying to make sense of the conflicting and cowardly advice I was getting from priests and fellow Catholics. They were afraid to suggest the risky, narrow road of faith, because they weren't walking it themselves. I am aware of how harsh this sounds, but feelings are seldom subtle in life-threatening situations. And I was still young and self-righteous.

I decided not to have an abortion. My decision was aided by the advice of another doctor who came to me after the first one had left. She said that we did have a small chance of survival if I stayed in bed the duration of the pregnancy, and I decided to take that chance. Don was also very encouraging, although before he had been reluctant to influence my decision because it was not his life at stake. I stayed in bed at my grandmother's for another four months. One day, I stood up to go to the bathroom, and I began to hemorrhage, just as had been predicted. I made it to the hospital, but I lost the baby. Again, I lay alone in the hospital bed considering the meaning of what had happened. I came up with nothing that made sense or comforted me. I prayed, but I felt utterly alone in my prayer.

In the end, I put the whole ordeal on a shelf in my soul and closed the door.

I returned home from the hospital to find my family in stress. My husband had hired a couple of men who had been recommended by our parish priest to help him with the children while I was laid up. He was desperate and had to accept any help he could find. I am sure that our priest didn't know anything about these men, other than that they were homeless. They turned out to be two alcoholics on the fringes of the left, men who spouted political invective against America, all authority and, in particular, "Catholic nonsense". They were highly intelligent, and we were exhausted from trying to make sense of everything. While swilling gallons of imported beer, they flattered and cajoled us with new and clever ideas that tired young parents of small children don't hear very often. "There's no such thing as hell", one of them scoffed. "Life is earth school, and if you flunk a class you get to take it over again." We started drinking right along with them, and that philosophy sounded pretty good to Don, a teacher in junior high school. It is amazing how brilliant drivel sounds when your neo-cortex is anesthetized.

Anyone who has become addicted to a substance knows how quickly and pervasively it can dominate one's life. I do not need to go into great detail about the levels of degradation to which we sank. Alcoholics Anonymous discourages emphasis on "drunkalogs" at the expense of how we came to healing. Anyway, after a while, everybody's story starts to sound amazingly alike. Human nature is human nature; substances are substances. At some point I made the transition from acting like Sue to acting like alcohol. And, as they say, "the higher the top, the longer the drop". But the whole time I was drinking and hating myself and drinking more to drown the pain and shame, I remained dimly aware of what Alcoholics Anonymous calls the God-shaped hole in my soul. I tried to capture that sense of oneness with God by drinking. The high of alcohol is a cheap and blasphemous imitation of a Holy Spirit high, believe me.

When I was in my teens I had an extremely close love

relationship with God. Often I would lose track of time in prayer and become so absorbed in His Presence that I felt as if I were leaving earth. I would leave for school in the morning and get so caught up in God that everything around me seemed to sparkle. The sensation is difficult to describe. I would simply bask in His Presence. It was a feeling or sense, beyond mere emotion, that left me suffused with peace and joy.

By the time I started drinking I had long ago abandoned my relationship with God on a conscious level. But having been so close to Him is not something one ever forgets. God hard-wires himself into your soul. My mind may have forgotten, and my feelings may have run cold, but my spirit remembered and ached for Him. I put Him on that shelf in my soul and took down the bottle god.

The day came, in July 1981, that I woke up and could not tie my shoelaces because my hands were shaking so badly. I had long ago abandoned any hope of not needing a drink. It may be hard to believe, but I had never heard of alcoholism, and I had no idea what was wrong with me. All I knew was that when I tried to stop drinking I would start shaking all over and become so sick that I thought I would die. I quickly discovered that alcohol kept me feeling somewhat normal, and that became my primary obsession. With five small children, I wanted to feel normal so that I could at least pretend I was there for them as a mother. But that morning in July I awoke with the horrifying awareness that I had not left enough booze from the night before to get me through to the time when I could go to the store for more. I crawled out of bed shaking and searched desperately through my dresser drawers for a bottle I might have forgotten.

Unknown to me, Don had called my grandmother to ask her if she could put up a down payment to get me into a thirty-day alcohol treatment center. I heard him talking to one of the counselors at the center, calling me an alcoholic. I looked in a mirror at the bloated and bleary-eyed face staring back at me. "Oh, my God!" I whispered, "You're an alcoholic!" I was immensely relieved that my condition had a name and, with hope, a cure. I went through the program and came out a month later sober and happy. Don didn't recognize me. He went to the same center a few months later.

When the dust cleared, I took a sobering look at the mess my family was in. The children had become sullen, distrusting, independent ragamuffins. They had picked up little street-wise friends whose moms were mostly single parents who were overworked or on drugs. They would send their kids to other people's houses so that they could rest or use drugs in peace. My children's language was tough and peppered with four-letter words. My heart broke when I saw how accustomed they were to making peanut butter and jelly sandwiches and instant macaroni and cheese. I did not remember that God forgives and restores. More accurately, I had never really done anything before that needed serious forgiveness. In my youth and pride I had thought I was well on my way to holiness. How tender and thorough is His love for us that He does not permit us to remain with such an illusion forever!

One evening, about six months into sobriety, the Mormons came to the door. We had been struggling mightily to put our family back together, with less than stellar results. We quickly became infatuated with Mormon wholesomeness and with their wonderful family activities. We were so blinded by their dazzling health that we did not at first concern ourselves with the increasingly nagging theological questions. Was Jesus really Lucifer's spirit-brother, as the Mormons taught, or was He the second, divine Person of the Blessed Trinity? Was it really possible to become a god? Does the God of the universe really live on a planet called Kolob, on which He spends his time procreating spirit children who then wait for a Mormon couple to have a baby so that these spirit children can get a body? Does Joseph Smith, and not Jesus, really usher us into the celestial Kingdom? Could all this be true?

I had always loved being a homemaker and a mother, and the Mormon women certainly validated that feeling. Our children had never, it seemed to us, been happier or healthier. Their friends were wholesome little Mormons with clean language and a work ethic. Our kids kept journals and wrote to their grandparents regularly. They gradually regained their sense of family and their security. They began to play and laugh again. They were sealed to us for time and all eternity when Don and I were married in a secret ceremony in the Oakland Temple. I canned and sewed, which I had loved doing since early youth. We did our genealogy so our dead ancestors could be baptized. We gathered a year's supply of food. How could all this be wrong? I would become incensed when Christians passed out flyers trying to show that Mormons were not Christian. After all, we were the Church of Jesus Christ of Latter-Day Saints! Of course, at that time I knew very little about how to define the real historical Jesus or the exact role He had in salvation history.

As we rose in the Mormon Church, I became a teacher in the Relief Society (for women only), and Don became a Stake Missionary. (A stake is equivalent to a diocese.) As we delved deeper and deeper into Mormon scripture, into the *Doctrines and Covenants*, *The Pearl of Great Price*, and, of course, the *Book of Mormon*, we became more and more disturbed by the harsh and legalistic God manifested in those pages. We began to notice contradictions no one could explain away. We wondered why God chose sixteenth-century King James English to dictate to a nineteenth-century boy. How can there be many gods when Isaiah quotes again and again: "I am the Lord, and there is no other?" (Is 45:5, 6). There was the unwillingness of fellow Mormons to talk about the strange ceremonies that went on in the Temple. The secret handshakes and gestures of self-mutilation began to irritate us. We loved the people, but something in our spirits knew that the secrecy was wrong. Jesus was not secretive. I knew nothing about Gnosticism, but I sensed a basic error.

I began to get a reputation for asking hard questions during Relief Society meetings, such that they rarely called on me when I raised my hand. One time I quipped testily, "So, Mother Teresa of Calcutta will not go to the Celestial Kingdom because she's not married to a Mormon priest?" I thought the idea was humorous. It seemed obvious to me that Mother Teresa was going to go to heaven, even without being a Mormon wife. No one laughed. Finally, a sister turned around to me and, with a voice oozing a kind of gaggy sweetness I have found only in self-righteous people, said, "Sister Sowden, you know, there are some things you don't understand yet, but you will not arrive at an understanding by asking questions." Heads nodded all around the room. "God will tell you the truth through a burning in your bosom", she added triumphantly.

After our rough, touch-and-go, three-year membership in the Mormon Church, Don's born-again sister quietly left a book called *The Godmakers*, by Dave Hunt, on our coffee table. Before finishing the book and before the end of the day, Don called the bishop and told him he was leaving the church and wanted his name stricken from the record. After I read it, I did the same. The book proved to our satisfaction that the Mormon Church was a cult and a hoax, so full of internal contradictions and outright lies that it seems impossible to me that the high leadership couldn't know these things.

At first we felt cleansed in a rush of self-righteousness, but we were again without a church. And there was something else we didn't know yet. You just don't get delivered from Egypt without Egypt having to be delivered from you. Unknowingly, we carried with us the Mormon underlying assumption of spiritual evolution to godhood that paved an unobstructed path right into the New Age movement.

One evening, after explaining things to the children and listening to their justified dismay at losing a big part of their social structure, we promised each other that we would never again get involved in organized religion. We found ourselves frequently quoting something we heard at an Alcoholics Anonymous meeting: "If someone claims to have the truth, hang on to your wallet."

In the void that followed, life went on pretty much the same on the surface. Don was still a teacher, and I was a mother who did some portrait painting and poetry writing on the side. I went back to recovery meetings. At the suggestion of some of my Alcoholics Anonymous friends and under the influence of my sponsor, I began reading books called *The Handbook to Higher Consciousness* and *The Course in Miracles*. These books and others like them began spoon-feeding me New Age doctrine before I had even heard the term.

I had not realized how isolated we were from mainstream Santa Cruz by being in the Catholic and Mormon churches. Our friends started opening our eyes to exciting new transcendental bookstores and to a different type of people who seemed peaceful and "together" and who wore Indian cottons and uncut crystals. As our ears opened to this enthralling new world, we began to hear self-empowering phrases like "take control of your own life", "visualize peace", "create good Karma", and "access the god within". Our fellow recoverees taught us meditation techniques at a Buddhist monastery. At one meeting, my sponsor helped me get in touch with my "power animal", whose identity would flash into my mind only when I was totally conflict-free and empty of any thoughts of my own.

Without realizing it, I was undergoing an exhilarating paradigm shift; my whole view of what the world was and should be was changing. It was as if I were looking at life through a camera with only one certain dimension in focus and everything else out. And then someone gently slipped in a lens of a different color and strength, throwing everything into a new focus, showing me levels and hues and shades of meaning I had never known before. My whole idea of the power structure of the universe turned upside down. Before, God was in control, and I could abandon myself to His loving sovereignty. Now, I was in control, and I had to do everything I could to get that Power out there to reside in me. I am convinced that the number one underlying difference between orthodox Christianity and the New Age movement is the locus of control.

As I became more and more immersed in the new thinking, my feelings, of course, also began to change. Our friends with the large family had long ago abandoned us as friends. During the last two years of our friendship, Don and I had been mostly drunk and foul-mouthed. So, we didn't have anyone around us challenging the wisdom of our new path or wondering why we seemed different. My new friends encouraged me to express what they considered valid rage at my parents for not raising me right and at God for allowing all my hardship. I had been a "Doris Doormat", they said, and now I was free to be me. Me, Doris Doormat? Anyone who really knew me would become hysterical with laughter at the suggestion. These all seem like such clichés to me now. It is hard to put myself in the place of hearing for the first time these encouragements to hyper-emotionalism and assertiveness or to feel again the tremendous rush of power I felt with the advice not to restrain myself.

Nobody in my circle of friends was just a mom at home; that goes without saying. Inevitably, I grew more and more restless, with a nagging sense that people who worked outside the home had lives while mine was passing me by. It seems incredible to me now that I, who had been almost militant in my dedication to being a homemaker and disdainful of women who abandoned their families to chase after worldly prestige or the American greenback, could have utterly forgotten the reasons for my commitment. But I had. Away from God, disconnected from all the ways He reveals Himself, even the most saintly (and I'm not!) devotee would allow every truth to slip through her fingers, as the water of the Holy Spirit did through mine. I had a college degree in Spanish and English literature—I allowed myself to be talked into doing something "professional" again. "Something worthy of your talents", as Don kept saying. He reminded me that one of the reasons he married me was that I was intelligent. (Well, I also laughed at his jokes.) I didn't really want to teach again. I had taught Spanish as a teaching assistant at the University of Washington and in a Catholic high school in San Francisco. I was only twenty when I taught, and I do not think I was a very successful teacher. Although I was academically advanced, I was too young, too ignorant, and too arrogant to be aware of my shortcomings.

I'm bilingual, which enabled me to gain employment with the Migrant Headstart program. My responsibility was to connect migrant workers with the social services available to them. I had not seen relentless poverty and dirt-floor homes since my childhood in Mexico. Now I was seeing them again in the labor camps of California. My job had me going daily to these camps to interview large families living in one-room chicken coops. I had to struggle with the old helpless feelings of where to begin. And although I was no longer a Catholic, I was again deeply moved by the migrants' quiet piety, their devotion to the Sacred Heart, their surrender to whatever God had for them. They were not people who fought for their rights, as romanticized as this sounds. They seemed like people who were just grateful they had a job picking strawberries that paid them twenty times more in one day than they made in a week in Mexico. I became angry for them, I guess, but their politeness stirred places in my heart I had long forgotten. One day I caught myself staring at a picture of Our Lady of Guadalupe in a migrant's house. My eyes filled with tears. And then, quite suddenly, I yanked myself from my reverie and put that rustling of my spirit on the dark shelf where I stored everything else.

My co-workers watched me work and decided that I had a gift for counseling and a heart for the poor. At that time I gave a lot of weight to what they said. They were sprites in gauzy dresses straight from a Botticelli painting. They were intelligent and had names like Crystal Dawn and Sunshine Moon. I was in the process of redefining myself, and they became my mentors. So, when they suggested I get a master's degree in counseling psychology, I did. I began a three-year degree program, which was academically excellent and utterly New Age. Along with psychopathology and personality theory, group dynamics, and sex-role stereotyping were the powerful underlying assumptions of relativism, pantheism, and feminism. The predominantly Buddhist teachers believed in the psyche above all, in accessing the god within, in empowering the client with neuro-linguistic programming and power visualization techniques. In 1987, I emerged a well-indoctrinated New Ager, anxious to go out into the counseling world to help brush away the Judeo-Christian cobwebs that were preventing most people from realizing their full potential.

For three years I worked in alcohol and drug units in hospitals and in family therapy centers. I loved it at first, and I was making a lot of money. I believed that I was making a big difference in people's lives. My children were increasingly involved in their own lives as teenagers. At least, that's what I told myself to justify my not being there for them very much. Parents in my group believed that children needed to be free to explore their own paths. I told myself that I was exercising existential courage by not taking responsibility for their reactions to my frequent absences. I felt I was modeling how to be independent. I truly believed all this. It was the darkest, unhappiest time of my life.

Then, while working in a hospital drug unit, I broke my back. This isn't as awful as it sounds. I had broken my back twice before. Ironically, the fusions rendered my back more susceptible to breaking. I probably turned awkwardly or lifted something a little too heavy. I don't really know. But I had to leave work for a few months to have my back fixed. While recovering, I had plenty of time to think about my work and to get in touch with how disappointed I was in the counseling field. I found myself remembering the number of times I saw a patient who left the hospital, victorious and hopeful, only to return a short while later in much worse shape than he had been before.

Of course, recidivism is in the nature of alcoholism. But I had a nagging feeling that we weren't reaching the heart of the problem. Alcoholics Anonymous says that it is a spiritual program because alcoholism is a spiritual disease. But our treatments were patently psychotherapeutic. One day, talking with a fellow therapist, I remarked, "I just want to get at the truth about this guy's self-destructive behavior!" The therapist gave me the look one usually reserves for an errant toddler. "Whose truth?" he mocked. "Yours, or his?" Another time a therapist wondered out loud if I wasn't perhaps becoming a bit too moralistic and didactic for the field. After all, she reminded me patiently, the solution to each person's problems lies within himself. It is inappropriate to superimpose one's own agenda on another. Her observation, by the way, came in response to my joking remark that our patient might stand a chance of getting better if she'd just stop sleeping around and having several abortions a year. As I made this remark, I was dimly aware that my thoughts were coming from a much deeper and truer place than I had accessed in years. My co-worker's final parting shot stung me through and through: "What are you, some kind of Christian?" My face burned. If you really wanted to embarrass me in those days, all you had to do was imply that I was a Christian or, worse, a Catholic Christian. I equated Christianity with self-righteous intolerance and rigidity, the polar opposite of the all-accepting free spirit, the non-judgmental healing balm I envisioned myself to be.

And so there I was, flat on my back and miserable. It still amazes me how quickly my love for my career evaporated as soon as I got some distance from it. I became aware of a growing distaste, then dread, for the idea of going back to that work. And then, one bright and shiny day, the phone rang, and my boss told me as kindly as he could that, because of insurance complications, they would not be able to have me back. I pretended to be shocked, even disappointed, but secretly I was thrilled. I felt a great weight lift from my spirit, and something inside of me whispered, "Be released . . . you're free." I lay there, ripped suddenly and permanently from my career. For a while I felt angry and then guilt-ridden for all the bad advice I had given, for all the things I hadn't said for fear they were not appropriate remarks for a counselor, yet a small hope began to grow in me that Someone out there had something better for me, although I had no idea what.

I took up portrait painting again to fill the weeks of recovery. As I filled in lines and shadows in the faces I was painting, I could feel something rearranging my insides, shifting things around, settling things that were in turmoil, stirring things up that were lying fallow. It was if I were being winnowed and sifted. I was not yet at the point where I was praying again, but, after so many years of ignoring my inner life, I was aware of a Presence in me vying for attention.

One day, toward the end of my convalescence, while I was picking through my jewelry box to find the mate to an earring, I found a Miraculous Medal that my great-grandmother, a convert herself, had given me when I first became a Catholic. Why was I so profoundly moved as I looked at that little aluminum medal? Why had I hung onto it for all those years? When we were Mormons, a

Relief Society sister had successfully convinced Don and me to get rid of our Sacred Heart statue, even though it was our wedding present to each other and we had had it enthroned in our home. The little medal was just too small to have been noticed. But now I stood there looking at it, and I was filled with a powerful yearning for my lost innocence and zeal, convicted to the quick of how I had lost my first love.

Quite suddenly I was overwhelmed with a desire to run back into the arms of Mother Church. I thought that Don would never understand. However, at the same time as I was experiencing a longing for the Church, Don was beginning to listen to his sister talk about her "born-again experience". During her first few visits, we both resisted her evangelization efforts. I rolled my glazed eyes or smiled with feigned patience. Don paced nervously and reminded his sister that he had nine years of college and a minor in theology. But, undaunted, she poured out her heart and her love for Jesus.

Gradually our resistance began to break down. I turned with renewed joy to Jesus through the Catholic Church. Don, however, made one last effort to save our children his way. He sold one of our cars for extra money, added it to our savings, and took the kids on a driving journey around the country. I stayed home to take care of my grandmother and an uncle, who had moved in with us earlier that year. In Arizona, Don began to suspect he had made a mistake. The kids were homesick and wanted to return to their friends and girlfriends. Don tried desperately to provide our children one last redemptive shot at a good education by showing them historical sites and

making them write about them. Finally, when he got to
Washington, D.C., he gave up. He had intended to drive
through New England and then back through the northern border states. He decided instead to make a beeline
through the middle of the country to get home quickly.
He got to Denver, where his other sister lived, and stayed a
couple of days to rest. She was also a "born-again" Christian, and, after listening to the outpourings of his dark
and confused soul, she recommended that he speak with
her pastor.

It was at that meeting that Don asked and received the
Lord back into his life. The pastor said, "Churches will
disappoint you, and people will disappoint you, but Jesus
will never disappoint you." As Don said later, "That day
the Holy Spirit witnessed to me of the truth of what the
pastor was saying", and he returned to California on fire.

So there we were. Don was a "born-again" evangelical
with pentecostal leanings who loved to turn every conversation around to Jesus. He watched anything on TV
about Jesus, no matter how southern the accent or out-
rageous the hairdo. I was attending daily Mass with the
Poor Clares, saying the Rosary, and reading everything I
could get my hands on that had to do with Our Lord and
His Church.

There was a time when I would go to Mass early Sunday
morning, and then Don and I would travel to his evangelical church. At that time, Don would not consider going
to Holy Mass with me. And, although our marriage had
improved immensely since our coming back to the Lord,
it began to be strained again. We couldn't talk very long
without disagreeing about some aspect of theology or lit-

urgy, or whatever. I couldn't believe that God wanted us to continue on those separate paths. Finally, after praying about it, I told Don I would stop going to the Catholic Church if he would let me choose the evangelical church that we would attend. He readily agreed. Thus began our six-year membership in a Foursquare church.

We were plunged again into a whole new world with an entirely new vocabulary and way of seeing things. The congregation worshipped with their hands held high in the air, swaying and clapping and often dancing to the Christian rock band that was the signature of that particular church. Since I have always liked rock music, I learned to look forward to Sunday just to sing at the top of my lungs with them. The worship was exhilarating and punctuated with people yelling "Alleluia!" and "Praise Jesus!" The pastor was young, good-looking, charismatic, and deeply in love with Jesus and the Bible. He did not have the southern pentecostal delivery I find objectionable, or I would never have gone back. (I realize that my objection is irrational, but it is one from which I can't seem to rid myself.) He was also very intelligent. I can't follow someone who doesn't know more or think better than I do. I don't think that's irrational.

Two ministries characterized the church. The pastor firmly believed in small home groups in which the individual could receive more intensive care and counsel, and he also had biblical counseling and deliverance prayer. As Catholics we are not usually accustomed to think in terms of deliverance. We have the confessional. But evangelical pentecostals believe that habits of sin are often caused by oppression by the devil (they call him "the enemy").

They make an important distinction between possession —which, by their definition, is impossible for a Christian, since he is already possessed by the Holy Spirit— and oppression—which is a certain type of demon pushing on a person and needling him from the outside. Because of my counseling background, I was very soon asked to be a member of one of the Women's Ministry teams, although being a professional was not a requirement. Don and I were also asked to be leaders of a home group, and then leaders of the leaders. We held these positions for the last five years of our membership in that church. We were elected to the church council, went on a mission to the red-light district in Amsterdam, and made a huge number of friends. We were very accepted, very busy, and very happy. I loved being so deeply involved in ministry and church. I was beginning to feel as if I was experiencing the fulfillment of my deepest heart's desire, the same one I had had when I wanted to be a nun.

Inevitably, however, things began to rub this relentlessly Catholic soul the wrong way. During our first year there, the pastor made an off-hand remark during a sermon about how he had been "fixed" to be sure he wouldn't have any more children. I was deeply jarred, but I held my feelings to myself for a while, struggling with my lack of charity and my judgmentalism. Finally, someone told me that one should not let resentments take root and become trees of unforgiveness, so I summoned up my courage and wrote him a letter. He wrote me a very kind letter back, but his explanation was inconclusive and reflective of the Protestant belief that birth control is a non-issue, like taking an aspirin for a headache.

Then I became increasingly disturbed by the nonchalant and minimal manner in which the Lord's Supper was handled. In the Foursquare denomination communion is only a symbolic gesture to remind us of the price Jesus paid for us and for our brotherhood of believers. It was given only once a month, and it would frequently be canceled for any one of many spurious reasons. Why did that bother me so much? Could it have been that I still believed in the Real Presence of Christ in the Holy Eucharist? My growing discomfort with isolated details did not improve when we got cable TV and discovered the Eternal Word Television Network (EWTN). Don would sometimes watch the network with me, but more often I watched it alone. I found myself riveted to it, soaking up Fr. Benedict Groeschel and Mother Angelica in the same way my starving ten-year-old spirit had soaked up the beauty of Concha's mother's words in Mexico.

Over the years, going to the evangelical church and watching EWTN, I began to develop an obsession with the issue of authority. No matter what subject I would bring up with my leaders—transubstantiation, apostolic succession, auricular confession to a priest, or the priesthood itself—the conversation always ended being about authority. I had several intensive counseling sessions with the pastor's wife and the head of Women's Ministry. I received deliverance prayer several times for "the spirit of religion" or my "problem with authority". I told them that I was begging the Lord to show me where I was wrong. "I really don't want to be a Catholic", I said. "I just want God to remove all the old, dead barnacles and demonic residue of Catholicism that are still clinging to a soul that just wants to stand before God, clean and washed in the blood of Jesus." But I said over and over again that it was my impression that they, not I, were the ones with the "problem with authority". They kept trying to argue to the person, and I kept trying to argue to the subject.

They said that my problem with authority was understandable and could be traced to the flaky absenteeism of my mother. I told them that my problem was that I wanted to be assured that the truths people were telling me actually came from God. They said that my problem with authority was really an inability to trust, which was understandable since my mother abandoned me in Mexico, when I could not care for myself. I said that I didn't think God wanted us to trust our own feelings and judgments or private biblical interpretations, and for that reason He must have set His Church up so that the source of authority would be above the whims of personal interpretation. They answered that my need to have one infallible central authority was a reflection of my discomfort with being the unique person God made me to be. I answered that I thought that over twenty thousand denominations contradicting each other on central issues would make the Holy Spirit out to be a liar. Remember, He promised to be with His Church always (Mt 28:20), and not to let the powers of death prevail against it (Mt 16:18).

I had many sessions with church members on many subjects. Finally, I received three pieces of advice. First, stop being so intellectual, because your heart is thereby deafened to what God is whispering to you. Second, you don't have to stay in this church, you know. Third, take everything off your shelf and give it fearlessly to God. Do whatever you have to do to get the answers you are looking for.

I have to give them credit for that last piece of advice. It was risky of them to suggest that I do the research. I began a frenzy of reading history and apologetics, all behind Don's back, of course. He was blissful at the Foursquare church, and I didn't want to rock the boat until I had arrived at a conclusion.

Every time I picked up a new book, I hoped that this would finally be the one that would set my spirit at rest, that would contain the magic idea or the clever turn of phrase or the inspired insight to which I could respond with a resounding "Aha!" Would I ever be freed from the Catholic ghost that haunted me? Once in a while I would read something by a Protestant apologist that would be reasonably compelling. I would read about corrupt popes or something of this sort, and I would come close to rejecting the Church. Then the next day it seemed I would read or hear something else that would clarify the issue. I do want to say that I am extremely grateful to God for putting me in a church that encouraged me to read the Bible carefully and frequently. I read it cover to cover six times in the six years I was in the Foursquare church. I believe Catholics really need to read their Bibles more. Let's face it, it is a Catholic book! I read in Jeremiah 17:9: "More tortuous than all else is the human heart, beyond remedy, who can understand it?" I was being encouraged to listen to my heart. I had done that before, and it had led me astray. I went on like that for a few more months, struggling and reading, praying and asking counsel, and struggling still more. And then, with a suddenness that I should have been used to by that time, it all came tumbling to an end.

It is curious how sometimes God ends a noisy tumult with a quiet and gentle orchestration of seemingly unrelated incidents that speak of His unbroken Presence in every detail of our mundane existence.

While searching through satins and laces at a fabric store (I make wedding dresses), I looked up and spotted two nuns, also shopping. I stood frozen where I was, intently watching their every move, trying to read their souls through their faces. One of them smiled at me as they left. My heart ached and burned. I stood by the lace with my brain blank, and then I heard myself think: "There's a Catholic church a few blocks from here."

I left the store without buying anything and pulled into the church parking lot. I suddenly felt silly and melodramatic. Maybe I was just overreacting to an irrational impulse. After all, I didn't really want to go back to the Church, did I? Talking about it, defending it, even studying it was one thing, but putting my body where my soul was was quite another. I finally overcame my resistance and got out of the car. More accurately, I surrendered to a powerful Magnet pulling my heart to the sanctuary, where I knew Jesus was waiting for me. I walked self-consciously through the side door into the empty church. As I sat down, I kept looking around. It felt as if someone else was in there with me. I wanted to cry, and I didn't want anyone to see. Then I remembered. There was Someone there, and it was safe to cry in front of Him. I sobbed with release, repentance, and a deep, deep longing.

The next morning over coffee, Don said that he sensed

something was wrong. He was somewhat aware of my search, but he had been hoping I would decide against the Catholic Church. Now everything I had gone through came spilling out, and he sat there dumbfounded. I regret not letting him in on things as I was dealing with them, but I was trying to avoid conflict. Don responded with characteristic courage and finality. He telephoned the pastor and the members of our home group, and he announced that we were returning to the Catholic Church. No one was as surprised as I thought they would be. Apparently my secret wasn't as much of a secret as I had thought. I think some of them were privately glad that I would no longer be pushing them into the corner over the issue of authority or the Real Presence of Christ in the Holy Eucharist.

I have to admire Don for sticking with me in the search for a parish. In the almost two decades since we had left, the Church seemed to have polarized between liberal remnants of the post-Vatican II rebellion who quoted the Dalai Lama and Jesus with equal enthusiasm and conservatives who attended church out of loyalty, but who participated at Mass by closing their eyes and saying the Rosary. It began to look as if we were going to have to choose between orthodoxy and being Spirit-filled. I had thought that the entire Church was like the one shown on EWTN. It was a rude awakening. We went from parish to parish. If the liturgy wasn't lukewarm to dead, it was the flamboyant Father So-and-So show, with what we considered way too much emphasis on the personality of the priest and not enough on worshipping Jesus. Had we made a terrible mistake? Had we not listened carefully enough to God? Were we once again going after our own idea of holiness, instead of God's? Why do most of these people either seem to take the Church's treasures for granted or to know so little about the truths of the Church that they don't notice when heresy is being spouted?

Just when we were despairing, we decided to give our old parish a try. We had to overcome powerful negative memories. But God is so faithful. He surprised us with two priests who were delightfully orthodox and Spirit-filled, Fr. Patrick Dooling and Fr. Thomas Foster. Both are intelligent and devout. It was a combination we had seen only on EWTN, and we were just about to write the TV station and ask them if we could make them our church (even though we knew better), when God showed us the place to call home.

God could not have possibly provided a more fitting pair of priests for our needs. Although both are scholarly and orthodox, one has the quiet patience to answer un-hurriedly all of our objections, and the other has the same angry edge Don has about the appalling biblical ignorance and seeming complacency of so many Catholics. While Father Tom provides the calming humor and perspective about the foibles of the historic Church, at the same time he cannot contain his passion for Mary and for the charis-matic gifts. Father Patrick exudes Don's level of energy and impatience (while never being uncharitable), and he said something that defined for Don what had been both-ering him without his realizing it. Father Patrick went to Italy and came back with this observation: "The Italians are sacramentalized but not evangelized." For Don, this voiced his objection toward American Catholics. In contrast, he realized that the evangelical churches are evangelized, but they need to be sacramentalized.

The piety and love with which these two priests celebrated Holy Mass, for us, redeemed the liturgical changes. Even daily Mass is well attended. Most of the ancient devotions — exposition of the Blessed Sacrament, litanies, and praying the Rosary — are regular parts of our parish life. And among other services for the poor, we open the parish hall to the homeless.

Yet Don was still confused about several issues. He gritted his teeth and white-knuckled his way through several aspects of what he believed to be Catholic theology.

Don had become something of a Scripture scholar in the last few years. Continuous and deep probing of the Bible is extremely important to him. Needless to say, when I began returning to the Church, his first concern was those several items of Catholic doctrine that are considered by Protestants to be extra-biblical — Purgatory, the Immaculate Conception, veneration of saints, and Tradition in general. He was, of course, accustomed to using the Bible as the sole source of guidance and inspiration. The notion of a teaching authority and apostolic succession did not seem to concern him at all. When I would exclaim, "But, how does so-and-so get the authority to say I'm wrong and he's right?" Don would become impatient and frustrated with me, as if I were asking a useless question that displayed a lack of faith in the Holy Spirit's guidance.

He was still questioning these particular doctrines after we left the Foursquare Church, and there were several occasions where our discussions got a little heated. I did not have clear answers myself, and, although I sensed his objections were wrong, I did not know exactly why.

One day, while standing in front of the church after daily Mass, Don was chatting with the priest about the Real Presence and asking whether he should be receiving Communion if he still had some doubts. The priest recommended two books, *Surprised by Truth*, edited by Patrick Madrid, and *Rome, Sweet Home*, by Scott and Kimberly Hahn. As we read these books, Don's eyes would fill with tears of joy as each of his questions was answered, one after another.

What settled all of his other objections were the points that (1) the idea that the Bible alone is the sole guide of faith and morals and (2) the belief that faith alone is enough to save are *not biblical*. Once he grasped those facts, the door was opened for him to accept Sacred Tradition, apostolic succession, and the teaching authority of the Church.

It seems incredible that those two little books could have so thoroughly brought all of Don's gray areas to light. He is finally at peace with all the Church's teachings and is full of the joy of a returned prodigal.

As for me, I had stopped defining myself by someone else's beliefs and had begun to let God define me. Not having had a normal and validating childhood with Christian parents to lay down my spiritual skeleton, I had spent years trying to build my own. My initial love did not hold up under my first big temptation, but God clearly had His hand over the whole process by which I finally came to the end of myself. We believe that Jesus in the Sacred Heart remembered that we had enthroned Him in our home. After all the years that I spent trying to find myself, even if it was the self that God made, I have concluded that the more one searches for the self the more one is going to find no one home. To look inside oneself is to look into a black hole with no bottom.

Instead, God is painting the willing and surrendered spirit as He goes along, filling in the lines and shadows and colors according to a pattern He had from the beginning of the world. We may grab the paintbrush from Him for a while, but when we finally hand it back He erases all the lines that we put in that didn't conform to His pattern. He brightens the overly dark shadows and clarifies the colors.

I know now that the best studio in the world to be in, the one that allows God to do the best job painting us, is the Catholic Church. It has the richest variety of colors and the best canvas; it hires the most skilled artists, artists who draw on the successes and failures of the great Masters, the saints. As I look over the whole canvas of my life to this point, I can see that God has always been painting me Catholic, and I am overjoyed that I have given Him back the brush.

The Lord called me back through the Eucharist, and I now sing with all my heart with the psalmist:

> How lovely is thy dwelling place,
> O LORD of Hosts!
> My soul longs, yea, faints
> for the courts of the LORD;
> my heart and flesh sing for joy
> to the living God.
>
> — Psalm 84:1–2

Handing on the Baton

Thomas J. Pillion

"And the award for excellence in religion goes to Thomas J. Pillion, Jr." As a graduating ninth grader from St. Mary School, Newington, Connecticut, in June 1961, I was honored to receive St. Mary's annual religion award. I shook hands with the pastor, who gave me a certificate and a twenty-five dollar savings bond, and I returned to my seat amid a polite round of applause from my fellow students and their parents. I was a committed young Catholic during an era when Catholics knew what being Catholic meant. In 1958, when I entered St. Mary School, 85 percent of all Catholics went to Mass every Sunday and believed in the Divine Presence in the Holy Eucharist; that is quite a difference from the drop to about 30 percent in 1996.

As I sat there, I wondered how my parents, both of whom were in the audience, felt. After all, my father was an inactive Catholic, one of the 15 percent who slept in on Sundays and who left the religious training in the family to my mother, a Protestant who had promised to "bring the kids up Catholic" in order to marry one.

Although my father never attended Mass except for special occasions, I believe he had a spiritual yearning for Christ. Many Sundays I would come home from Mass to see him in front of our television, absorbed in the preaching of a quiet but convicting man with a strange beanie. As a second grader, I never quite understood the messages of Bishop Fulton J. Sheen, but I know my Dad placed value in them because he would become angry if we interrupted him. I don't know the impact Bishop Sheen made on my father, but I have faith that, in some small way, he contributed to Dad reconciling with the Lord when he received the last rites just before he passed away in 1991.

My third-grade catechism teacher was a Marine named Sgt. Richter. (Back in those days we called our instruction catechism, rather than CCD or CFF). In the third grade, I was a bit of a wise guy. My friends and I knew Sgt. Richter's tough-guy reputation, and we often would see how far we could push him during class. He would justifiably reprimand us; I couldn't decide whether or not I liked him. Then word got out that Sgt. Richter was a judo expert who was scheduled to give a judo demonstration on a local television show. During the next class, in a smart-alecky tone of voice, several of us pressed Sgt. Richter to tell us how he was going to dazzle everyone on TV. His response? He humbled himself before the Lord and us. He asked us to pray that he would perform well, because without Jesus whatever he did was doomed to fail. I was amazed that this grown man would ask us little kids to pray for him, as if the prayers of third graders could actually make a difference. I said a prayer for Sgt. Richter, and from then on I was respectful in class and listened to the lessons he taught.

I watched Sgt. Richter on TV, but I don't remember a thing about the show. I do remember his conviction, his example, and many of the simple but powerful lessons he taught us, such as the following:

— The proper way to make the sign of the cross;

— To affirm silently the words of St. Thomas, "My Lord and my God", during the Consecration of the bread, and to beg, "My Jesus, mercy", during the Consecration of the wine.

— When you fold your hands for prayer, note how your thumbs intersect to make a miniature cross, and use it as a reminder that Jesus loved us enough to die for our sins.

Sgt. Richter taught by his example that a real man will submit himself to Jesus.

I graduated from elementary public school in sixth grade and entered St. Mary, the new parochial school that served grades seven through nine. Later, my elderly eighth-grade teacher, Sister Anthony, taught me Church history in a way that I readily accepted the doctrine of apostolic succession and papal authority, as well as the need for the Church to remain loyal to the pope during the divisions of Martin Luther's day. She also planted seeds that kept me from totally relinquishing my faith when I questioned it years later.

During my eighth-grade year I went on my first retreat. I don't remember how I was "recruited", but I went by myself, in late winter, and joined a small group of teens at a retreat house somewhere close to the Connecticut shoreline. Several priests led discussions and gave us time to spend alone in prayer. At one point they asked us to consider the priesthood as a vocation. During one of the few recreation times, I was shooting baskets by myself in the cold March air, and a priest joined me. I can't remember the substance of any of the discussions; I only remember feeling proud to be a Catholic.

I was confirmed while at St. Mary School. During the bishop's homily, he asked those of us who felt led to do so to make a commitment to refrain from drinking alcohol until the age of twenty-one. He must have moved me in some way, or the Holy Spirit was immediately working in my heart, because I made the promise and held fast to it, with the exception of having one glass of wine at dinner on Christmas Eve in 1967, when I was twenty years old. I believe that commitment, together with the self-discipline I gained from always giving up something during Lent, was a major factor in my being able to resist "near occasions of sin" in high school and college.

While at St. Mary School I heard that those who wore scapulars and those who attended nine consecutive First Friday Masses were guaranteed to go to heaven, and those who attended five First Saturday Masses would be guaranteed to have Our Lady present at their death. My sources may have been distorted, but I liked the challenge, so I successfully completed nine First Fridays and wore a scapular for a long time. I can't remember if I made five consecutive First Saturdays or not, but I know I attended at least several. Later in life, evangelical Bible Christians caused me to question Catholic Marian devotion, but on graduation day from St. Mary School I credited my religion award to an outpouring of God's love in response to my devotion to Our Lord and His Mother.

In September 1961 I began my sophomore year at Newington High School, from which I graduated in 1964. I spent most of my after-school hours learning to play the guitar and working out at the nearby New Britain YMCA. One afternoon I met Jim Havlick, who introduced himself to me as the associate physical director of the YMCA. Jim had recently graduated from Springfield College, Massachusetts, and while not Catholic he was a committed Christian dedicated to youth. Jim became my role model. He would post excerpts from his file of "words to live by", sayings such as "No one stands so tall as he who stoops to serve another." I was impressed with those simple but powerful sayings and later on developed a similar file, which I still maintain. My relationship with Jim was a major factor in my decision to attend Springfield College.

During my time at Springfield, through no fault of the college, I began to drift from my Faith. While my intentions were good, my commitment to the Catholic Church resembled the analogy of a frog boiling. You know the analogy: if you put a frog into a pot of hot water, it will immediately jump out; but if you put the frog into lukewarm water, where it is comfortable, it will get lazy and sleepy. You can then slowly turn up the temperature and boil the frog. My Catholic Faith similarly became endangered during a ten- to twelve-year process that began at Springfield.

At Springfield Mass was not celebrated on campus, but the school was quite helpful in seeing that Catholic students were given information about the nearby parishes.

The closest church was a short ten-minute walk from campus, and my roommate and I would regularly attend Sunday Mass together . . . at least for the first six months or so. The homilies were poor, the priests were old and not very dynamic, and the parish family was somewhat impersonal. Those factors, combined with a few late Saturday nights, eventually gave way to my missing Mass intermittently, then more frequently.

Nineteen sixty-eight was a time of turmoil in America. In addition to the Robert Kennedy and Martin Luther King assassinations, anti-war sentiment was at an all-time high. So were defiance and a "God-is-dead" mentality. More and more of my peers were questioning their religious faith, and I was having a harder time holding on to mine. New college graduates were being drafted by the score and sent off to Vietnam, and I would soon be eligible. As an alternative to being drafted into the Army, I applied for and was accepted into the Naval Flight Program. The whole idea of being in the military was foreign to me, but I was sworn in on November 19, 1967, although I wouldn't have to report for duty until after I graduated in June 1968.

In the spring of 1968, I began my final semester of college in fieldwork training at the Cambridge, Massachusetts, YMCA, amid the subculture of colleges such as Harvard, the Massachusetts Institute of Technology, and Radcliffe. While there I met Linda Duncan, a student nurse and my future wife. Linda was a devout Catholic whose faith played a major role in her life, especially when at the age of thirteen she had lost her father. Unfortunately, after knowing each other less than one month,

I completed my training at the YMCA and returned to Springfield for graduation.

The day after I graduated, I reported to Aviation Officer Candidate School in Pensacola, Florida. After a whirlwind ten weeks of intensive training from Marine drill instructors, I was commissioned an ensign and began naval flight officer training. In June 1969, I received my wings. The following September, after a year or so of heavy correspondence interspersed with only a few visits, Linda and I were married and settled near my Navy base at Patuxent River, Maryland.

As I look back on twenty-six years of marriage, I believe our marriage is stronger now than it has ever been. Likewise, as I look back, I see a direct correlation between the strength of our marriage and the strength of our commitment to Christ. As I drifted from God, our marriage weakened. As I drew closer to Christ and to the Catholic Church, our marriage prospered. Unfortunately, we didn't recognize this correlation as we were going through those experiences.

Linda and I took seriously the concept that marriage is a three-way union of the two of us with Christ. However, even before the wedding ceremony took place, we unknowingly sowed seeds that would later reap heartache and a falling away from the Faith. In spite of our Catholic commitment and our pledge that our marriage would transcend the commonplace, in truth, we had both been affected by the liberal attitudes and defiance of the '60s, some of which had crept into the Church and into our hearts — mostly into my heart.

First, in preliminary planning and discussion for our

marriage, we had rationalized that the Church's teaching on birth control was out of touch with reality and the times. Linda and I both believed in and practiced chastity before marriage, as we had been taught by the Church. In my selfishness and pride, though, I decided that, because we had followed God's will and saved ourselves for each other, we deserved to have no restraints within our marriage. At St. Mary School I had never questioned the Church's authority, but in the late '60s, I wondered if the Church really had a right to dictate when and how we could express our love within our marriage.

Humanae Vitae was published in 1968, but I never thought to read it. We were fortunate, we thought, that the young priest who married us at Linda's hometown parish was "with the times", and he could relate to young couples like us. When we asked him about birth control, his answer was, in effect, "Well, the Church teaches that it is wrong, but, in the final analysis, you have to follow your conscience. So, if you don't believe it's a sin, it's not. God will understand." In essence, he told us we could use birth control if we could rationalize it. And we did. We were happy to hear what we wanted to hear—what we interpreted as the big "go ahead".

I was on my way down the slippery slope. First, Satan convinced me that we were not bound by the Church's teaching on birth control. Eventually I reasoned that if the pope was confused on birth control, maybe he was out of touch in other areas, too, and I came to doubt papal infallibility in general.

With our "consciences as our guides", Linda began our marriage using "the pill". She used it for about six

months, during which time she had difficulty controlling
her weight, and she became more irritable than I was used
to seeing her. We finally decided, for medical rather than
spiritual reasons, to stop using the pill. A short time later
God exercised His will in our lives, and our first child, Jennifer, was born in June 1971. We wanted children, so we
were elated with Jennifer, even though we had not planned
her arrival time.

Shortly after Jennifer's birth we moved to Jacksonville,
Florida, with my Navy P-3 aircraft squadron and developed friendships with other couples. The spiritual dimension of my squadron mates was varied. I gravitated
toward those who believed in male leadership in the family. In and of itself, I believe this concept is supported
in Scripture. Unfortunately, in many cases, Navy males
limited their leadership to economic or financial aspects,
such as what houses, cars, and "toys" to buy. Due in part
to husbands being gone for extended periods of time, the
responsibility of raising the family, including the spiritual
leadership, was often left to the wife.

I found myself caught up in this scenario, and, under
the influence of my peers, I became more and more like
them. Many rarely attended church, and my attendance
at Mass became increasingly intermittent. Our parish was
made up of few young adults and several uninspiring elderly priests. I would mutter cynical comments to Linda
during Mass and complain that I felt worse after Mass
than before I arrived. "Why couldn't these guys, whose
full-time job it is to preach," I reasoned, "come up with
some substance that we can apply to our daily lives."
Rather than focus on the Eucharist and my need to wor-

ship Christ, I put the onus on the priests to perform, with an attitude that seemed to demand, "Well, entertain me."

Like my friends, I spent money on my hobbies and left the remainder of my paychecks for my wife, along with the responsibility of getting the bills paid. I hadn't imbibed until I was twenty-one, but now I found "happy hours" and social drinking increasingly acceptable. When we went out in public with our married friends, they often made jokes at their wives' expense, just to get a laugh. I sometimes found myself acting in the same manner. Many of the wives, who were playing the role of both father and mother, felt unappreciated, eventually developed hardened hearts, and left. They became ripe candidates for the feminist movement, which was gathering steam in the early '70s. Much later in life I learned that if husbands would assume leadership in the way that Ephesians describes it—based on the same sacrificial love that Christ has for the Church—women would feel more inclined to "complete" their husbands rather than "compete" with them.

In the early '70s, however, I knew nothing of the feminist movement or its agenda. My first personal exposure occurred when, deployed to Iceland, I met a broken-hearted Air Force officer who had returned to the States to find his wife had left him to join what he called the Women's Liberation Movement. I felt bad for him because he was a faithful husband and a decent guy who loved his wife. Looking back, I wouldn't have blamed Linda for adopting a feminist attitude too, but fortunately God was working in our lives.

While I was deployed to Iceland, Linda made friends

with some women in the Jacksonville area who attended a weekly Bible study with an emphasis on husband-wife relationships, Proverbs 31, and so on. In addition to the Bible, they recommended a book called *The Total Woman*. When I returned from Iceland I saw the book on Linda's nightstand and concluded, based on the title, that she was going the route of my Air Force friend's wife. The exact opposite was true. Linda, in spite of her frustration with me, learned to focus on my positives rather than my negatives; she treated me the way she "saw me in the future". She supported me unselfishly, and, in short, gave me room to grow. She kept asking herself what she could do to make herself the best wife possible rather than trying to change me.

I credit Linda's biblical approach to our relationship and her unselfish attitude, which she learned from those sessions, as the main reasons that our relationship survived during the 1970s. Unfortunately for Linda, positive results were not immediately forthcoming. Fortunately for our future and our family, Linda had faith and perseverance.

Although we delighted in Jennifer, we were in no hurry to have another child. To plan more intelligently, we decided we would again use artificial contraception. However, God worked His will in our lives whether we liked it or not, and in June 1973 Linda gave birth to Jon, our first son. Since we had talked about having two children anyway, Jon was a welcome addition. Maybe we would have a third one "some time down the road a number of years, as sort of a backup," I would jokingly tell my friends, "if the cost doesn't interfere with my hobbies", which were handball and playing in a local area rock-and-roll dance band.

After Jon was born, we decided we needed a birth-control method that really worked. A change of orders had moved us back to Patuxent River, Maryland, and we had become friends with a young Navy doctor named Ken and his wife. Linda went to Ken for advice. He installed an IUD called the Dalkon Shield, which eventually became dislodged; Linda became pregnant with the IUD floating in her uterus. The baby could become strangled, we were told, should his head grow through the shield. Surgically removing the shield was considered dangerous, therefore abortion was a recommended option.

Linda, who, following Jennifer's birth, had become a qualified Lamaze childbirth instructor, was aware of *Roe vs. Wade* and had strong convictions against abortion. On the other hand, I had never heard of *Roe vs. Wade* and was pretty much out of touch with the issue. I was not personally in favor of abortion, but, based on the amoral influence of many of my pro-abortion peers, I had developed a rather apathetic, laissez-faire attitude. Linda would challenge me on the issue from time to time, and I would retreat to my music room and refuse to discuss it. Suddenly we were faced with personal circumstances that demanded a verdict. Linda flatly refused to consider an abortion, and I supported her. But we were both concerned over her and the baby's welfare, especially since we had heard rumors about women dying from infections caused by use of the Dalkon Shield.

Linda's prayer time escalated during the course of her pregnancy, and mine did too, somewhat. Fortunately, the

Lord never took His hand off us, and in May 1975, He again delivered a healthy baby to us, in accordance with His will, not ours. You would think that we'd have been astute enough to recognize that "maybe God is trying to tell us something", but we were not. We did, however, in our gratefulness to God for keeping Linda safe, welcome Thomas J., III, whom we nicknamed "T. J." I joked with my friends and co-workers that "our backup came earlier than we expected". We were starting to be singled out as "they must be Catholic" because our three children were the most of all the junior officers in my squadron. "If they only knew", I would chuckle to myself, too apathetic to stand up for my Catholic Faith and too lazy to explain that being Catholic had nothing to do with why we had three children.

In 1975 we had another home port change from Patuxent River to Jacksonville and from there to Sigonella, Sicily, ten months later. Linda, ever "The Total Woman", was very supportive of me and looked to the bright side of life in Sicily: an opportunity to see another culture and travel in Europe. Our two years in Sicily had some advantages and were in many ways enjoyable, but the pace drained our relationship.

In Sicily I worked an average of eighty hours per week and rarely saw my family. The divorce rate took its toll on many of the eighteen officers assigned with me. Linda and I never considered divorce, nor was the topic even raised, but several times she indicated that she didn't like our relationship. Our marriage was at its lowest point since our wedding day, although I probably would not have admitted it.

In retrospect, our mediocre marriage was directly proportional to my failure to keep our relationship Christ-centered. From the outside looking in, we appeared to be doing well; even from the "inside looking in" we got along, but we really didn't communicate much. When we did things as a family, my mind was usually preoccupied with music, work, or what it would be like to be unmarried and have no family responsibilities. In short, I was in my early thirties but, in some ways, more selfishly immature — and much less in tune with the Lord — than I had been at twenty.

After T. J.'s birth, we again were faced with the birth-control issue, which I viewed with much less of a sense of humor than previously. I issued tactless instructions to Linda, such as, "You better not get pregnant again", but I had no real solution. We were both negative toward artificial birth-control devices, I more from disillusionment than from any great allegiance to Church teaching. Reluctantly, we agreed to practice a form of rhythm method whereby we would abstain even during the first and last days of the supposedly safe period, just to be overly cautious. Neither of us had heard of Natural Family Planning. I became bitter, refraining not out of sacrificial love and respect for Linda, Christ, and the Church, but because I considered us too incapable of coming up with a workable secular solution. I felt cheated.

One night in June 1977, Linda's brother called to tell us that Linda's mother had suddenly died of a cerebral hemorrhage. Linda, who had always been close to her mother, was more upset than would ordinarily be expected under the circumstances because she hadn't seen her mother since we departed the United States the previous summer.

I took emergency leave, and we traveled to Massachusetts for the funeral. While there, unbeknownst to us, the emotional trauma on Linda's system disrupted her menstrual cycle, and she became pregnant. Once again, God had his way with us whether we liked it or not. Linda, already totally distressed over the loss of her mother, became even more upset. And I, bitter because I had to abstain from sexual relations more than I felt was fair, became more resentful because my abstaining was not even effective. Well-intentioned friends suggested to Linda that she could always get an abortion. We never considered that option, but neither did we consider the pregnancy a blessing. Then my mother, who at T. J.'s birth had indirectly implied that we ought to do something about our inability to prevent pregnancies, changed our hearts. She suggested to Linda that perhaps the baby was God's way of replacing her loss. From then on, Linda and I mustered a welcoming attitude toward Amy, who turned out to be a lovely baby and a major blessing in our lives.

Over the long weekend of Thanksgiving 1977, we went to Rome with one of our ski couple friends and toured St. Peter's Basilica and the Sistine Chapel. I was most taken with Michelangelo's work, especially the statue of the Pietà. Although the experience wasn't enough to reconvert me to become a committed, active Catholic, I believe it kept me from further sliding in my faith and gave us a spiritual lift during Linda's pregnancy.

About the time Amy was born, I was promoted to the rank of lieutenant commander. In July 1978, with orders in hand and Amy just several months old, our family moved to Washington, D.C. I began a three-year tour on the staff of the chief of naval operations, and we eventually settled in the suburb of Burke, Virginia, just outside the Capitol Beltway. Linda registered us in the nearby parish, Holy Spirit Church, in Annandale.

The pace of work in Sicily had left me little time for music. I was determined to change that, and, in early 1979, I joined a country-rock band that played weekend nights in Moose lodges, firehouses, and big dance halls in the rural areas outside the Beltway. Because of the distance we traveled to many of our gigs, I would often get home at 2:30 to 3:30 A.M. On Sunday mornings, I had difficulty getting up for Mass and, as in my days in Patuxent River, again became lax in my attendance.

The priests at Holy Spirit Church were older, like those from some of my previous parishes, and they spoke broken English. I thought that their homilies were bland and that they weren't earning their keep. When Linda complained about my apathetic attitude, I would draw an analogy to my band: if we were good, we'd attract a crowd; if we weren't, people would vote with their feet and leave. Likewise, I argued, "Why should a priest who gives a mediocre homily expect anyone to come, let alone put money in the church basket?" This kind of thinking made it easy for me to roll over on Sundays and go back to sleep. Somewhere in the recesses of my mind I buried all that I had learned at St. Mary School about the meaning of the Mass and the Eucharist.

Meanwhile, I worked all week, prepared music on weeknights, and slept away most of the weekend daylight hours. Linda raised the kids, kept the household going, and served as an area coordinator for natural childbirth classes. We were busy but had little in common with each other, and our marriage was unfulfilling to me. I refused to ask myself how much I was putting into it.

I began getting less satisfaction out of my Navy assignment as a small cog in a big bureaucratic wheel. I decided that if I worked in civilian life the kind of hours I worked in Sicily, with the same dedication, I could make a fortune. So I dropped out of the band, took some graduate business administration courses at George Washington University, resigned from the Navy, and joined a company that provided engineering and management services to the military — a "Beltway bandit". After about six months, I realized I was not going to become independently wealthy; further, I was unfulfilled both professionally and personally in my marriage . . . and I had quit the band!

In October 1980, a former Navy friend invited me to look at the Amway business. Dissatisfied with my job and lured by the promise of "financial freedom and a business of my own", I signed up. Linda, at first sceptical, was attracted by the idea that couples build the business together. The strong relationships she witnessed among the people we met gave her hope that perhaps we could improve our marriage.

We actively built the business and, in the process, rebuilt our relationship. The business involved attending seminars and rallies. Little did I know that these functions would be the bridge eventually to lead me back to the Catholic Church with a faith stronger than I had ever known before. The road back, however, was neither smooth nor straight.

In May 1981, we attended our first area-wide leadership seminar in Norfolk, Virginia, along with fifteen thousand other excited distributors. Our sponsors explained that we were part of the Bill Britt organization and that Bill was a strong Christian who had built one of the largest and most successful organizations in the country. We listened to business leaders Friday night and all day Saturday and were impressed. Our sponsors encouraged us to attend Bill's nondenominational Sunday morning service. "You'll witness a miracle", they told us.

The service opened with several distributors' testimonial witness of how they couldn't succeed in their businesses until they had their hearts right toward other people, and they couldn't do that until they had their hearts right with God. With a hint of cynicism, I thought to myself, "How nice." Eventually, Bill himself came on stage and told us that he was not a preacher but he felt a responsibility for spiritual leadership of his group because he attributed all his success to his relationship with Jesus. Bill emphasized that the service was non-denominational. He quoted Scripture to show that we are all guilty of pride and that we all need to put Christ first in our lives rather than worshipping money, power, sex, hobbies, or anything else that could come between us and our Savior.

Bill then asked Jesus to work on the hearts of those in attendance. He challenged couples to turn to each other in forgiveness and humility, to commit to each other, to give up their selfish ways, and to ask Jesus to be their personal Lord and Savior. He asked those who would make a commitment to step forward toward the stage and visibly stand up for Christ. To my amazement, hundreds of couples around us began turning to each other in tears and starting for the stage. Bill kept on. He challenged all who were addicted to drinking, sex, or drugs to turn over their burdens to Jesus and to come forward. Hundreds more flocked toward the stage.

Two questions crossed my mind as I sat there taking in everything: First, is this a cult, with Bill seeing if he could manipulate and guilt-trip all of us out of our seats and onto the coliseum floor? Second, what should I do? I kept mentally arguing with Bill that I did not need to make Jesus my personal Lord and Savior because I already had done that back in the second grade at my First Communion. Then, for the first time since my days at St. Mary School, I started praying silently, directly to Jesus. "Lord, you know I gave you my heart back in second grade. I don't have to walk forward to prove it, do I?" A small inner voice seemed to respond, "Where have you been, Tom?"

I decided that Bill could not guilt-trip me. I stayed put, refusing to look at Linda, who seemed pretty comfortable with the whole process. Finally, sensing that no more attendees would be having a born-again experience that day, Bill explained to all who had come forward that they were now Christians and what it meant to be in Christ. He further explained that they had taken only the first step; next they must find a good Bible-believing church and grow in the Word. He cautioned them to avoid New Age denominations or churches that were steeped in legalism; that taught that salvation was earned through good works; or that added to the gospel such things as Purgatory. He mentioned no names, but I sensed Bill criticizing the Catholic Church. I mentally defended the Church as Bible-based; I wasn't sure about Bill's other accusations.

Afterward we got into heavy discussions with our sponsors and a couple we had sponsored, both of whom were Catholic in name but going through similar soul-searching regarding their allegiance to the Church. Were we offended or impressed? Was Bill trying to start his own religion? Was a service like this appropriate at an Amway rally? We decided to stick around and find out. More significantly for me personally, over the next days and weeks I kept replaying many of Bill's questions over and over in my head and heart: Catholic Church notwithstanding, was Christ really the Lord of my life? Was my pride keeping me from Him and from a good relationship with my wife? What had happened to my spiritual life over the past ten or twelve years?

I developed some Amway role models, all of whom had solid marriages and a correct "vertical alignment", which was how they referred to their priorities of God first, wife second, family third, then business, hobbies, and so forth. My vertical alignment was way out of whack, so I decided to follow their example; I read the books they read and listened to the tapes they studied. They led me to books such as *How to Win Friends and Influence People* and to tapes by positive-thinking preachers such as Robert Schuller.

I found that Bill Britt was a well-intentioned Christian whose business associates' denominational affiliations ranged from evangelical to pentecostal to fundamentalist, with the Bible as the common denominator. Although many in the business were Catholic, few, if any, of the leaders were practicing Catholics. Several of the most successful leaders were former Catholics who had switched to merge their beliefs with their business partners. The "prosperity gospels" and faith messages preached by Kenneth Copeland, Kenneth Hagin, and Charles Capps influenced many. I was never coerced into practicing any of these teachings, but since all the successful distributors attributed their success to biblical faith principles, I decided to study Scripture.

In our local business circle, my borderline Catholic associates talked about how Britt's non-denominational services were full of life compared to the lackluster Catholic Masses we had attended. Britt's people were excited about their faith and free from ritualistic legalism, we decided; they praised God from the depths of their souls, grateful that they knew Christ personally and that He loved them. Most Catholics we knew seemed dead in their faith. They dragged themselves to Mass, then showed no life once they got there. I convinced Linda we should take Britt's advice and find an exceptional Spirit-filled church.

The gospel message we learned from the Britt organization, simplified, said that we can never be good enough to earn heaven on our own. Through our sins, we owe a debt that we could never pay; but sinless Jesus paid it all for us, and we can receive eternal life through faith in Him. For the first time in my life, although I had had a good Catholic upbringing, I began to catch a glimpse of why Christ died for us, and I began to appreciate the magnitude of His gift. I had always been taught that Jesus died for our sins, but I could never correlate how His dying on the cross was tied to our salvation, or why He needed to be crucified. Despite the shortcomings I would later discover about the Protestant gospel, I am grateful that, in its simplicity, I came to appreciate what Christ did for us. I wondered if Catholics understood salvation in the same light. If so, why weren't they more excited about the gift they have? Maybe they were, but I just never noticed. Linda, who was still regularly attending Mass, could not answer my questions and also had to admit that the Protestant explanation helped to clarify her understanding of what Jesus did and why.

We attended another leadership seminar the following fall, at a resort in Pennsylvania. Another non-denominational service was held, and again all were invited to make Jesus their personal Lord and Savior. I decided that, even if I had already considered myself "born-again" as a baptized Catholic, it certainly wouldn't hurt to make a visible recommitment. Linda and I stepped forward for the altar call. So did many of the people we brought. Afterward, business leaders recommended some good Bible churches in our home area.

We attended a few of the recommended churches with our friends. Each had positive elements, and one in particular seemed to resemble the "alive" spirit of Britt's services: good music, good preaching, uninhibited praise worship, and good fellowship. Some of our friends chose to leave the Catholic Church for another church. Linda and I discussed the issue at length because of our common interest in getting our "vertical alignment" correct. We had actually begun really talking to each other and rebuilding our relationship. We decided that some of the criticism of the Church was true, but we elected to stay with the Church for two main reasons; one was Linda's and one was mine.

Linda said, "You know, all those people seem to have a genuine love for Christ, and it's been contagious. But I could never imagine joining a Church that wasn't focused on the Eucharist, even if their preaching is better and their people are more enthusiastic." I agreed. I also decided that, prior to my leaving, I would give the Catholic Church the benefit of the doubt that the doctrines for which they were being criticized were not contrary to Scripture. I would find out how the Church viewed salvation and assess the Catholic response to the accusations that were being levied against the Church by my well-intended business associates. I had already determined that some of their information might be in error just from what I could hazily remember from Sister Anthony's eighth-grade Church history class. Perhaps my mission, I told Linda, would be to remain loyal to the Church and bring my newfound enthusiasm into our parish.

Unfortunately, I had difficulty finding good Catholic teaching on Scripture, and I even found some so-called Catholic material that seemed to lend credibility to fundamentalist criticisms of the Church. I visited the bookstore at Catholic University of America and was astounded by the amount of material that was laced with humanistic philosophy, feminism, liberation theology, and very liberal interpretations of Scripture. For example, I saw in print that Paul was a woman-hater and a chauvinist, which is why the Bible is so sexist. Other books on the Bible, while perhaps true to Catholic doctrine, were intellectually deep but beyond what the average reader could understand, let alone apply in practical terms. I couldn't find Catholic views on salvation, especially in terms of Protestant teaching on radio shows like John MacArthur's "Grace to You", Chuck Swindoll's "Insight for Living", and Charles Stanley's "In Touch". I'm sure that good Catholic books were there, but I had difficulty separating the wheat from the chaff. Everything I read by and about Pope John Paul II appeared consistent with Scripture, but many American Catholic leaders seemed overly focused on liberal social issues and relative ethics.

Many Catholics, I decided, might not have physically strayed from the Church the way I had, but they have never mentally and spiritually made an adult commitment to Christ. They may have gone through the motions of confirmation as an eighth grader but have never really made the Faith their own. In one sense, evangelical Protestants are right in their belief that some Catholics are a product of their own legalism and don't understand the magnitude of the saving action of Christ. They come to Church to fulfill an obligation, but they have no joy when they are there because they don't know why they are there; they do not make a personal connection with the Real Presence of Christ in the Eucharist; they don't know Him in the Now. Maybe, I thought, having been through this myself, I could help reach these Catholics through my music. I knew that while true faith is not based on feelings, good music could elicit emotions and prepare a person for a personal relationship with Christ. Perhaps I could musically contribute that.

About that same time, in the summer of 1983, I received a call from the New Spirit Singers, a talented Holy Spirit Church folk music group, saying they were in need of a guitarist. I decided I needed to give back to Christ what He had given me in the way of musical talent over the previous twenty years, so I joined the group. I took over the leadership of the group in 1986. In 1988, I also accepted leadership of a fledgling teen choir. Both groups began to take up most of my free time, and I gradually became less active in the Amway business.

Many of the Britt leaders considered their business to be their ministry. By sponsoring people and bringing them into the business, they believed that they were also bringing them to Christ. I had always applauded the Christian principles upon which I felt the business was built, and I felt comfortable with the idea that I could potentially bring people to a saving knowledge of Jesus. However, as I renewed my fervor for the Catholic Faith, I became less and less willing to be an evangelist for an organization that was, albeit subtly and perhaps not intentionally, undermining the Catholic Church. Although I still view the Amway business as a great opportunity for someone willing to put forth the effort, I would caution Catholics who place value in their Faith not to change their beliefs in order to duplicate the "success patterns" of their mentors.

A significant turning point in my journey home to the Church also occurred in 1983, when I attended a videotape presentation of Dr. James Dobson's series, "Focus on the Family". The third tape of the six-tape series was entitled, "Where's Dad?" It discussed the need for fathers to take responsibility for spiritual leadership in the home. Dobson compared life to a relay race, with fathers and sons on the same team; in order to win the race each father had to complete his lap with the baton and hand it on to his son without dropping it. A lap was a lifetime, and the baton was Jesus Christ or, in my case, the Catholic Faith. Dobson asked, "Have you received the baton, will you carry it, and will you hand on the baton to your son without dropping it?" Somehow, through the grace of God I had received the baton, but, if I hadn't already dropped it, I was certainly fumbling with it. Dobson's message slapped me alongside the head, and I was determined to do something about it.

I owned up to my obligation as spiritual leader of my home. Linda, also a student of the Dobson material, had been complaining about the public schools and their amoral effect on our children, the oldest of whom was Jennifer, then about thirteen. Concurrently, our parish received a new pastor who impressed us. Monsignor McMurtrie was a strong proponent of Catholic education and promoted our parish elementary school. After hearing Dobson and Monsignor McMurtrie, I immediately enrolled our children into the Holy Spirit School, and I made a commitment to attend Sunday Mass regularly and be a Catholic role model for my children.

In addition to giving back my musical talents to Christ, I decided to invest in tomorrow's youth the way Sgt. Richter and Jim Havlick had invested in me. In fall 1984, I volunteered to teach tenth-grade CCD, and I have continued to do so. I found that most Catholic tenth graders knew *about* Christ but didn't *know* Christ. I made it my goal to transmit the "Catholic gospel" with the same fervor as the evangelicals spread their "Have you been saved?" gospel. My approach has been to focus on the simplicity of the gospel message — that God loves us, that he wants us with Him, that "He is alive", and that we must make Him real in our lives. I explain how the evangelicals come to Christ through their "born again" experience of committing to make Jesus their "personal Lord and Savior". I further explain that, as Catholics, we are born into Christ at baptism but that we should continually renew our commitment and "personal" relationship with Jesus through confession and the Eucharist. I had never actually seen this "Catholic gospel" in print, but, having talked with Father Albertson, a parish priest and friend, I decided that as long as I didn't contradict Scripture or the teachings of the Church I would be safe.

In 1985, Jennifer graduated from the Holy Spirit eighth grade and enrolled at a local Catholic high school. While in that school, she participated in a "Life in the Spirit" seminar, became a team group leader, and joined a team prayer group. Her prayer group had occasion to visit the Franciscan University of Steubenville. I was impressed with her "Life in the Spirit" materials and especially the materials she brought home from Steubenville. Because the material complemented my teaching, I started incorporating it into my CCD lesson plans. I liked the fact that it was scripturally based, it emphasized the need for life in Christ, and it leaned away from the "feel-good" wishy-washy text material that had been offered through our CCD office at the time.

In 1985, Linda and I attended a Natural Family Planning seminar. We liked what the Couple-to-Couple League had to offer, and we believed their teachings to be more true to Scripture than those of some of the evangelical radio Bible teachers to whom I had been listening. In the middle of our trying to learn the program, Linda suddenly became pregnant for the first time in seven years. This time, however, unlike our days in Sicily, we both resigned ourselves to God's will. We had total peace of mind throughout the whole pregnancy, even during Linda's emergency caesarean delivery, at which time we almost lost Mark, our fifth child. Well-intentioned friends told us how sorry they were for us because Mark interrupted a life pattern in which all our older children were in school and we would have finally had some time to ourselves. We focused on the blessing, and Mark became a unifying factor in that our older children rallied to support the family more than they ever had in the past.

Less than two years later, Mary Beth was born, and in 1990 our seventh child, Christopher, arrived. During both pregnancies, because she was in her early and mid-forties, Linda was encouraged by doctors to have an amniocentesis so she could consider abortion if necessary. In both cases she refused, and, in faith, we prayed and turned over the situation to the Lord. We were blessed to have both babies born healthy, and we thanked God, who, we believe, keeps us growing closer and closer to Him.

One Sunday after Mass, in the fall of 1991, I happened to pass a table set up outside the church by the parish pro-life committee to promote their materials. My eye caught a tape called "Protestant Minister Becomes Catholic". Having always enjoyed hearing testimonial stories from back in my active Amway days, I decided to purchase the tape. When I heard Scott Hahn talk about his days of criticizing Catholics for believing in Mary, Purgatory, the pope, and all the elements of the Faith for which I had been searching for answers, I became excited! After ten years of searching I had finally found what I had been looking for: good Catholic teaching from someone who had questioned every element of the Catholic Faith, studied all the historical documents in light of Scripture, and convinced himself that the Catholic Church in her totality is true. At last, here was someone who could provide sound answers to evangelical Protestants' criticisms.

Imagine the further injection of excitement I felt when I found that Scott, in addition to having hundreds of tapes on the Bible from a Catholic perspective, was a professor at the Franciscan University of Steubenville. Scott's tapes and the source materials he referenced easily removed any of the doubts I had developed about the areas of Catholic faith that had been criticized by the Protestants. Scott's wife, Kimberly, also a convert and an outstanding speaker, helped restore my love for the Blessed Mother to the kind of childlike faith I had had back in St. Mary School.

Scott and Kimberly led us to other quality Catholic source material, such as the works of Karl Keating and Bishop Fulton J. Sheen. I also had found over the past years that our diocese was very loyal to the Magisterium, and that every graduating seminary class seemed more solid in their faith than the previous class. I was given a copy of the book *Surprised By Truth*, which contained conversion stories of others like the Hahns. One story I especially enjoyed was that of Tim Staples, who had followed many of the same radio ministries as I had. I attended a live seminar by Tim the weekend he came to town to attend his brother Terry's ordination. These experiences have made me realize that the Holy Spirit is truly working in the Church today!

And the Holy Spirit is working in our family. Despite our continual battle with Satan for the souls of our children, we have some bright spots. In the early '90s, then in his late teens, our "Dalkon Shield" child, T. J., went through several years of passive rebellion. After barely graduating from high school, he renounced his Faith and left home to live with some heavy-metal band buddies. Almost a year later, while attending a party, he overheard an argument between a Bible-believing non-Catholic and an atheist. Although not a party to the conversation, T. J. was taken with the gospel message of the Christian, asked him some questions, had a "born-again" type of experience, and began going to the friend's evangelical Church.

T. J. renounced the vices he had acquired, began daily Bible reading, and attended Bible study groups with church members. Although Linda and I wished he had returned to the Catholic Church, we were happy that he had at least returned to Christ. Linda attended daily Mass to pray for him. Soon, former band members and friends, some of whom had become Muslims or Mormons, were all vying for T. J.'s allegiance. In his search for truth, T. J. came to me for answers, and I introduced him to my Scott Hahn tapes. T. J. was interested but stated, "I sure wish I could ask Scott questions to his face." I told him that Scott was a professor at Steubenville, and perhaps he ought to go there and ask Scott the questions personally.

Today, T. J. is a student on the Dean's List at the Franciscan University of Steubenville, where he majors in theology and plays in the music ministry. He loves the school, Scott Hahn's classes (and others), and his Catholic Faith. Linda and I keep praying for him, for each other, and for all our children. I keep active by teaching tenth-grade CCD, directing the adult and teen choirs, and studying our Faith. I thank God for the Catholic Church, and I pray that I will be faithful to hand on the baton.

God in the Passing Lane

Rick Strom

Ever since I can remember, after watching my first football game at age four, I have always wanted to play professional football. My earliest memories of watching football on television were that there was a big pile of people and one lucky person with a football got to jump on top. It looked like a lot of fun. My dream came true when I became a member of the 1989 Pittsburgh Steelers. It was a very difficult journey into the National Football League, and, although I have managed to be in the league for seven seasons, it has been anything but easy and stress-free. Foot surgery, a broken leg, a broken finger, torn rib cartilage, and a mid-foot sprain have all seemed to be career-ending injuries, as well as major setbacks to my football career. As I advanced to the various levels of competition, however, those injuries, along with the desire to play in the National Football League, have driven me to my knees and helped to wake me up to the reality of Jesus Christ and His Church.

I have to begin by saying my awakening to our Lord

Jesus Christ and his Church was only enhanced by the love, support, and example given by my mom and dad. The prayer group that my mom regularly attends invited me to speak one night about my journey of faith, and the line that got the strongest reaction was, "Well, I guess I cannot stand before you and tell you that I had to overcome my parents." It is my hope to be able to be as loving and faithful to my wife and children as my parents were and still are to each other and to us.

During the summer of 1978, I noticed that at night my right foot ached with pain. The pain was greater when I was more active during the day. One night I made a startling discovery. I could move my right foot up and down but I could not turn it in. I showed this to my mom and dad. They were puzzled. A few days later they scheduled an appointment with an orthopedic surgeon. During the time leading up to the appointment, they decided to stop in my room and say a short prayer with me at my bedside. Now, we always prayed before meals, sometimes the traditional "Bless us, O Lord", but more often it was a prayer of our own thoughts and words. We also prayed, each one of us individually, our own prayer out loud as we departed for vacations, and we always went to Sunday Mass. Missing Mass, whether at home or on vacation, was never an option, illness being the obvious exception. I mention this because at age thirteen I am sure that I had thoughts that just maybe my parents were being a little juvenile and excessive by stopping in to pray at my bedside on a nightly basis.

We went to see a doctor. He ordered some X rays,

looked at them, and proceeded to show me where a calcium bar had grown over a joint in my right foot. This
was the cause of the pain and the immobility. He went on
to say that there really wasn't much to do for it except to
fuse the joint when the pain became too great. I had yet
to play one down of organized football, and here was a
doctor telling me that at best I would probably be able to
walk normally once the surgery was performed. Running
normally was not a possibility. We left discouraged.

My parents continued to pray with me. Several weeks
later, someone mentioned to them the name of another
orthopedic surgeon, Dr. O'Malley, who was greatly respected. We made an appointment and went for the examination. Dr. O'Malley had seen this condition before
and had learned a new surgical procedure to remove the
calcium bar, replace it with other tissue, and free up the
joint. He was one of only a few surgeons in the Pittsburgh
area who knew how to do this procedure. We scheduled
surgery. My parents continued to pray with me.

After the surgery, I was in a cast for four weeks. On
the day my cast was removed, the doctor warned me that,
although he believed the surgery had been a success, I
could expect several weeks of painful rehabilitation before
my foot returned to normal. Initially, my foot and ankle
felt a little stiff but relatively pain free. I soaked my foot
for twenty minutes for two nights before announcing that
my foot was pain free, and I was ready to go catch up on
all the activity that I had missed while I had been in the
cast. My foot never bothered me again. I never had any
pain. I thanked God for healing my foot and never forgot

the example of faith and persistence in prayer that was demonstrated to me by my parents over that six-month period.

Unfortunately, even with my healing so fresh in my mind, the Catholic Faith grew to be more of a set of rules and obligations designed to limit my freedom rather than a path to happiness, fulfillment, and an encounter with the living God. I did not have an openly outward rebellion where I stopped going to church, stopped believing in God, and ventured off into a life of drugs, alcohol, and sex. My rebellion was subtler. My rebellion was one of neglect and irrelevance. During my high school years, God became someone I turned to when I needed a favor, and church was something I did on Sundays. My motivation for staying out of trouble was that I had dreams of gridiron stardom, not that I loved God and desired to spend eternity with Him in heaven. Athletic success, social status, and my own view of right and wrong were the gods I allowed to take center stage in my life. My athletic, academic, and social life flourished, but my faith became stagnant and merely an obligation. I did not resent God or shake my fist at Him. I still went to Mass and said an occasional prayer, but few things were as boring as my high school religious education program, and God seemed to be so distant. Imperceptibly, I became a Catholic in name only.

As I entered my senior year in Fox Chapel High School in Pittsburgh, Pennsylvania, I was looking forward to great success on the football field. I had played well enough during my junior football season to receive recruiting letters from the likes of Pitt, Penn State, Ohio State, and even

UCLA. We had a good team, and with a few good breaks we were thinking championship.

Fall camp began in the hot and humid month of August. We had just finished our first week of practice and were ready for a pre-season scrimmage against Valley High School in New Kensington, Pennsylvania. Fox Chapel and Valley had a great rivalry whenever they competed against each other in any sport. In this scrimmage, since it was just a pre-season scrimmage, we played by the rule that each team's quarterback was not supposed to be hit. It was toward the end of the scrimmage when my head coach stepped into the huddle with me and said, "This is his last play. I don't want anyone to touch the quarterback." I called a play action pass, broke the huddle, and approached the line of scrimmage with the thought, "Hey, coach, where've you been for the first part of the scrimmage?" (Everyone seemed to have forgotten about the special lay-off-the-quarterback rule.) I barked out the signals, took the ball, faked a handoff, and dropped back to pass. I spotted my receiver twelve yards down the field, and the throwing lane was clear. I stepped and delivered the pass. Earlier in the play, while I was looking downfield, the nose guard had beaten his blocker around to the left and was racing toward me. The right offensive guard spotted him and dove to cut him at his knees. The nose guard leapt for me, was hit in his knees, and struck me with his shoulder pads just below my left hip. My foot was planted in the ground, and my knee was locked in place.

The ball had just left my hand when the hit took place. Immediately, as if in slow motion, I felt my knee sliding apart as I was knocked to the ground. I grabbed my leg, looked down at it, and saw my foot pointing east when it should have been pointing north, and my knee not looking anything like the knee I had had just moments before. I began to scream, "O my God! O my God!" For the next five minutes it was all I could say. I had to wait at least ten minutes on the field before I could be taken to the hospital because my good friend and wide receiver had broken his foot in five places earlier in the evening and the ambulance had not returned from dropping him off at the hospital.

As I lay there on the field in a great deal of pain, fearful that my football career had just ended, many questions began to race through my mind: "Why, God? Why now? Why this? What about those prayers I prayed before this scrimmage about safety, health, and success? Didn't you hear those? Don't you care? Where are you?" I was lifted into the ambulance and taken to the local hospital. I was sedated and quickly moved into what I thought was the operating room. When I awoke several hours later, I felt the cast around my leg and wondered how badly I had damaged my knee. To my somewhat pleasant surprise, I discovered that my knee was completely intact. The sliding sensation had been my femur, my thighbone, breaking just above my knee. The prognosis was good: six weeks in a cast, twelve weeks of rehab, and I should be able to join my basketball team early in the season.

Since I had been injured so early in the football season, I held onto the slightest hope that I could be ready to play again by the time the playoffs rolled around in November. When it became apparent to me that I would not be ready to play football until next year, I returned to the questions that first crossed my mind when I was injured. "Why, Lord? Why this? Why now?" If nothing else, I had a great deal of time to think while I was hobbling around on crutches. Why does God, who is supposed to be so good and so loving, allow us to suffer? I was concerned primarily with my own situation but, while I was thinking about it, what about everybody else in the world? My mom has a favorite saying, "Praise God in all circumstances." That had a nice ring to it when I was being named to all-star teams and being recruited to colleges, but what about with a broken leg and a lost football season?

At the low point of my physical therapy, after I had failed the test I needed to pass in order to play again that year, I confided to my mom that I believed God was punishing me for things I had done earlier in high school. She didn't believe that was the case. She reminded me just how much God loves me and how much He wants me to trust Him, even when things do not go as I planned. The questions I had to answer were: Can I trust the Lord with His plan for my life? Can I praise Him even in this circumstance? Do I really believe in Him?

I was cleared for athletic competition on the day of our first regular season basketball game in late November. In December I received my first football scholarship offer, from the University of Pittsburgh, and within a couple of days three other schools had contacted me to say they thought enough of my football skills to extend scholarship offers to me. I made four recruiting visits, and in February 1983 I signed a letter of intent to attend Georgia Institute of Technology in Atlanta on an athletic scholarship.

I had it all planned out by the time I arrived at Georgia Tech for fall camp in August 1983. I figured I would spend my first year as backup quarterback, start by my second year, rewrite the record book by my final year, be named to various all-American teams during any and all of my playing years, and, who knows, even win the Heisman Trophy. I would do all of this while thoroughly enjoying Atlanta's social life, remaining perfectly healthy, and picking up a first-class education in the process. Needless to say, it didn't exactly work out that way.

I did not anticipate playing much as a freshman because I didn't anticipate the senior quarterback suffering a season-ending knee injury in the third game of the season. I played in a couple of games versus North Carolina and Tennessee that year, but I did not play very well. Tennessee had a defensive lineman named Reggie White who hit me so hard that I lost the feeling in my face for a minute or so. We struggled as a team. I struggled as a quarterback. We finished with a disappointing three wins and eight losses.

I would have to say that my faith in God had become very impersonal by the time I entered my college years. I felt very grateful to God for the healing of my broken leg, for the scholarship that I had received, and, most important, for my family. I believed myself to be a Christian; after all, I was Catholic, but in no way did I ever understand that Jesus was personally interested in every aspect of my life, every day of my life. It certainly had never occurred to me to share my faith or to talk about God with others. My faith seemed to be a private matter, and I wasn't certain how much I wanted others to know about my personal beliefs. Truthfully, I am sure that I could not have clearly articulated what I believed or why I believed it. This made me uncomfortable when others talked about God. I usually tried to avoid these situations.

During my first year at Georgia Tech, I made three significant discoveries. The first was that I was seven hundred miles from home, and very few people in Atlanta, Georgia, knew my parents or me. The second was that I was a little more homesick than I thought I would be. The third was that not everyone in Atlanta was Roman Catholic or thought highly of Catholics in general. This last discovery became apparent during a ride to a retreat in North Carolina during my sophomore year. More on that later.

Like many eighteen-year-olds, I probably would have defined freedom as the distance between where I lived and where my parents lived. Now, please don't get me wrong. My parents were wonderful to me even when I was a teenager. I did not fully realize how far Atlanta was from Pittsburgh when I decided to go to Georgia Tech. I had flown to Atlanta with my parents to visit the campus when I was being recruited. To me, Atlanta was only an hour and a half away from home by plane. In reality, it was approximately a twelve-hour drive, depending on how much of a hurry I was in to get home. My family dropped me off for the fall football training camp in August 1983. I was not able to return home until mid-December. Those few months seemed a long time to be away from family.

Football camp began. There I was, eighteen years old, away from home for the first time, exhausted from two practices a day in sweltering heat and humidity, and it was

Sunday morning. No one was there to wake me up to be sure I wouldn't be late for Mass or to ask me which Mass I would like to go to. As I languished in bed, I tried to rationalize my not going to Mass. I knew that God would understand if I caught up on my much needed rest. Fortunately, the old habit was hard to break: I dragged myself out of bed and managed to get to Mass that Sunday and every Sunday that followed.

During that first year, I often thought about my freedom. I was far from home and could do just about anything I wanted, good or bad; I could decide for myself. Sometimes, while on my way to Mass, I would wonder why I was even going, especially when I had to get up after a particularly late Saturday night. Was I simply going out of habit? Was I going out of a sense of obligation to my parents? Whose faith was I living, theirs or mine? I really didn't have much of an understanding of the worship of God in the sacrifice of the Mass. It occurred to me that if anyone had asked me why I went to Mass or even why I called myself a Catholic, I would have been hard-pressed to give a compelling answer. I simply continued attending Sunday Mass because I believed that it was the right thing to do. I was Catholic, Catholics went to Mass, therefore I went to Mass. Another reason for my Mass attendance was because I enjoyed going. When I was homesick, Mass provided a link with my family. It was also a refuge from all the pressures of football and the stress of college. I would walk out of Mass feeling a little less burdened and a little less lonely. I could not have explained these feelings at the time. The answers to these and other questions did come to me in a slow but steady process of prayer and study, but not until a few years after I graduated from college. For the time being, I went to Mass.

During my sophomore year at Georgia Tech I went on a Fellowship of Christian Athletes retreat in North Carolina. Four of us drove together, three guys and a girl named Jill. The conversation in the car was very lighthearted at first, but then it began to move to matters of faith. Someone asked the rest of us, "What's the Lord been doing in your life?" I wanted to say none of your business, but I knew that wasn't a proper response. I simply remained silent. Jill started speaking. I wasn't paying much attention until I heard her say if she ever met a Catholic, she wouldn't know what to say to him. I sat up a little straighter and asked what she meant. She went on to explain that she heard Catholics do not read the Bible, do not understand the Bible, and do not believe in the Bible.

I tried to explain to her that I thought Catholics had this thing called Mass and during daily Mass there are three passages from the Bible and during Sunday Mass there are four passages from different parts of the Bible, so she must be mistaken. The two guys riding with us in the car started laughing at our conversation. When Jill asked what was so funny, I knew I had been discovered —I was one of them, a Catholic. Jill said she was very sorry if she had offended me and then proceeded to ask how often I read the Bible. I sheepishly began to explain to her this thing called the Mass where I hear the Bible read every Sunday. She asked me what was my favorite passage. I replied I really liked the Gospel. She reminded me that it was all the Gospel. I was at a loss for words, and scriptural passages. I do not think she said, "See what I mean?" but in my mind that was all I heard. I do not remember much more about that retreat except my resolution: "I am going to read the Bible systematically from cover to cover."

I got back to campus and immediately went to buy a notebook so that I could write down each day what I read. I started in Genesis but quickly realized I was biting off more that I could chew. I went to the New Testament, beginning with Matthew, and read all the way through Revelation. I had two rules for myself during this time. The first was that I had to read from the Bible every day. The second was that I had to read a minimum of one chapter a day. I finished reading the New Testament in about four months.

I was amazed at how familiar I was with most of the four Gospels (daily Mass while attending St. Edward's elementary school had done that for me). St. Paul's letters were more understandable to me now, when read in their entirety rather than as short excerpts read during Mass. Many of the Gospel stories, such as the parable of the talents in Matthew 25, or the Bread of Life discourse in John 6, or even the teaching on lukewarmness in Revelation 3, became very thought provoking for me. It was the beginning of a daily prayer time. A few minutes a day was all it took, but I have been reaping the rewards from that exercise ever since.

I wound up as the starting quarterback my final two years at Georgia Tech. We were an average football team during my redshirt junior year and finished with a disappointing five wins, five losses, and one tied game. My senior year we were worse. I was hurt after the sixth game, causing me to miss all but seven plays of our final game of the season. We finished with a dismal two wins and nine losses.

I was injured during a Wednesday practice. For all intents and purposes the practice was over. At that time our record was two wins and four losses, and the offense was putting in some extra time making sure we knew our assignments for the upcoming game. The play we were working on was a pass versus a blitz. I dropped back, the strong safety blitzed, and I had to get rid of the ball quickly. I took the ball, dropped back, and threw it in the right flat to my fullback. The safety blitzed and tried to bat the pass down. He missed the ball but did manage to hit my hand. As my hand was going forward, he caught my little finger while running in the opposite direction of my hand. I felt a snapping sensation and immediately looked at my hand. My little finger, to my horror, was at a ninety-degree angle pointing sideways, hard left. I was taken off the field for an X ray. The doctor looked at it and counted eight bone fragments within a one-inch area of the middle of my little finger on my right hand. It looked as though my season and possibly my career were over.

I could not help but ask Our Lord why. This whole situation had such a familiar feel to it. I had been in a similar situation before with my leg in high school, and things had seemed to work out quite nicely. Could I now pray, "I trust You, Lord. I offer this suffering to You. I unite it to the cross"? Quite frankly, no! I was too disappointed, too upset at being injured and not accomplishing the goals that I had set for myself. I wanted to mope and feel sorry for myself, and for a time I did.

One of the reasons I chose to attend Georgia Tech was its excellent academic reputation. Because I had already experienced a potentially career-ending injury in high school, I wanted to be sure that, if for some reason I was unable to play professional football, my academic degree would mean something in the "real world".

Within the first few months of classes during my freshman year, I began to hear the grumbling of several upperclassmen who were taking management classes from a professor named Dr. Phillip Adler. Apparently, this professor taught socratically, and his students underwent daily question-and-answer sessions that left many with bruised egos. As a student who much preferred silent listening to vocal participation, I privately vowed never to take a class taught by Dr. Adler.

During the end of the fall quarter of my fourth year at Georgia Tech, I scheduled my classes for winter quarter. In filling out the computerized class schedule form, I mistakenly put in a wrong number on a computer sheet and wound up scheduling a senior-level chemical engineering lab as one of my electives. I was a management student. I did not discover the error until the day before the first day of classes for the winter quarter. As soon as possible, I canceled the chem-e lab and tried to schedule a class that would count toward my degree. I ran into one major problem. The only classes available to me for winter quarter 1987 that counted toward my degree were taught by Dr. Adler. With fear and trepidation, I scheduled the class.

Dr. Adler wanted his students to operate successfully in a highly competitive, highly pressurized environment because that's what they would face when entering the job market, and the stakes are higher outside the classroom than inside. Above all, he wanted his students to know how to think and make decisions. He taught a decision-making process he referred to as the conversion of information to knowledge. Within the process he gave four study questions: (1) What was said? (2) What does it mean? (3) Why was it said? (4) How does it affect me in the real world? If you take the four study questions and apply them to the information that you have taken in, the result will be knowledge and a knowledge base. If your knowledge is solid and springy, you can make decisions that will lead to a better life. Scheduling that chemical engineering lab turned out to be one of the best mistakes I ever made. I scheduled Dr. Adler four more times after that first class. I latched onto this process, and it began to change the way I thought, the way I played football, the way I socialized, and the way I prayed.

I had been passive for so many years about being a Catholic. Yes, I went to Mass on Sundays. Yes, I made it to confession once a year—whether I needed it or not. Yes, I prayed at least before I ate, and yes, I had even read the New Testament a couple of years ago. All of that being said, did I ever seriously consider, seriously think about, seriously investigate what the Church was or at least claimed to be? Did I know for certain what the

Church taught about Jesus Christ, about salvation, about the sacraments, about the Eucharist, about grace, about the Blessed Virgin Mary, about the saints, about abortion, and about birth control? As Dr. Adler would say, "My knowledge base was full of cracks, big ones."

I took this active method of thinking to my daily habit of Bible reading. I looked especially at some specific passages that I had highlighted from the past couple of years. One passage I went to almost immediately is in the sixth chapter of the Gospel of John. I applied the four study questions.

1. What did Jesus say? Beginning with verse 50, Jesus said four times that you must eat His flesh and drink His blood. Many of His disciples murmured at this saying, but Jesus never backed away from it.

2. What did Jesus mean? Was he merely speaking symbolically? Obviously, His disciples did not think so. They murmured at this saying, and many of them stopped following Jesus because of this teaching. He was being very serious. He must have been referring to the Last Supper when He held in His hands the bread and the cup filled with wine and said, "This is my body" and "This is my blood. . . . Do this in remembrance of me."

3. Why did He say it? It must have been very necessary. It must have been very important, or else why did He allow so many people to stop following Him? He even turned to His closest disciples and challenged them as to their intentions.

4. What does this mean to me in the real world? In John 6, Our Lord told everyone present that they must eat His flesh and drink His blood. He must also be speak-

ing to me and every other follower of Christ through the Sacred Scriptures. One day it dawned on me: when I go to Mass and receive the Eucharist, I am fulfilling Our Lord's command to eat His body and drink His blood in remembrance of Him. Furthermore, when I go to Communion, I am receiving the most powerful Being in the entire universe and beyond. He is the one who created every thing that I can see and not see. Moreover, when I open my mouth or hold out my hands, I am receiving or holding the Author of all life, including my own. Did I really believe this? Did I act as if I believed it? I began to pray more like this: "Lord, I believe, but please help my unbelief."

My broken finger did heal in time for me to play in the 1987 Blue-Gray All-Star football game in Montgomery, Alabama, on Christmas Day. It was also a chance to show the pro scouts that I had the ability to play in the National Football League. After the game, I looked forward to the draft.

Although I wasn't overly confident that I would go early in the draft, it never occurred to me that, in a twelve-round draft, twenty-eight teams would make the same mistake twelve times and not draft me. At a little after 5:00 P.M. of the second day of the draft, toward the end of the twelfth round, I called my parents in Pittsburgh to tell them that I hated football; I was tired of the frustration, the injuries, and the disappointments. In other words, "I quit." While I was expressing my frustrations, my parents were saying things like, "God has a plan, and you do not know what God has in store for you." In the middle of our conversation my mom interrupted me, saying, "Hold on a minute, Honey. It's the other line." (I have since forgiven her for answering call waiting during this "darkest hour".) A few seconds later she came back and said, "Hang up the phone. It's the Steelers", and she hung up on me. Seconds later, my phone rang in Atlanta, and on the line was an official from the Pittsburgh Steelers. He was offering me a chance to work out in hopes of signing me to a free agent contract. Suddenly, my dreams of playing professional football were alive again. Two days later, I signed a contract to play football for the hometown Pittsburgh Steelers. I was ecstatic. My boyhood dreams of playing professional football were becoming a reality.

I went to my first Pittsburgh Steelers' training camp at St. Vincent College in Latrobe, Pennsylvania. In July 1988, I competed for a spot on the roster with Bubby Brister, Todd Blackledge, and Steve Bono. To my disappointment, I never played in a pre-season game. When the day came for mandatory cuts to a sixty-man roster, I got the dreaded knock on the door. The official who gave me the bad news also told me that I had impressed them enough that they would like me to come back next year and try again. I promptly responded with a "thanks, but no thanks" answer.

I felt that I had failed. Not only that, but during training camp I had been setting aside twenty minutes a day in the afternoon to pray. As I prayed, I began to tell Our Lord how much I wanted to make the team, but, more important, I wanted what the Lord wanted. If He wanted me on the team, then I would be there. If not, He had something better for me, and that would be OK. After I was released, I could not believe that was really what the

Lord wanted. Could He possibly have made a mistake? No, that was not possible.

I quickly left Pittsburgh, moved back to Atlanta, and a few weeks later took a job with the Federal Reserve Bank of Atlanta in Jacksonville, Florida. I owe a debt of gratitude to Jim Hawkins and the people at the Fed for allowing me to work for a short six months before I eventually returned to try out again for the Steelers in 1989.

While I was in Jacksonville, a good friend and former teammate of mine at Georgia Tech, Mike Travis, was trying to get involved with the Fellowship of Christian Athletes in the Jacksonville area. FCA was having a weekend retreat, and he invited me to go along with him to observe.

We arrived in time for breakfast on Saturday morning. The kids on the retreat were great to be around. During breakfast, one of the counselors shouted, "Attitude check!" The response would be a thunderous "Praise the Lord!" This occurred several times during the retreat, and it made me think seriously about my own response to the cry of "Attitude check". The skits and talks were very good, and by Sunday afternoon the challenge was laid before us all: Remove one obstacle in your life that is affecting your attitude and your relationship with the Lord. We were challenged to confess that sin to God and receive His forgiveness. I resolved to confess that obstacle, that sin, as soon as I could get to confession, and so I did. It was the shortest confession I ever made, and when I heard the priest say, "I absolve you from your sins . . .", I knew I was forgiven, and I was very grateful to God.

I returned to Pittsburgh in the spring of 1989 to begin my second attempt at playing football for the Steelers. During the summer of 1989, I started going to weekly charismatic prayer meetings in the Pittsburgh area. As I was growing in my faith, it was becoming more important for me to meet other people my age who were enthusiastic about living the Christian life.

Earlier, in August 1985, I had met my future wife, Karen Elizabeth Craze. We met in a restaurant in Sandy Springs, Georgia. I happened to be there with a fellow Georgia Tech quarterback, Todd Rampley. I had told Todd that I wasn't interested in meeting his old high school buddies, but I wouldn't say no to meeting one or two of the girls he knew. Karen just happened to be praying for a similar intention, to meet dedicated Christians.

Karen was a beautiful woman with a smile that made her face light up. She had a lively personality as well. I had a great time being with her that night. I left the restaurant with every intention of seeing her again, and we began dating a few weeks later. Karen attended the University of Georgia, so we were able to see each other only every second or third weekend. I knew very quickly that she was someone very special, although it took me a long time to tell her. She was not a Catholic at that time, and little did I know that God would use her as the catalyst to awaken in me the desire to grow in knowledge, love, and awe of what is, now for both of us, the Catholic Faith.

In 1989, I invited Karen to attend the prayer meetings in Pittsburgh, and we attended for six weeks. We saw a number of people our age there, but we were never introduced to them or talked to any of them. It probably did not help that we practically sprinted out of the meetings as soon as they were over. At the end of the sixth meeting, which was also the eve of the first day of training camp, we met two guys who introduced us to numerous other people who were about our age and enthusiastic about the Lord and about being Catholic. These friends were wonderful examples, supports, and sounding boards for both Karen and me. The Lord has continued to bless us with strong Christian friendship with many of these same people.

Training camp went very well. I was finally able to play in the pre-season games, and, considering that it had been over a year and a half since I had last played organized football, I played pretty well. I made it past the cut to sixty; the final cut to forty-seven was next.

On the morning of the final day of cuts I awoke confident that I had made the team. I drove to the stadium, went to my locker, and proceeded to the 9:30 team meeting. Chuck Noll walked into the room and began to address us. He started off by telling us that we were the forty-seven men he was going to war with in the National Football League, and our goal was to win a championship. I was in the room. I was sitting in one of those chairs. Chuck Noll was talking to me. I had made it! I had actually made it! I practically floated to practice and could not wait to race home to celebrate with Karen and my family.

After practice I was walking back to the locker room when I was stopped by one of the Steeler scouts. He asked me how I was doing and then went on to tell me about some changes in the injured reserve rules, some injuries on the offensive line, and how they had wanted to talk to me before practice but didn't have a chance. In short, I was being released, but they wanted me to sign a developmental squad contract. I argued with him, but it was no use. I was gone, and I wanted no part of the developmental squad. I drove home.

My family had heard the ten announced cuts and that there were still two to come, but they were sure I was not one of those two. They were ready to celebrate. As I pulled into the driveway, my family came out to greet me. I walked into the garage, up the basement steps, and I met Karen in the kitchen. I looked at her and barely managed to get out the words, "I got cut." There was a lot of disappointment, frustration, and tears in that house that day.

About an hour after I broke the news to everyone, we all gathered in the kitchen to commiserate. A short while into our gloomy conversation, my mom spoke up with her thoughts on the situation. She would not give up trusting God or praising Him for His perfect plan for all of our lives. She reminded us, as only she can, that we must praise the Lord in all situations, even in our disappointments, and she was unwilling to give in to sadness and discouragement. Jesus is still Lord and King! She was right, and we all knew it. A few minutes later we all joined her in giving thanks to God for all the opportunities and joys He had brought me through athletics, all the highs and lows that went along with football. Everyone in the kitchen that afternoon spoke a prayer of praise and thanksgiving to God.

I did sign a developmental squad contract a few days later, and I began practicing with the team. Five weeks into the season, our starting quarterback, Bubby Brister, sprained his knee, and I was activated to the forty-seven-man roster. I finished the season as backup quarterback in the first of five seasons that I would spend with the Pittsburgh Steelers.

During that first season with the Steelers, I started attending a prayer meeting at the University of Pittsburgh. It was being run by some of the same people Karen and I had met at our final summer prayer meeting. At the prayer meeting, a "Life in the Spirit" seminar was being offered. I was invited to attend, and so I did. When the time came for the prayer for the baptism of the Holy Spirit, I hesitated. I fully expected changes to take place if I invited the Holy Spirit to come into my life and lead me, but I was not sure what I would become. In the end, I did go and pray for the Holy Spirit to empower me to lead a fully Christian life. Nothing magical happened, but I knew that I had just recommitted my life to Our Lord, and He would make the changes he saw fit. Our Lord was becoming much more personal.

On April 28, 1990, I made one of the greatest moves of my life. I asked my girlfriend, Karen Craze, to become my wife, Karen Strom. On April 6, 1991, she did just that.

Our period of engagement was also a time for Karen to inquire more formally about the possibility of being received into the Catholic Church. She joined RCIA classes given by the Oratory parish at the University of Pittsburgh. I went with her as a sort of moral support. I never intended to go to all of the sessions, but after three weeks I was hooked. I was going whether she was going or not.

My last formal instruction concerning the Catholic Faith had ended with my confirmation in eighth grade.

Yes, I did manage to attend a few high school religious education classes, but I probably did more clock-watching than listening and learning. I was now twenty-five years old. I believed in God and had an active, growing faith. I prayed fairly regularly and was trying to improve my personal relationship with Our Lord. I just had a dismally low appreciation for being Roman Catholic. As I sat through those adult education classes as a "cradle Catholic", I was a little embarrassed to discover how much I did not know about the Blessed Trinity, Sacred Tradition, justification, the sacraments, the saints, the Blessed Virgin Mary, prayer, Purgatory, liturgy, the liturgical year, liturgical colors, feast days, sacred time, sacred space, infallibility, authority, councils, creeds, and a host of other issues.

My academic studies had enabled me to receive a college degree in management; my athletic pursuits had enabled me to play in the National Football League; but my understanding of the Faith was childish and limited, rather than mature and full.

I was to be married in a few months; my fiancée was possibly going to become a Roman Catholic. We had some important decisions to make, and the catechetical knowledge base I was using to make my decisions was no better than a fourth-grade level. Fortunately, the Holy Spirit was active in our lives, and He gave us a hunger to know the truth and the teachers to show us the way.

With six months to go before our wedding day, we began talking about children—when and how many. As a lifelong Catholic I must have picked up the idea somewhere along the way that contraception was not an option. I really did not know for sure. Had the Church changed its teaching? Is avoiding contraception an ideal to strive for? Could you use contraception for serious reasons? As we began to ask other people about it, the issue grew even cloudier. We heard a lot about following our conscience. We were told that some forms of artificial contraception were OK, while others were not. It was very frustrating trying to get a definitive answer.

Finally, we met with Fr. Fred Byrne, O.S.B., who was going to celebrate our wedding Mass. We told him our thoughts, our concerns, and our fears regarding contraception. He sat back, thought for a moment, and then very gently said, "I guess it's all a matter of whom you trust: God or some contraceptive." God bless Father Fred!

Karen was furious. The idea that using artificial contraception was somehow in violation of God's plan for marriage and that it demonstrated a lack of trust in God—this was a teaching that she had never heard before as a Protestant evangelical Christian. Father Fred was not the one who was going to have to carry a baby for nine months or to care for it later. She considered this to be the dumbest teaching she had ever heard. She wondered why the Church couldn't get a grip on reality. After all, this was the '90s.

Despite her concerns, Karen was received into the Catholic Church in February 1991, two months before our wedding day. Since we were now both Catholic, we decided to call upon Our Lady through the Rosary for the forty days of Lent just prior to our wedding day on the weekend after Easter. We prayed the Rosary together with the intention of asking for Mary's intercession to enable us to do God's will regarding the whole issue of family planning. Remarkable things happened and continue to happen as a result of the intercession of Our Lady.

First and foremost, by our wedding day we were given the grace and faith to follow the Church's teaching regarding contraception even though we still had doubts. Within a couple of months after our wedding day, we were 100 percent convinced of the truth and wisdom of Mother Church. We discovered the clear and prophetic teachings of the Church through Pope Paul VI in the encyclical *Humanae Vitae* and Pope John Paul II in the apostolic exhortation *Familiaris Consortio*, the "Magna Carta" for family life. We found John Kippley's book *Sex and the Marriage Covenant* to be of tremendous help in understanding the covenant of marriage that the Church has proclaimed to the world to be a covenant of love and life, a covenant of total self-giving.

In addition, prior to our wedding day, on our way to a Natural Family Planning class, we heard a former Protestant minister on a Christian radio talk show explaining the Catholic Church with such beauty and clarity that we just sat in the car in amazement and listened to him speak. That former minister was Dr. Scott Hahn. On that show, he made the comment that many Catholics were living like poor beggars, not realizing that they were sitting on Fort Knox and that they had the keys. That was a word picture that has stayed with me ever since, and it has been wonderful discovering its truth. A short while into our marriage, we began listening to some of his audiotapes. We have found them outstanding!

Our initial plan was to delay conception for at least the first year of our marriage. Several months later, we began to reconsider our plan. One of the advantages of practicing NFP is that couples must continually evaluate and then reevaluate their plans for a family. We discovered that the Bible only mentions children as blessings. We found that children are meant to be the incarnation of the love between the husband and wife. Finally, we listened to audiotapes by Scott and Kimberly Hahn that teach that in the marriage covenant two people become one flesh, and the one flesh they become is so real that often nine months later you have to give it a name. So far, we have named ours Mary Katherine, James Richard, and Elizabeth Grace Strom. Kimberly Hahn explained that the issue of family planning is in reality the issue of the lordship of Jesus Christ. If we can trust the Lord with our time, our talents, and our money, shouldn't we also trust Him with our family? If we have serious reasons to postpone having a child, then we practice self-control (a fruit of the Holy Spirit), not contraception. This is what the Church has taught for almost two thousand years. On a practical note, we learned that the divorce rate of couples who follow the Church's teachings for marriage is under 5 percent, compared to the national average of above 50 percent. Following Jesus' teachings on marriage is safe, healthy, and beneficial — and with God's grace, possible. We must get this word out.

The fame that has come from playing professional football has given me a unique platform for sharing with others what I have discovered by following Our Lord Jesus Christ and His One, Holy, Catholic, and Apostolic Church. I often wondered what God wanted from me and how I was supposed to hear His voice among all the other voices. I found that the answer is very simple. He gave us the Church. "You are Peter and on this rock I will build my church, and the gates of Hades will not prevail against it" (Mt 16:18). "The pillar and foundation of the truth is the church" (1 Tim 3:15).

I am now in the process of retiring from professional football and beginning a career in commercial real estate. As I look back on my career in professional football, I am very thankful to God for giving me the talent and good fortune to play for five years with the Pittsburgh Steelers and for one year with the Buffalo Bills. I would be less than truthful if I said that I wasn't bothered by my lack of field success. I never became a starter or set any records or won a championship. Yet, from a supernatural point of view, I am very pleased with my years in professional football and with the opportunities I have been given to grow in my faith in God. When things have looked hopeless, God has been there for me. Life goes on, sanctification continues. I hope and pray that I will remain even more faithful to the call to holiness in my next career.

I am often asked to speak to junior and senior high school youth groups, adult "Life in the Spirit" seminars, men's conferences, and prayer breakfasts. I hope the message that they hear from me is that the Lord whom we claim to love, the Lord in whom we believe, the Lord who has a plan for our lives, the Lord whom I have so often asked, "Why, Lord?" is in our midst today. More important, He is in each and every tabernacle of each and every Catholic church throughout the world. When we go to Mass and receive Holy Communion, we receive the Lord and King of the Universe. We should never pass up the chance to see or visit Jesus in person. If He were giving a talk locally, would we go to hear Him? I hope that the answer is a resounding yes. Well, guess what? He is present, He is here, and He is giving a talk anytime we want. All we need are faith and effort. We can be as physically close to Our Lord as were Peter, James, and John. This isn't just good news: it's good news beyond expectation.

Finally, I hope my listeners hear me say: "God — the Father, Son, and Holy Spirit — is to be found in fullest possible earthly expression through the bride of Christ, the One, Holy, Catholic, and Apostolic Church. The sacraments are essential to living a holy life, and the Eucharist is the source and summit of the Christian life."

OK, I'm ready: Attitude check — "Praise the Lord!"

Someone Really Is Listening

Terese Norris

As the third child of seven, I had the best of everything in life. I had two older sisters who did a fine job of "breaking in" my parents to the art of child rearing, and there was a five-year span between myself and the four younger children. I had the benefit of being the youngest for five good years as well as being old enough to watch and help the last four grow up.

We were the typical Catholic family of the '60s, in the then rural community of Camarillo, California. We went to the local parish school, studied our *Baltimore Catechism* questions, attended Mass at least on Sundays, and watched *Lassie* and *Get Smart* on television on Saturday nights.

In the early '60s, the Catholic Church had the "best of everything", too. We had lovely, Immaculate Heart of Mary (IHM) sisters teaching in nearly every grade, and they were in full habit. What an inspiration they were to us young girls! Yes, we always wondered if they had ears or if they poked those straight pins right into their heads to keep their veils on. They were something special. I was impressed, and I believe that more than one of us girls harbored thoughts of becoming one day like them.

Our school choir sang parts of the Latin Mass in Gregorian chant. We always celebrated the first day of May as a day of games, processions, and a May crowning of the statue of the Blessed Virgin Mary. Meatless Fridays, stuffy Lenten afternoons making the stations of the cross, Benediction, all the verses of "Pange Lingua" sung on Holy Thursday by our school choir while the third-grade girls processed in their year-old First Communion dresses — all these gave us a strong sense of Catholic identity. With the saints and martyrs as our examples, we also were ready to die for our Faith.

It wasn't until I was in the seventh grade that things began to change. The sisters' habits became a thing of the past. Gregorian chant was no longer sung during Mass; instead, we sang songs such as "They'll Know We Are Christians by Our Love", while the younger kids swayed back and forth to the beat.

No, I wasn't shocked. It was new and different, but I really didn't have an opinion on it one way or another. I remember my eighth-grade IHM teacher asking me once what I thought about the change in their dress. I responded, "May I tell you tomorrow?" I was planning to ask my dad that night what "my" opinion should be on the subject. In our family, Dad was the one with the opinions.

I don't recall Dad being particularly concerned one way or another with the changes in the Church. We participated in the church choir as a family, trying to fill in the gap left by the IHM sisters, who were eventually asked to leave the parish. Dad chose the songs from the missalette, my sister played the organ, and my other sisters and I took turns leading the singing.

And so passed the '60s. I went to public high school in the early '70s. Life was full of activity — band, plays, speech club, sports. I never really critically looked at what it meant to be Catholic. Our family still attended Sunday Mass and followed the Ten Commandments and the laws of the Church as best we could.

My high school religious training took the form of CCD classes where we learned to find meaning in the lyrics of songs by groups such as Simon and Garfunkel and the Beatles, songs that my parents did not allow to be played at home due to their countercultural nature. I felt that my being Catholic really didn't make me much different from the other kids at school.

During high school, I had the opportunity to attend a couple of retreats where I felt the presence of God more closely. I spent two summers in Mexico, traveling and working in small villages. That's where the seed to become a missionary was planted. I began to think seriously about becoming a missionary to some developing country. I took pre-med classes at the local junior college after graduating from high school and corresponded with several missionary orders.

After two years of junior college, I decided to check out a missionary order called the Medical Missionaries of Mary, in Massachusetts. I told the Mother Superior that God had given me so much, I wanted to give something back. I had a lovely month-long stay with the sisters. They were active and happy and sang a beautiful "Salve

Regina", the melody of which haunts me to this day. It was fall, and the trees were showing their brilliant colors.

My stay there was perfect except for one thing. Almost daily I received letters from "the boy back home" telling me how much he missed me and making me terribly homesick and lovesick. When Mother Superior asked me to return home for a year and earn a dowry, I was a bit disappointed but at the same time relieved to be able to go home for a while.

I was employed that year in a convalescent hospital, and I really enjoyed working with elderly people. From that experience, I decided to become a nurse in order to have the opportunity for hands-on bedside care. The Medical Missionaries had said that I could either go to nursing school before entering the order, or I could enter first and then attend school. This proved to be a very important decision in my life. I longed to enter right away, but I agreed to finish college first in order to please my parents. I decided to attend the Catholic University of America to earn my nursing degree. I still remember the feeling of foreboding I felt as I left home for the airport. I just ignored the feeling, passing it off as "butterflies". I gritted my teeth and went ahead.

Catholic U was full of surprises. Aside from feeling a bit disoriented during the lengthy registration process, the real shocker came at the student Mass. It was held in the student lounge. We all sat on the floor. When it was time for the reading of the Gospel, no one moved to stand. I thought to myself, "This isn't right," so I stood. Everyone continued to sit during the entire Mass, even during the Consecration!

At Communion time, I noticed that the students were receiving Communion in their hands. This was 1975, and Communion in the hand had not yet been officially authorized by the Church.

It took me a while to get used to some of the irregularities. One of my roommates was a religion major. She explained that the people are the Church and that the Magisterium is always quite a bit behind the times. "The people set the trends, and the Magisterium will eventually follow them." So, we were merely setting new trends! Was that why there were no curfews in the dorms, and my roommate occasionally had her boyfriend spend the night? Or why the nursing department taught contraception to the nursing students as an option for their clients? Were these simply other new "trends" that would be sanctioned by the Church at a later date? Who decided which trends to set? Was that the job of the students who were now "experts" in moral theology because of taking classes taught by moral theologian Fr. Charles Curran? Curiously, Father Curran was eventually asked to leave the university because his teachings were not in line with the teachings of the Catholic Church, but that was some fifteen years later. How many "trends" had been set by that time? All this was a bit mind-boggling to someone who virtually had only an eighth-grade religious education, a structured childhood, and a very simple faith.

I had to take two religion classes in order to graduate. One of the required courses for incoming freshmen and transfer students was called "Modern Critiques of Religion". I remember having to study such works as Sigmund Freud's *The Future of an Illusion*, which held that religion was an invention of the mind. We also studied a work by philosopher Albert Camus that expounded the message that society today has come of age and doesn't need to be bound by the shackles of a man-made religion. The bottom line was that in our modern society we have now progressed enough to make our own choices and reach our own decisions. These philosophies sounded very plausible and liberating to a young student who had never really been allowed to voice her own opinion while growing up. I was now faced with many a moral dilemma. The old Jesuit priest who taught the course systematically refuted arguments against religion. Yet, I don't recall any of his counter arguments in support of religion. I do remember that the counter arguments made much less sense than the critiques. The works of St. Thomas Aquinas or St. Augustine were never cited as possible answers to the questions raised by the religion critics.

I continued to attend Mass and go through the motions of being a practicing Catholic throughout my first year at the university. Looking back, I can see that my relationship with God was suffering, but at the time I really didn't notice. I was too busy with college life. We continued to have Mass in our dorm lounge. Occasionally, my roommate would bake a delicious honey loaf that would be consecrated (or so we *thought*) for Communion. We continued to remain seated throughout the service, along with the priest. The priest didn't wear vestments and was usually addressed by his first name or nickname. For example, Father Curran was called "Charlie". My roommates referred to priests as "clerics" in a slightly derogatory sounding tone.

Things didn't really fall apart until my second year. I enrolled in a class on the Gospel of John. You wouldn't think that there would be a problem with that one, would you? This class was taught by a highly intelligent Jesuit priest who had a strong background in Greek. He could translate Bible passages directly from Greek to English. This class really challenged my simple belief in the truth of the Bible. For example, he taught, contrary to Church Tradition, that John's Gospel wasn't actually written by the apostle, and he stated that the author changed facts to support his points and to fulfill Scripture prophecy. I remember being challenged because I believed in the "myth" of Adam and Eve. I had always tried to have the openness of a child concerning matters of faith, but now I reasoned that the time had come for this little child to grow up. When I allowed myself to doubt, everything snowballed, and I no longer knew what to believe. I became angry and confused. Angry because, if so much that I had believed and trusted to be true for so long was just "myths" or made up, what could I really believe? Was religion just some man-made scheme to keep me in line? Was everyone in on this deception — teachers, parents, priests? Was there really a God or was He made up too?

I began to believe that I had been lied to and that I had fallen for those lies, hook, line, and sinker. It was hard to find anyone to confide in at this point. My parents seemed threatened when I shared my doubts with them. They just didn't want to discuss them. I asked the university to recommend a spiritual director, and so I met with a nun and told her my story. I remember her telling me that I was "throwing the baby out with the bath water" and that "God is a good God." Unfortunately, at that point, I couldn't tell the baby from the bath water, and I really needed to be reassured of God's existence before being told of His attributes. I got nowhere fast and finally realized that I had completely lost my faith. Not surprisingly, I felt free. I could now live my own life and make my own decisions and not feel guilty. Perhaps I had wanted this for a long time and just needed a good excuse finally to break away. Catholic University made an excellent scapegoat. This was the 1970s, when many priests and sisters were being encouraged by modern psychology to find new ways of expressing their faith, which led to many leaving their vocations. It was also the beginning of the age of feminism, when women were encouraged to leave unfulfilling marriages in search of self-actualization. I can see now that all these philosophies gave people license to release the bonds that tied them to lives of faithfulness and self-sacrifice. It would be easy to blame the university for my loss of faith, but I can only blame myself for allowing my sense of God gradually to slip away. I had disregarded His rules and rationalized my own behavior. All this left me like a sitting duck when my then weakened faith was tested.

Where did all this lead me? I couldn't be a missionary now; I had nothing to offer. So, when I was offered a scholarship to join the Air Force as a nurse, I reluctantly accepted. The Air Force scholarship was very good; it paid for my books and tuition. In return, I agreed to serve for four years. I was used to following orders, so I didn't have very much trouble adjusting. In fact, I was happy to find out that once I started working in the Air Force hospitals some of the uncomfortable formalities, such as saluting and calling each other by rank, were not strictly enforced.

With the exception of hospital work, Air Force life was great. There were so many places to go, things to do, and lots of great looking men. The four years turned into six years full of adventure and travel. Of course there was quite a bit of work, but I enjoyed the nursing profession.

I didn't think about God much during those years. I was too busy playing and seeking pleasure. Lacking an imposed system of ethics, I allowed myself to create my own. It had three precepts, to be applied more or less strictly according to the situation. One, be honest; two, don't hurt anyone; and three, try to help others if you can. These seemed to work pretty well as guidelines to live by.

I still admired the teachings of Jesus, even though I couldn't believe He was really who "they" said He was. I was also interested in studying the teachings of Buddha. Buddhist teachings are similar to Christianity in that both advocate self-sacrifice and charity toward one's neighbor. More and more, though, I felt an increasing sense that my life had become devoid of any real meaning. Could self-pleasure be all that life is supposed to be?

Looking out at the stars one clear evening in northern Japan, I felt very alone. It was as if I were just an insignificant bump on the earth, and there was really no one who cared whether I lived or died. I remember thinking that if there really was no purpose for my life, I might as well just quit the struggle and end it all. Who would care? Fortunately, I rejected that idea since, well, just maybe, I could be wrong and there was a God. I also reasoned that, because I didn't create my own life, I really had no right to destroy it. So my life went on, but the question of the meaning of my life was not answered.

I was working in the obstetrics department of the hospital. From time to time I felt a little bit of jealousy over the young, unmarried, enlisted women who were having babies. Some of these women, it seemed to me, were just babies themselves. I believed that I would make a much better mother than most of them. Of course, though, I had my career goals, and a child really wouldn't fit in with them very well. However, those young Air Force women were handling both motherhood and a career, or so it seemed. And there was such a thing as day care. Welcome to parenting in the '80s!

I had a few initial reservations about becoming pregnant. I soon decided to look at it as another adventure. Perhaps it would give my life a little purpose and show off what a great person I was. Remember, this was the 1980s, the era of the autonomous female who could have a career and raise a family without having to depend on anyone else, least of all a male.

I wasn't going to let a little thing like pregnancy change my life. So, after an active pregnancy and an exciting delivery, I found myself with the cutest little baby boy. If there was a God, He sure wasn't punishing me for my sins. Somehow, everything worked out very well for me.

When my son David was a month old, I took him to the base chaplain's office to see about having him baptized. You might ask why, if I didn't believe in God, I wanted to get him baptized. Well, I had thought about that and decided that I would like him to have all the opportunities for a wonderful life that I enjoyed as a child.

I had had a happy childhood, growing up in the Church, so I didn't want to deny these experiences to my son. If he decided to make a choice at a later date, at least he would know a bit about what was available. Fortunately, the deacon at the chaplain's office didn't see it that way. He told me that he could not baptize my son because I was not a practicing Catholic. He said that it would be like handing a child an ice cream cone and then not allowing him to taste it. We talked for a little while, and he told me how he had done "everything in the book", but that Jesus had forgiven him and he had come back to the Church. Then he looked me in the eyes and said something for which, to this day, I am eternally grateful. He said very kindly and sincerely, "Jesus loves you so much!" Something in his voice touched me, and I began to cry. He seemed so open and honest. Perhaps someone out there did care? I had tried to be so strong, so independent, for so long. I had had to make my own decisions — to be a super mother, to be a career woman, and at the same time to make certain that I didn't fall back upon the "crutch" of religion. The one thing that didn't fit into my plan was the emptiness I felt in my heart. I had tried to fill this void with adventure, travel, romance, even motherhood, but without God that deep place in my heart remained empty.

For the sake of my child, I promised the deacon that I would go to confession and try to begin to believe in God again. In exchange, he agreed to baptize my son. I gave no guarantees, and we left it at that.

I kept my promise as best I could. I attended Mass regularly and went to confession. Yet, my life was far from sinless. But how to start believing? I tried to pray. But how does one pray to a God one does not believe in? I supposed that if this was going to work, I had to take the first step. That step, I figured, was to start with the basic assumption that there was a God and work from there. I no longer allowed myself the luxury of doubting. That strategy seemed to work fairly well. With God's existence as a premise, I saw myself as a creature, not an autonomous being. I didn't have to depend on myself for everything. At least now I could pray. Little by little, the other pieces of my life began to fall into place. I still had many questions, however.

For example, I was still too proud to admit that I had been lost. The dimming of my conscience had been so gradual that I had never really felt it happening. I told myself that I had merely been honest with myself, trying not to be hypocritical by outwardly practicing a faith that I could not accept intellectually. I had enjoyed being my own boss and calling the shots. So, if I hadn't been lost, what was the purpose of redemption? If we didn't need redemption, why did we need Jesus, and what was the Mass all about? I tried to read books written by Catholics, but it seemed as though I'd heard all those clichés before. I tried to accept the truths that intellectually and logically evolved from the major premise of God's existence. But what had happened to that feeling of closeness with God that I had once taken for granted? That feeling, unfortunately, was going to take many years to regain and would never be quite the same. I suppose that, as my conscience had dimmed, so had my sense of God. I was now rediscovering God as an adult. I was not the same person I had been in college before I had lost my faith. Even if I found it now, I could not expect everything to return to the way it was.

During those years of questioning, I also found out that baby-sitters, day care, and being a working mother were definitely not in the best interests of my son. I began to realize that an Air Force career was just not compatible with the life of a single mother. Occasionally we had surprise disaster drills, usually in the middle of the night. During these drills we had to report to our duty stations at 3:00 or 4:00 A.M. and sign in. In lieu of awakening the neighbors at that hour, I once left my baby sleeping soundly and rushed to the hospital to sign in, intending to return directly. When I arrived at the hospital, the full impact of what I had done hit me. How could I have left a helpless infant alone like that? What if this had been the real thing?! I didn't wait to find out; I signed in and hurried back home without waiting for further orders. I filled out my termination papers the next day.

Moving back in with my family in Camarillo was a real blessing. I could work as much as I needed, and I had no problem getting the best of sitters — my family. Fortunately, they were very willing to help.

Staying home and being a mother was wonderful, perhaps even more fulfilling than a career. I found that I enjoyed the little boring jobs like cooking and doing laundry because I was doing them for someone I loved.

Looking back, I realized that I had been lied to. What made me believe that godlessness, ambition, and adventure were the paths to happiness and fulfillment? Here I was, perfectly happy, taking care of a little boy and doing housework. I also had time to pray and to do more reading.

In the back of my mind, I still carried some regrets that I had never become a missionary. That had been my desire since I had been a young girl. Now the missionary field would have to wait until I had finished raising my son. I felt that I had really missed out on what I had been called to do. Then I heard about the Los Angeles archdiocesan-sponsored Lay Mission Helpers. Entire families went to serve in the missions through this program. When I wrote to the Mission Helpers, they wisely turned me down, advising that I concentrate on raising my son, who was now three years old. I was disappointed. It wasn't so much that I wanted to bring the Faith to other people but more to work with them and, I hoped, to find out how people living in such poverty could manage to have any faith at all.

It was one thing for me to have faith in a good God when I had everything I wanted and was so richly blessed. How could someone who had nothing, who seemingly had been forgotten by God, still believe in Him? What was the secret? Two years later, I had the opportunity to find out. While reading a copy of the *Catholic Digest*, I ran across an advertisement for a sponsorship organization known as the Christian Foundation for Children. They were asking for volunteers. I wrote to them and was invited to spend a weekend in Kansas at their headquarters in order to discern if we would be compatible. After an enjoyable and informative weekend, I was offered an opportunity for myself and my son to live and work for a year in Guatemala. This was really a dream come true. I had had a special love for the Hispanic people and culture ever since I had spent those summers in Mexico. Guatemala sounded wild and primitive, and that made it all the more exciting. Now I could learn first hand the secret of the strong faith of these people.

The Foundation was very helpful. They even timed our arrival to correspond with a foundation sponsored retreat for other Americans who arrived at the Guatemala City airport on the same day. After the retreat, we were driven for five hours over winding mountain roads to the town of San Pedro, where we would be staying. I had no idea what my job or jobs would be, and I was still struggling to understand the Spanish language.

San Pedro was a much more modern town than I had anticipated. We stayed in a two-story stucco house with indoor plumbing, a gas stove, and an electric refrigerator—not quite roughing it. Downstairs was the business office for the project and the clinic where the children and their families could receive medical care. Much of my work was done in the clinic, where I assisted the project doctor with medical examinations, or in the office, where I translated letters written by the children to their sponsors. The best part of my job, though, was traveling two or three times a week, usually on foot or in a taxi, over the dusty pot-holed roads into the neighboring mountain villages to meet with the parents of the sponsored children. I was able to bring my son with me on these visits, and he always had a host of curious Guatemalan children surrounding him. It was the first time most of them had ever seen a *gringito* (little *gringo*).

Here in these villages life was a bit tougher. Some villages had no electricity or even a road passable by car. The people had to walk two to three hours to town carrying the fruits and vegetables they raised to sell. Some families lived in huts made entirely of corn stalks, with thatched roofs. The sponsored children were provided one hot meal daily, which was prepared in the project kitchen. These meals were cooked over an open fire in a makeshift, leaky, tin-roofed wooden hut. The smoke in these kitchens was unbearable, which caused some of the cooks to suffer eye problems. I bought one of the cooks a pair of safety goggles, but she said the smoke just came in anyway. I really wished I could have done more to help.

The men building roads through the mountains to their villages with shovels and wheelbarrows asked me to send them a tractor. Even if we could have afforded a tractor, there was no way to get it to them in the mountainous terrain. At least they didn't seem to be starving, since the projects provided them with the essential food they needed to survive through co-ops and the income from the sponsors that served to help the entire village.

I found that these people did have strong Catholic faith. They were cheerful, gracious, generous, and very hospitable. Every time I visited one elderly lady, she gave me an orange or a treat of some kind. I eventually found out that, in addition to being poor, she suffered from severe arthritis. She had a very difficult time carrying her groceries home from the market and could carry only a few at a time. Each item was hard won, yet without a moment's thought she willingly shared what she had with a stranger.

One thing I loved about Guatemala was the way the

people expressed their faith. They held colorful and joy-
ous processions through the streets on all the major feast
days. Nearly the whole town participated. Passion Week
was exceptionally festive, with great floats carried through
the streets by twenty to thirty people. Even Dave, now six
years old, got to take a turn carrying one of the floats.

It seemed that the people's whole lives centered on the
Church—at least those who remained Catholic despite
the efforts of the evangelical and Mormon missionaries.
When someone died, there was a large funeral procession
and a nine-day Rosary novena, which was repeated on
the first anniversary of the death. It was very upsetting
not to be able to afford refreshments for all the neighbors who came to the home for the nine days. People
in the remote villages walked miles to attend Mass on
Sundays, and when they prayed it was evident that they
were putting their hearts into their prayer. They depended
on God to provide for their needs. Their faith was not a
contradiction or a question of "Where is God in all this
poverty?" Their faith was a refuge, a source of hope in a
seemingly hopeless situation. With nothing else to depend
on, they had to depend on God. Their faith was very simple, unconfused by theological controversies, and as practical as it was simple. I was soon to have an opportunity
to experience this kind of simple faith for myself.

During the Christmas season I had to travel to Guatemala City to renew my visa. In addition, my father had
sent vitamins for the children who were suffering from vi-
tamin A deficiency. He had arranged with a friend from
the California National Guard to fly the vitamins to the
Guatemala airport while on a mission to Central America.

Dave and I were to meet the plane, pick up the vitamins, get our visas stamped and then return home to San Pedro.

We missed the 5:00 A.M. bus, so we had to wait for the 6:00 A.M. bus. This put us at a slight time disadvantage. We would not arrive in Guatemala City until 11:00 A.M. We would have to find the consulate and get our visas renewed, then go to the airport to meet the plane at 2:00 P.M., and, finally, catch the last bus to San Pedro by 5:00 P.M., all using unfamiliar public transportation. The bus ride winding through the mountains was brutal with all the curves and, predictably, Dave got sick. He always suffered from motion sickness while traveling those roads. The only reason he wanted to come with me was that I had promised to buy him a McDonald's hamburger while we were in the city. It was a treat he really looked forward to, since there were no McDonald's anywhere near where we were living.

We managed to find the consulate, and, after waiting in line, we were told to leave our visas and come back and pick them up in the morning. I explained that this wouldn't be possible, since we were not prepared to spend the night. I had brought only enough money for transportation, fees, and Dave's hamburger. I believe that God intervened, because the clerk then said that we could return late that afternoon to pick up the visas. All that took only about an hour or so. I thought we'd be in good shape for meeting the plane at 2:00.

So off we went. I was feeling quite smug as we boarded the bus to the airport. We might even be early. We arrived at the airport a half hour early. I went to the information booth and asked about the National Guard plane, and, much to my chagrin, I was told that the plane was not coming in at this airport but at the military airport across the runway. "How do I get there?" I asked. I was told that I couldn't get across the runway, but I could take a bus around. Time was getting short, so I thought I'd splurge and hire a taxi to take us. The driver quoted us a price of about $5.00. This was an exorbitant fee for merely going across the runway, so I dragged David out to the street to await the bus. I suppose the taxi driver thought we were rich *Americanos*! Dave was hungry, and we hadn't had a chance to go to McDonald's yet, so while we waited for the bus I sat him down to eat the small sandwich I had brought for him. Just as he unwrapped it, along came the bus. I grabbed Dave, and we jumped on the bus. It was so crowded that we had to stand. Dave was unable to eat his sandwich. I saw a man in uniform and got off when he did, only to find that we had gotten off too soon and would have to walk the rest of the way. The clock was ticking as I hurried Dave along.

Eventually, we found the gate to the military base. It was closed and guarded, and it was almost 2:00 P.M. Amazingly, when we asked for the terminal, the guards just waved us past and directed us down a road. We walked and walked for what seemed like miles. Dave was trying to be so good, although he still had not had a chance to eat. It was past 2:00 P.M. now, and I thought I could hear the rumble of the National Guard's C-130 in the distance, so we kept on. Eventually we came to another guarded gate and, again miraculously, were allowed to cross. Somehow we found the military terminal, but it seemed to be deserted. The plane we had heard a while back should have been down for a long while by now. I finally found someone in the terminal and gave him the name of the flight operator. He acted as if he'd been expecting us and led us through the terminal, right out onto the runway. It seemed as if I were being led by an angel as closed gates and doors were miraculously opened before us. I had almost given up hope of meeting the plane's crew. Usually flight crews are in a big hurry to leave after a completed mission. The runway seemed deserted of people, but about one hundred yards away sat the big green C-130.

As we rushed toward it, I wondered if everyone had already left. Breathing a little prayer, I looked up to see movement under the wing. Was it the maintenance man or could it be . . . ? He waved. It was my friend Major T., from the National Guard. And beside him was a gigantic box. He was surprised to see us.

"How did you know which day we were coming in?" he asked. I told him I had just asked flight operations for the time the National Guard mission was arriving from Panama. Major T. informed me that there had been three National Guard missions from Panama that week. How I had found the right one was another miracle. "Now," he said, "how are you planning to transport this box?" I told him I had brought a little baggage cart and that we were planning to return the way we came — on the bus. Looking at the size of the box we both realized that it would be impossible to get it onto a city bus. That meant another taxi. Would I have enough money? And why were those vitamins so heavy, anyway?

Major T. helped us to hoist the heavy box onto the cart.

It was awkward and top-heavy, but it rolled. We walked that box right down the runway and through the terminal. I was pulling and Dave was pushing, and no one stopped us or asked for a customs inspection. Thank goodness, there was a group of taxis not very far away, so we headed toward them. The driver wanted about fifteen quetzales to take us to the consulate and then to the bus station on the other side of the city. Taxis certainly were more expensive here than they were in San Pedro. I told him that I had only ten quetzales left, which was true. It was all I had. I hadn't anticipated having to take a taxi. He agreed to take us for the ten quetzales and loaded the heavy box into the trunk. The trunk lid wouldn't close.

While we were driving, I told him that the box contained vitamins for the children in the villages around San Pedro. Finally, Dave piped up, "When are we going to go to McDonald's, Mommy?" I had totally forgotten my promise. When I told David that we were out of money, he started to cry. He had been so good throughout this whole ordeal. I had practically starved him and run his little legs off. Now I was going to have to break my promise. That was the last straw. His little heart was broken, and so was mine as I watched him sobbing. I knew that McDonald's was on the other side of town and there would be no way of making it now, even if I had the money. I have heard it said that the guardian angels of children stand before the face of God, and that must be true because, as I was explaining that we could not possibly make it to McDonald's, I looked out the window and there were the unmistakable golden arches. Who would have thought that Guatemala City would have two McDonald's?

In a flash, I remembered that my Dad had put a small stack of quarters in the corner pocket of my shoulder bag for emergencies. I felt for them — they were still there after six months. I negotiated with the cab driver to exchange some of the quetzales I had paid him for the American quarters. Not only was the driver happy to exchange the money, he also drove us right through the drive-through window. Dave got his hamburger without wasting any time. This was beginning to be too much to pass off as coincidence. I could see holding a plane until we had a chance to meet it, but what kind of God would concern himself with a mother's promise of a McDonald's hamburger for her son? Only a very real, involved, and loving God. I was beginning to realize that it is when we have nothing that we can best perceive God's actions in our lives. When everything is going smoothly, we may not even notice God's caring.

Our adventure was not over yet. When we got to the consulate, I told our driver that I would meet him in front in about ten minutes. The driver was also in a hurry, as he had to be back at the base at 5:00 P.M. for another fare. To my amazement, our visas were ready. We were able to be at the prescribed meeting place in exactly ten minutes. But where was the taxi? All of a sudden I had a sickening feeling that I had been very stupid. How could I have left that big box of vitamins in the trunk and have expected the driver to return and pick me up? He had already been paid, and that box of vitamins could be sold for a lot of money. Anything from the United States is considered precious in Guatemala, and vitamins are very expensive and hard to get. As the minutes ticked by, I felt worse and worse. After all that we had been through to get the box, to have lost it through stupidity was tragic. Dave was happily munching his hamburger, oblivious to our predicament. Children are so trusting. Their prayers are also efficacious, so I asked Dave to pray with me that the taxi driver would come back. Dave didn't have time to take another bite of his hamburger before our taxi arrived —with the box safely sticking out of the trunk. The driver said he had been caught in a traffic jam as he drove around the block. I mentioned that I had been worried about the box and thanked him for coming back with it intact. He told me that he had been tempted, but he realized that he was registered with the base and could be traced. He also said that he had grown up in San Pedro. I can't say for certain, but I bet that our prayers were what caused him to turn around and return to us.

We were exhausted when, at 10:00 P.M., we finally arrived in San Pedro. We made quite a sight, noisily bumping that box over the cobblestone streets, very thankful for all the blessings we had received that day. We surely couldn't have done it without God's help. This sequence of events helped me to take a giant leap in my faith journey. As simple as it may sound, it enabled me to realize there is Someone who listens to our prayers, even those left unspoken. We opened the box the next day, and, to our surprise and delight, it was loaded with Christmas presents from our family and our neighbors back home. There were also many other treats —peanut butter, cheese and crackers, and, of course, lots of vitamins for the children. What a wonderful Christmas we had! Little did we know, while in Guatemala City, just how valuable that box really was.

This is only one example of the excellent care we received from God during our year in Guatemala. It certainly makes it easier to pray when you know that Someone is really listening. Having prayers answered so readily and in such amazing ways gave me a great boost in faith. It seemed that the worse off I was and the more I had to depend on God, the more He would reach out to help and provide so many, many blessings. That, then, is the secret of the poor. The poorer one is, the more one must trust God to supply one's needs. The more one trusts, the more blessings one receives. This very simple point took me a year to begin to understand and will take a lifetime to put into practice.

After I returned home from Guatemala, my faith continued to develop, and gradually the old clichés seemed to take on new meaning. Somehow the Gospels at Mass seemed new and vibrant. Then the Mass itself began to make more sense. I saw a wonderful goodness in the Catholic Faith that I had seen before but never fully appreciated. I enrolled Dave in a newly formed, small Catholic school and learned a bit more about "orthodox" Catholicism. We didn't have to give up all the wonderful devotions that had strengthened me as a child. I read about St. Louis DeMontfort and started to say the Rosary again. How full the Catholic Faith was becoming for me! There seemed to be no bottom to its depth. The more I read, the more fascinated I became.

I wanted to experience real Catholic community life.

My Protestant friends had annual family retreat camps.
Our church didn't have that kind of community life. We
attended an Episcopal camp one summer. It was lovely,
but I couldn't really feel one with this community. That's
when I heard about the Apostolate for Family Consecration. The Apostolate holds Family Fests each summer at
their 850-acre "Familyland" in Ohio. That seemed to be
what I had been looking for. Dave and I went there and
were impressed with the wonderful Catholic families we
met and the spirit of true community. Prayer was part of
daily life as we worked and played together. The children
even stopped swimming in the pool at 3:00 P.M. to say the
Chaplet of Divine Mercy.

I brought home a set of video tapes on Marian consecration for parish evangelization. Through these tapes,
along with several members of our parish, we began the
process of consecrating ourselves to Jesus through Mary.
I learned about the spirituality of Pope John Paul II and
what *Totus tuus* (Totally Yours) means. My parish ran a series on the "Living Eucharist", a program that deepened
my appreciation of the Blessed Sacrament.

I will always be extremely grateful to the Catholic
Church and to the wonderful deacon at Hill Air Force
Base in Utah who would *not* baptize my son until I had
made the commitment to return to the Church. It has
been a remarkable journey for me, and I now express my
gratitude by being very active in my parish. One ministry
that I especially enjoy, in addition to family holy hours,
is teaching the baptism class to new parents. It is fun to
send these families off on an exciting journey of their own.
Most of them, like myself, have a long road to travel.

I have to watch myself, though, and be careful not to become so involved in parish ministries that I neglect my personal spiritual life. I now realize how important it is to remain close to God through prayer, private and communal, and the sacraments. When my next trial of faith comes along, I plan to be well prepared and ready to meet it through God's grace. My Catholic Faith is very precious to me, and I don't want to risk losing it, ever again!

The Sacrament of Reconciliation and an Examination of Conscience

Jesus, before ascending into heaven, gave His apostles the power to forgive sins. Bishops and priests, acting in the person of Christ, continue this mission of mercy through the sacrament of penance. Through these human instruments, the Lord forgives our sins in virtue of His Cross and Resurrection. In completing our return to God, we must seek sacramental forgiveness of our sins. For sin is an offense against God; it sets itself against God's love for us, and it turns our hearts away from God's love.

We should experience God's merciful love often by partaking in the sacrament of reconciliation. An explanation of the form of confession is provided below to serve as a guide in celebrating this sacrament. An examination of conscience is provided to assist you in preparing for it.

A Form of Confession

1. Enter the confessional and kneel down (or sit for a face-to-face confession). The priest may read a brief passage from Scripture.

2. Make the Sign of the Cross: "In the name of the Father, and of the Son, and of the Holy Spirit. Amen." Then say, "Forgive me, Father, for I have sinned. My last confession was _____. These are my sins. . . ." (Note: All mortal sins must be confessed according to kind and number. It is good to confess venial sins, but it is sufficient to have sorrow for them.)

3. Signal the end of your confession of sins and by saying: "I am sorry for these and all the sins of my past life" [(optional) add: "especially for _____", here naming some sin confessed in a previous confession that has been forgiven but for which you still have sorrow].

4. The priest may counsel you and ask questions about what he may not have understood clearly. He will assign you a penance consisting of prayers or other good works to do.

5. You say an Act of Contrition (see various forms below).

6. The priest says the prayer of absolution, which ends: "I absolve you from your sins in the name of the Father, and of the Son, and of the Holy Spirit." You answer: "Amen."

7. Dialogue: Priest: "Give thanks to the Lord, for He is good." You say: "His mercy endures forever."

8. The priest may say: "God bless you" or "Go in peace." You answer: "Thank you, Father." Then, leave the confessional.

Three Forms of the Act of Contrition

A.

My God, I am sorry for my sins with all my heart.
In choosing to do wrong and in failing to do good,
I have sinned against You, Whom I should love above
    all things.
I firmly intend, with Your help, to do penance, to sin
    no more,
and to avoid whatever leads to sin.
Our Savior Jesus Christ suffered and died for us.
In His name, my God, have mercy. Amen.

B.

O my God, I am heartily sorry for having offended
    You,
and I detest all my sins because I dread the loss of
    heaven and the pains of hell,
but most of all because I have offended You, my God,
Who are all-good and deserving of all my love.
I firmly resolve, with the help of Your grace, to confess
    my sins,
to do penance, and to amend my life. Amen.

C.

O my God, I am heartily sorry for having offended
  You,
and I detest all my sins because of Your just punish-
  ments,
but most of all because they have offended You, my
  God,
who are all-good and worthy of all my love.
I firmly resolve, with the help of Your grace, to sin no
  more,
and to avoid the near occasions of sin. Amen.

Adults' Examination of Conscience
according to the Ten Commandments

Examine your conscience by reviewing the Ten Commandments. A list of sins against these Commandments
is provided to help stimulate personal reflection in preparation for the sacrament of confession.

*I. "I, the Lord, am your God, you shall not have other gods
besides me."*

— Doubting the existence of God;

— Abandoning the Catholic Faith or joining any other religion;

— Disbelieving any truths of the Catholic Faith, or any
  teachings of the Church;

— Failure to profess or defend the Catholic Faith when required to do so;

— Denying that one is a Catholic or ridiculing the Church or its practices;

— Being ashamed of the Faith or failing to give external signs of it out of human respect;

— Reading literature that endangers your faith, or consorting with anyone who may endanger your faith;

— Joining secret societies or organizations opposed to the Catholic Faith (e.g., Freemasons, Communist party, pro-abortion groups);

— Witnessing or taking part in a marriage of a Catholic in a wedding not approved by the Catholic Church;

— Failure to make the Easter season Communion every year;

— Neglecting to go to confession at least once a year;

— Failing to fast and abstain on the appointed days;

— Failure to fast for one hour before receiving Holy Communion; failure to confess privately mortal sins that were previously forgiven in a general absolution service;

— Negligence in fulfilling the penance assigned by a priest in confession; praying without attention or while permitting distractions;

— Receiving Holy Communion without reverence or thanksgiving;

— Neglecting regular prayer;

— Remaining ignorant of the Catholic Faith or failing to seek necessary counsel from the Catholic Church regarding a problem in faith or morals.

II. "You shall not take the name of the Lord, your God, in vain."

— Blasphemous talk about God, Jesus, Mary, angels, or saints;

— Irreverent language about holy persons, places, or things;

— Cursing (or calling down evil upon someone or something);

— Swearing an oath without sufficient reason;

— Failure to keep vows or promises.

III. "Remember to keep holy the Sabbath Day."

— Missing Sunday Mass or missing Mass on a holy day of obligation through one's own fault;

— Coming to Sunday or holy day Mass late or leaving before it is finished without just cause (absence from Offertory through Communion is mortal sin); willful distractions during Mass;

— Doing unnecessary servile work or shopping or conducting business on Sunday.

IV. *"Honor your father and your mother."*

— Disrespect, disobedience, or insult to one's parents, grandparents, or guardians;

— Disrespect of spouses or family members toward one another;

— Parent's failure to have children baptized soon after birth, educated in the Catholic Faith, make confession, First Communion, or confirmation, or go to Sunday Mass;

— Parent's neglect of their children's needs: material, educational, disciplinary, moral, or emotional;

— Mistreatment or abuse of children;

— Failure to provide for one's parents in time of their necessities;

— Failure to do one's duty according to one's state in life, at home, at work, or at school;

— Disobedience to the lawful demands of one's superiors, teachers, or employers; student's neglect of studies;

— Disrespect for the elderly;

— Disobedience to the civil law or to the officers of the state;

— Failure to have patriotism.

V. *"You shall not kill."*

— Unjust killing (or murder);

— Abortion;

— Counseling a woman to have an abortion or assisting in an abortion; participation in surrogate motherhood;

— Artificial insemination; participation in sperm banks;

— Obtaining surgery for the intended purpose of sterilization;

— Mutilation of the body;

— Attempted suicide;

— Violent behavior;

— Needlessly putting your life or the life of another in danger (e.g., reckless driving); physically fighting or striking another;

— Excessive drinking of alcoholic beverages or excessive smoking;

— Abusive use of prescribed drugs;

— Using, distributing, or selling illegal drugs;

— Too much or too little sleeping or eating (e.g., laziness, gluttony, wasting one's time, vain preoccupation about diet);

— Not taking reasonable care of one's health; excessive concern over bodily health or appearance;

— Taking revenge;

— Anger, hatred, aversion, coldness, or resentment toward another;

— Name calling or abusive or harsh language toward another; rude or impolite conduct; inconsideration for the feelings of others;

— Mocking the physically or mentally handicapped or those of another race or religion;

— Giving bad example for others to imitate;

— Lack of compassion for someone afflicted;

— Failing to help another in danger or serious necessity;

— Boasting of one's accomplishments;

— Stubbornness in one's opinions;

— Favoring opinions contrary to Church teaching (e.g. on abortion, divorce, sterilization, contraception);

— Impatience;

— Cruel treatment of animals.

VI. "You shall not commit adultery."

— Fornication (where both parties are unmarried);

— Adultery (where at least one party is married to someone else);

— "Petting" (masturbation involving others or arousing sexual passions of another, e.g., by passionate kissing, embraces, or touch);

— Impure actions by oneself alone (e.g. masturbation, touching, exposing oneself; inducing erotic sensations);

— Homosexual acts;

— Unnatural sexual acts (oral, anal, incestuous, or involving animals);

— Using contraceptives or premature withdrawal;

— Refusing the marriage right to one's spouse without a sufficient reason or making an unreasonable demand of it;

— Dating someone who is civilly divorced but is yet bound by a valid marriage;

— Causing an unnecessary separation from one's spouse or children;

— Immodesty in dress;

— Sinful entertainments (e.g., immodest dancing, books, magazines, pictures, video, TV, internet, certain musical groups);

— Offensive or impure language (profanity, vulgar speech or stories);

— Consorting with companions of bad moral character who are or may be an occasion of sin.

VII. "You shall not steal."

Notes: (1) The amount or extent of the sin must be confessed. (2) The sin is mortal if the worth of what was stolen or damaged is equivalent to a daily wage; otherwise, it is venial. (3) For the forgiveness of mortal or venial sin, there must be the intention to restore or repay.

— Stealing goods or money;

— Damaging or destroying public or private property;

— Accepting or buying stolen property;

— Cooperating with another who steals;

— Smuggling;

— Filing an unjust lawsuit or making unjust claims in a lawsuit;

— Dishonesty in business dealings;

— Charging exorbitant prices;

— Concealing defects of goods offered for sale;

— Not paying a worker justly;

— Failure to do the right amount of work for which one is paid; working poorly;

— Failure to pay income tax or the right amount of tax;

— Offering or accepting bribes;

— Excessive gambling or betting;

— Not paying one's debts;

— Neglect or needless delay in paying bills;

— Borrowing without permission of the owner;

— Not reporting incorrect change to a cashier;

— Failing to return something borrowed;

— Using money in a selfish or irresponsible way (e.g., needless or extravagant spending or shopping);

— Not sincerely seeking out the owner of something that was found;

— Failure to contribute to the support of the Church according to one's means;

— Not making restitution for goods stolen or damaged;

— Cheating on tests, schoolwork, or homework by students;

— Violation of copyright, any kind of fraud;

— Cheating in games or sports;

— Wasteful or abusive use of goods or food.

VIII. "You shall not bear false witness against your neighbor."

— Deliberate lies;

— Perjury (lying under oath);

— Not keeping lawful promises or oaths;

— Swearing to do something sinful or unlawful;

— Deliberately trying to overhear another's confession;

— Harming another's reputation (slander or gossip);

— Telling the faults of others (detraction);

— Revealing secrets that should be kept; betraying trust;

— Reading another's letters or private documents when one has not the right;

— Boasting of our sins;

— Uncharitable criticism;

— Rash judgments and false suspicions;

— Deliberately misleading or deceiving another;

— Refusing to forgive another who asks pardon, or holding a grudge;

— Failing to make an apology to one who has been offended.

IX. *"You shall not covet your neighbor's wife."*
(See also the Sixth Commandment).

— Willful thoughts or desires of impurity.

X. *"You shall not covet anything that belongs to your neighbor."*

— Loving any persons or things more than God;

— Failure to have charity for one's neighbor;

— Greed (excessive desire to possess material things or too great a preoccupation with them);

— Selfishness; self-pity;

— Wanting to keep, take, or damage the property of others;

— Desiring to possess, control, or restrict another unlawfully;

— Jealousy or envy of another's good fortune, good looks, reputation, or possessions; delighting in another's disgrace or misfortune;

— Wishing evil for others;

— Pride; vanity; desiring to be praised;

— Failure to do something that ought to be done;

— Fully intending to commit some sin by giving internal consent but not succeeding in accomplishing it by an external act.